Not like other
boys

Books by Marlene Fanta Shyer

FICTION

Weekend
Never Trust a Handsome Man
Local Talent

Not like other boys

boys

Growing Up Gay: A Mother and Son Look Back

Marlene Fanta Shyer
and Christopher Shyer

alyson
books

LOS ANGELES • NEW YORK

Authors' Note
In the investigation of our past we have tried to be truthful as well as discreet.
All names in the book have been changed, except for those of family members and a few public figures.

Manufactured in the United States of America.
Printed on acid-free paper.

This trade paperback is published by Alyson Publications Inc.,
P.O. Box 4371, Los Angeles, California 90078-4371.

First published by Houghton Mifflin: 1996
First Alyson edition: September 1997

01 00 99 98 97   10 9 8 7 6 5 4 3 2 1

ISBN 1-55583-449-3
(Previously published with ISBN 0-395-70939-3 by Houghton Mifflin.)

Library of Congress Cataloging-in-Publication Data
Shyer, Marlene Fanta.
    Not like other boys — growing up gay : a mother and son look back /
Marlene Fanta Shyer and Christopher Shyer
    1. Shyer, Christopher. 2. Gay men — United States — Biography.
3. Mothers and sons — United States. I. Shyer, Christopher. II. Title.
HQ75.8.S48A3 1996
305.38'9664—dc 20   95-35698 CIP

The quotation in Chapter 33 is taken from the Dear Abby column by Abigail Van
Buren, © Universal Press Syndicate. Reprinted by permission. All rights reserved.

For Joanna and for Jim

- - - - - - -

Also, in memory of Paul Monette,
whom I never met, but whose
resonating words have inspired mine

C.S.

For Larry and for Marjorie,
and for Jane, who would have
loved this book

M.F.S.

ACKNOWLEDGMENTS

We wish to thank Helen Robinette, Robert Mayetta and Rose Dinolfo for their interest, help and encouragement. We owe special gratitude to Alice Martell for her early enthusiasm and push, to Gail Winston for her extraordinary dedication to our work, and to all the friends who have shared their experiences and insights, which enriched our memories and our book.

IT WAS SEVERAL years ago, sitting at lunch, when Chris suggested we write this book.

At first it seemed like an imprudent idea. Although I'd come a very long way in accepting my son's homosexuality, we had to think of the universe in which we lived. Was he ready to open up his life to the public? Was I ready to come out of my own closet, which was filled with the shame of years of intolerance? We tried to imagine repercussions and worst-case scenarios. There was Chris's father to think of, Chris's siblings, and their in-laws. What about the neighbors, Chris's colleagues, his varied and sundry cousins and aunts? What about the family business?

We talked and talked. It finally became clear that the good would outweigh the bad. If we shocked some people, stepped on some toes, revealed some family lore others might feel was private business, it would be worth it, and not only for our own catharsis.

Like Chris, I suddenly understood that we had a job to do. I had to put down in writing the painful steps I'd had to take to ascend my personal Matterhorn. There the air was pure of my own homophobia, of the pollution of societal censure and of my own failure as a parent. What follows in these pages includes all my slips and stumbles, for which my son has thankfully forgiven me and from which I hope others can learn.

My movement upward, into acceptance and respect for my son's way of life, did not escalate in one straight line. As Chris was growing up, I was growing little by little too, but each step I took was greatly weighted by my own insecurities and the atmospheric pressures of my time. It wasn't only Anita Bryant, the voices from the pulpit, or suburban conservatism seeping into every aspect of our lives. A great deal of our attitudes had to do with the absence of gay heroes anywhere in our culture. No matter how talented or accomplished or famous, the homosexuals on the world's honor roll had that invisible asterisk next to their names. If their sexual orientation did not diminish their work, it instantly diabolized them. They were a source of amusement or derision; their sexuality was a stain universally deplored. In those days, being "less than a man" meant being "less than a human," so as the mother of a boy who wasn't stereotypically boyish enough, who didn't want to fit into the macho clothes I'd psychologically prepared for him, I felt — for too long a time — as if I had failed to do my job. I couldn't seem to redirect this little dissident, who was destined to stand forever apart.

I didn't expect the constant churn of emotions as we wrote our chapters. It tore at me to learn for the first time of the life Chris had been living sub rosa for all those terrible years. And I berate myself. Why didn't I ask him at eleven, or at thirteen, "Do you think you might be . . . ?" It was an unthinkable, out-of-the-question, horrifying inquiry to put to a boy who might, after all, be heterosexual. An insult! A condemnation! Or worse, it might tip the scales, give him The Idea, tempt him into being "that way." In any case, the query would certainly devastate and traumatize the boy.

That's how we were thinking then.

Now, when I allow myself to imagine how that question — followed by an assurance that being gay was fine with us, his parents — would have saved my son fifteen years of desolation, assuaged a childhood and adolescence of torment and freed him from the pathology of self-hatred, I become distraught to the point of tears.

This book is my confession, a tract and a briefing all in one. And it is, above all, an apology to my son.

MARLENE FANTA SHYER

I AM AN AMERICAN MAN, an individual, neither proud nor ashamed of my sexual orientation any more than I am proud or ashamed of my eye color, race or unique fingerprints. I am who I am, and I'm finally ready to face life's music as a homosexual. Because I am linked to other gay males through the accident of sexual orientation and its invariable concomitant of heartache, I approached my mother to write this book. I am not telling my story to get pity, but to shorten the distance between acknowledgment and self-confidence in others like me. Hell, as I discovered, is oneself after all, and so what follows is aimed particularly at those who are still behind the closet door. Those like me who emerged, but found the rapids of struggle to get out almost unnavigable, may see themselves in these pages as well.

The book is also for anyone dear to them, to help them understand that coming to terms with being part of a minority group that is viewed by a great part of the world as heretical and disgusting is as wrenching for the macho jock as for the delicate artist. Am I capable of opening parents' eyes and softening their hearts? I am writing this with that fervent hope.

Stereotypes die hard. I have gay friends who are bond traders, physicians and dentists, football fans. Just last month, one of the men who came to give me an estimate on repointing the chimney bricks, a mason, was homosexual. I've had my car repaired by a gay mechanic, there exists today a gay household moving firm, and a close friend was seeing a railroad engineer who had just come out of the closet. We don't all love Judy Garland; we don't all lisp.

Also, not all boys who were school scapegoats turned out to be homosexuals. To the contrary, many gay men have a record of athletic excellence and a history of popularity with peers. So, my story is simply my story, with, I think, many universal elements.

In looking back, I'm not necessarily pleased with my own reactions to some events in my past. Recently I came out to a college friend. I was no longer as tentative about making that consequential announcement as I'd once been, but I was still apprehensive.

I'd waited ten years, afraid I'd lose him over this issue, something that shouldn't matter to our friendship. The happy ending should not have been a surprise; he immediately accepted me and, not long after my disclosure, invited me to his wedding, with my companion. Expecting a bad reaction from someone straight, I saw myself, too, as a victim of ingrained stereotypes.

Over the years, I jumped the gun many times to judge heterosexuals, occasionally misreading innocent comments or an indecipherable demeanor. Nowadays, I give everyone more of a chance.

I am still finding my way in a world that offers a wide assortment of human reaction, but there is a big difference now. I am hopeful for a more enlightened future, and I'm no longer lost. I know where I belong. It's my world, too.

CHRISTOPHER SHYER

Not like other boys

1

- - - - - - - - - - -

IT WAS ON LONG ISLAND, the summer I was sixteen. My cousin and I were changing into bathing suits in our beach club cabana when she whispered that she'd heard the rumor that our cabana boy was a homosexual.

"What's a homosexual?" I asked her.

"Men who fall in love with other men," she explained. Not a word about sex; that would have been much too far-fetched for two teenage girls in the era of black-and-white TV and black-and-white values. "There are lots of them, and they all live down in Greenwich Village. There are special bars you can go to see them." She'd actually spotted some on the street, holding hands, but I had a hard time believing all this. It sounded totally improbable, and as far as the possibility of "one of them" ever touching my life, well, marrying a prince and getting my face on a postage stamp were more likely possibilities.

Fifteen years, four presidents and what seemed like lifetimes later, I sat in a little chair in a New Rochelle kindergarten classroom waiting my turn for a conference with my son Chris's teacher. It was a standard-issue parent-teacher meeting, which in the enlightened sixties had replaced the yellow report cards of my day. This was my second child, so I already had a few school conferences under my belt, but this was my first meeting with the stellar Deb Gilmore. The only black teacher in a principally white school in a very white but "socially responsible" neighborhood, she had surmounted the suspicion that she might have been hired less on merit and more because of her color and had become tremendously popular. She was young and eager, with a reputation for warmth and sparkle. We considered ourselves lucky to have been granted the best of all good eggs to begin Chris's academic career.

My turn came, and Miss Gilmore turned her perpetual smile on me.

Chris had adapted beautifully to kindergarten. He was obedient-mature-bright-cooperative and a whole slew of predictably flattering incense I inhaled deeply and happily. "A pleasure to have in class" — over the following ten years it was the phrase I heard from the mouths of teachers young and old. The good, good boy. It was a predictable and wonderful first school conference, which I would share with Daddy at dinner that evening.

I asked about class activities. Did he play with the cars and trucks over there? What about the big building blocks? And the playground? Did he join the other boys in their games? Well, sometimes, but mostly he enjoyed setting the table. That was what he seemed to like to do best — arranging the plates and napkins and cups at snack time. Forks and knives instead of trucks and baseball; my heart sank. On the other hand, he didn't play with dolls. I remember asking, and the answer was no. Christopher did not play with dolls.

Chris's modus vivendi had been bothering me for almost a year. I went to bed worrying about it, and it was the first thing on my mind when I woke. It was the cinder in the eye of my view of our perfect life: our second son was turning into an odd little fellow. His sweetness, tidy nature, attention to wardrobe and cleanliness were charming but worrisome. The super-obedience, his non-cutup personality, his ability to sit quietly, the soft nature that had won him the Best Rester Award in nursery school — weren't these unnatural behaviors for a five-year-old boy?

"I've been worried about Chris," I told Miss Gilmore.

"In what way?"

Saying it aloud for the first time took courage. "I'm afraid he may grow up to be a homosexual."

If she thought I was deranged, she gave no sign and took me seriously. I explained that I had not a bit of solid evidence, but was just drifting in on one of those ephemeral mother-hunches. We had another boy, I said, who was a fully actualized, three-dimensional male, indifferent to clean hands, homework, etiquette. The older one had rough boyish edges. He knocked things over or was knocked over by them. Kirby, three and a half years older, was no stranger to the hospital emergency room, where I'd sat waiting for stitches, bandages and casts again and again over the years. My older son — not a bad boy — was committed to wholesome acts of mischief and damage, and totally uninterested in table settings. A real boy.

"I'll keep my eye on Chris," Deborah Gilmore promised. We'd keep in touch and have another conference in a month or two. She had not picked up on anything unusual about my son thus far. I went home relatively relieved. In any case, Chris was only five years old, and whatever I saw in him that was not pure, one hundred percent man could certainly be redirected, molded or changed. If the kid could be fixed, it seemed to me to be a perceptive and loving mother's — and father's — mandate to fix him.

My husband and I lived our first year as a married couple in a dogpatch of a battleground. I was embarrassed to meet our next-door neighbors in the elevator of our apartment building; I thought they must be hearing the nightly verbal fireworks right through the walls. I have thought many times that in today's climate of love 'em and leave 'em, we would have been divorced within the first six months. Try as I have to remember what those mongrel fights were about, I can't. Not in-laws. Never money. Maybe how wide to leave the windows open or what to watch on television. Once I burned the bacon and he ranted like a madman in the smoke-filled kitchen. I do know that my husband, even at the peach-fuzz age of twenty-two, had very strong opinions, a loud voice and a nitroglycerin temper. I came from a background of parents tiptoeing around each other and having virtually no disagreements in the twenty-seven years before they divorced, while my husband had grown up the son of two screamers who were dedicated to and loved each other unconditionally. It appalled me to hear his father shriek at his mother about things like having bought the wrong kind of herring. It offended me equally when she — after waiting until his wrath had subsided — let him have it back, both barrels. I found this type of emotional engagement wacky and disgraceful. Secretly, I considered it ghetto-caliber low class.

His parents lived in the decorator-done, matching-Cadillacs environment of the parvenu, while I came from some hazy Czechoslovakian lineage that featured ancestors who had been judges, oil paintings, opera recordings, threadbare Orientals and second-hand Buicks. We were the genteel folks, not poor but never rich, and my in-laws were first-generation wall-to-wall, with hearts of gold and pockets lined with it.

They were good and simple people in their warm and non-judgmental way. A not very Jewish family, they were paradoxically very ethnic-minded. They looked at people of other religions with faint suspicion, like the drinking water in third-world countries. Once they got over the shock of my having been raised as a Catholic (although I had lapsed long before we met), and once I'd married their older son, I was not only safe, I was delicious. My mother-in-law called me every morning of my life at ten minutes to nine, till death did us part, and although we might have come from different planets, we managed to connect in solid good-will and friendship over the thirty-five years we were family.

I did not want to replicate my in-laws' scrappy marriage, and after the first year a sort of miraculous calm settled over ours. My husband and I were now best friends, intensely dependent on each other and basically inseparable. When I became pregnant with Kirby, the ballistics stopped and Bob became saintly — the only way to describe a husband who wrapped his love and attention around me in a selfless and protective way, uncomplainingly putting up with the agoraphobia that limited our social life and plagued me during my twenties and early thirties. It didn't have a name then, my inexplicable attacks of paralyzing nausea, and going to a "head doctor" for help was out; in our world, only "mental cases" went to psychiatrists. Instead, my husband, unbelievably tolerant and caring, coddled me, with never a word of complaint about my bolts out of restaurants, theaters, parties. If we had to leave plays and movies, half-eaten meals and family celebrations, he put up with the burden of my social handicap with equanimity and not even the hint of reproach.

Until the children came and — in time — the phobia went, we were pretty much stay-at-homes, and there were no divisive issues between us. Our values, views and tastes meshed in everything from friends to contemporary art. We grew together as if we'd been spliced, becoming as much of a duo as the couples we loved watching in black and white: George and Gracie, Steve and Eydie, Lucy and Desi.

Every night I waited for my husband's return from work at the picture window of our living room in our small third-floor apartment. If he was late, I was traumatized with anxiety. He drove twenty-five miles each way to work in his father's optical manufacturing plant. What if he was in an accident? How could I live without him? He began calling me just when he was leaving the office so I'd know what time he'd be home. That thoughtful courtesy continued throughout our thirty-two-year marriage, almost until our separation.

With the clarity of hindsight I see now not only how my dependency endeared us to each other, but how it worked against my having any strong dissenting point of view. It is not necessarily that we didn't agree in our opinions about our children, it's just that this loving symbiosis precluded either of us from forcefully standing our independent ground, and surely fostered timidity in me. If I fell into step behind my husband later, when it came to his views about Chris, it was certainly not his fault. Perhaps good marriages have a way of "rounding the edges" of both spouses, and I might have been particularly frail in the early days. It was due to my inordinate desire not to shake the foundation of our excellent partnership.

Kirby was born in 1957, and while the birth of a baby sometimes has a deleterious effect on a marriage, it didn't on ours. Despite an infant that drove us crazy screaming out his lungs from six to ten every evening and woke me intermittently during the night and at five every morning, the novelty and fun, the daily surprises of babyhood charmed me into the hassled joy I remember as early motherhood. And my best buddy husband and I grew even closer.

There was a clear division of labor, a fact that women of my generation never took as unfair. Mommy toted the bar and lifted the bale on the domestic shores. Daddy worked at work, not at home. It was the way it was done in those days when man was his nibs, the king. In spirit, though, Daddy *was* a potent part of the domestic scenery. He was interested in his family, home every night, and frantic when baby's temperature rose or a rash appeared. Then and now, the kids have his full concern when they are under the weather. A sneeze or cough gets his immediate attention. He is in love with medical symptoms and always has some of his own to share with the world.

On the other hand, Bob was more of a hands-off father than even the most distant, career-oriented breadwinner papas of his generation. Not for him playground duty. Not for him a quiet chat with one of his children. There were no heart-to-hearts, piggyback rides or bedtime stories. Never in his long career as father did he read a book to a child. If Bob took one of the children to his office for the day, the idea sprang from my head or theirs, and although he was occasionally willing, it was up to the office staff to keep the kid busy once on the premises.

Still, if it meant their life or his, he would have given his. Peeling away his irascible, top-sergeant layers and the cut-down wit, forgiving the inattention and irritability, the aching shoulder or hurting back, the children knew he had a soft heart, an inherent goodness that went to the marrow, and I knew it too. He was difficult and funny, lovable and intolerable, aggressive then remorseful, a Jekyll-Hyde package incarnate.

This porcupine with a marshmallow heart went with me to open-school nights, teacher conferences, school concerts and Disneyland. At my insistence, he went on family vacations when he'd just as soon have kept it a twosome. All the while he was irritated, tense, nervous, controlling and overbearing, never sick but forever ailing, but he went. And although he could never buy anything for himself, he was generous to his family. His motto was, "If they need it, buy it."

One wonders about the family configurations of the homosexuals throughout history: the wisdom of my day had it that deviates were made that way by strong mothers and weak or absent fathers. Was this the case in the lives of Tchaikovsky, Isaac Newton, da Vinci, James Buchanan, J. Edgar Hoover and Lawrence of Arabia? What about John Milton, Hart Crane, Julius Caesar, Popes Leo X, John XII and Paul II? What kind of a mother did Michelangelo have? André Gide? Horatio Alger? What was Jean Cocteau's papa like? Somerset Maugham's?

Did they have a Bob for a father? At the time Christopher was born, we had segued into a three-way dynamic of Mom, Dad and Firstborn that I thought might have been to blame for the detour Chris seemed to be taking from heterosexuality. I was no longer the object of my husband's wrath; Kirby had taken my place. There was no cruelty intended, few physical blows, but the repercussions of my little son's small sins shook the walls. Homework skipped or sloppy, a key misplaced, boots left at school, the tricycle blocking Daddy's car in the driveway — Daddy trumpeted his anger in thunderous discharges while toddler Chris, traumatized and trembling, put his arms around my neck and held on for dear life.

My tot shook in fear during these domestic tempests. Much later I realized that it was possible the baby saw a connection between the detonating punishment and boyishness. Could he instinctively have assumed that since I was feminine and exempt from Daddy's verbal bombardments that it might be safer to be feminine too?

That was my reasoning for years afterward, but I vacillated. The jury was still out.

Twenty-five years later, my husband and I sat in the office of a marriage counselor. He had come highly recommended, was

forceful, direct and seemed evenhanded. It was a funny thing —
throughout our entire marriage and despite all other dissension,
we were in total accord in our evaluations of other people. And so
we agreed that Dr. Lowey, although crude — "no one we'd have
to a dinner party" — seemed efficient at hitting bull's-eyes in his
office. Bob got to like the man, began calling him by his improbable first name, Ramon, but later said that "if it weren't for the
marriage counseling, we'd still be married." Perhaps he meant the
sort of delving we endured the time Dr. Lowey zeroed in on
Chris's homosexuality:

He turned to me. "You blame Bob for it." It was not a question
but a statement of fact.

I looked at Dr. Lowey, who was holding his customary mug of
coffee, took in the crumbs from the doughnut he'd eaten earlier
that were still decorating the front of his shirt, and I shook my
head. "No, I don't."

Dr. Lowey stared me down. "You think it's his fault," he insisted.

Putting it mildly, I wanted to knock the cup of coffee out of
his hand. Would I ever stop being intimidated by men who sat
in black leather swivel chairs and had "Dr." in front of their
names? Maybe he was right. Did I? Didn't I? All of a sudden, I
didn't know. Was homosexuality nature? Was it nurture? A mix?

Dr. Lowey had his opinion, but felt that the only thing that
mattered was that I blamed Bob.

It wasn't until much later that it occurred to me that Bob might
also have blamed me.

When I went back to Miss Gilmore for a second conference, she
told me she'd been observing Christopher very closely. "He has
not approached any other little boys and tried to kiss them, or
anything like that," she said.

It was meant to be comforting, but she'd missed the point.
Five-year-old kindergarten heterosexual boys didn't go around
making passes at five-year-old girls, did they? All I wanted to
know was whether or not he behaved like the other boys in the

class. I kept asking the same question in different ways, so anxious to get the answer I wanted to hear. Did he fit in with his peers? Was he different? Too much of a sissy? Accepted by the others? One of the bunch?

He was doing just fine. Joining in the games, at ease with boys and girls. No sign of any sexual deviation whatsoever.

Well, hooray. I sailed out of Miss Gilmore's classroom, on top of the world. I'd obviously been looking for a spider when there weren't even cobwebs. So what if he really loved setting the table? For all I knew, Ted Dietrich, his little friend across the street, was doing the same thing in *his* class. It didn't mean a thing in kindergarten.

"So, maybe he'll open a restaurant," his father said. At that time, he still thought it was pretty amusing.

2

- - - - - - - - - -

I WAS HOME sick from kindergarten that afternoon when my mother wrapped me in a woolen blanket and carried me to Ted's house, depositing me into the warm maternal care of his mother. I was getting over the mumps and he had just come down with them, convenient timing for a couple of five-year-olds, quarantined and getting lonely on either end of the street. You could say Ted Dietrich was assigned to me by fate, by the circumstance of our physical proximity, by our parents' neighborly friendship and by the accident of our both being born in 1961. The Berlin Wall went up that year, a fitting metaphor for the walls that invariably arose during all my same-sex friendships, including this earliest one. We were inseparable after-school friends for a while, Ted and I, learning to ride bikes with training wheels together, sledding down Mulberry Lane on those heaven-sent snow days, and sitting across the table from each other through numerous tuna salad lunches and hot dog dinners.

Now Mrs. Dietrich warned us not to exert our sick little selves and established us on a couch in front of the TV. Then, while she busied herself in the kitchen, Ted and I embarked on what I consider my first sexual experience.

Under a blanket on the living room couch, no more than twenty feet from the unsuspecting Mrs. Dietrich, we pulled up our shirts and began to rub our stomachs together. We called it "playing tum-tums," and even then, at age five, I knew it felt too good, and knew without being told that it was wrong.

The fate of Ted's sexual orientation I don't know, but the fate of our friendship was to slide inevitably downhill, like our winter sleigh rides. It was unspoken, but the schism grew as Ted began acting out the role of true jock, while I, the second-class kindergarten citizen, was left behind to make the best of it with the neighborhood girls.

We did occasionally play together, Ted and I — when it rained; when no ball games were available down the street; and now and then, in a dark closet, in the attic and behind the locked bathroom door, we resumed our game of tum-tums. Three years after his family moved away, Ted's parents brought him to our new house for a visit. We were eight-year-olds then, light years away from kindergarten. Ted's parents occupied the beds in my room, and we were put to bed in sleeping bags under the dining room table.

With the lights off and the house quiet, Ted moved toward me, pulling up his shirt and beginning to pull down his pants. "Remember tum-tums?" he whispered.

Suddenly the lights flashed on and there stood Ted's mother, framed in the doorway and looking ten feet tall.

"Ted!" Her voice ripped through the room as if it were electronically amplified. "I told you not to do that!"

In one whoosh of emotion I was confounded, relieved, scared. Had he done this before? When, with whom? And then the relief: *his* mother had caught him, and she *knew*. My mother hadn't, and didn't. But then again, what if Mrs. Dietrich *told?*

But she didn't, and the incident passed and was forgotten. Well, not really forgotten. At the back of my mind, for years afterward, I thought about the episode, because I felt that no matter how far away Ted moved, wherever he was, he and I shared a deep and unforgettable secret I could tell no one else in the world. We exchanged no letters, postcards or telephone calls, never spoke again for three years, but the phantom Ted was as close as I came to having a confidant for most of my prepubescent life.

When I was eleven, I finally visited the Dietrichs in upstate New York. I had thought about this reunion for years, planning — what? I didn't know for sure, but in some hopeful corner of my heart, I imagined that my kindred spirit and I, in some wordless way, would unwind the dangerous barbed wire we were both wrapped in. By that time I knew its name, knew what it meant.

Mrs. Dietrich made up the trundle bed for me in Ted's room. As soon as it got late enough, dark enough, quiet enough, I gathered up my courage. Ted was lying in his bed, one intimate elevated foot from mine. "Do you remember tum-tums?" I asked tentatively.

Ted had forgotten, knew nothing about the game, had blotted it out of his memory. Or so he said. I had waited three long years to see him again, and he seemed to recoil under his covers, roll as far away as he could from me. I went to sleep feeling as if there were a billion people in the world and my shameful secret and I were all alone in it.

The fear of my parents' finding out followed me like a sinister shadow through my childhood and adolescence. If I heard my parents whispering in another room, I thought, They've figured it out, they're discussing me. If they looked at me too long, or with an expression that appeared suspect, I thought, They've guessed my secret. This ongoing fear propelled me into creating an obedient child persona, as if somehow that would overcome the blow that would ultimately come — their finding out.

Going to the pediatrician's for a routine checkup was, for me, an extravagantly formidable event. For sure, when he looked into my ear, he would see something different, would find me out. Certainly when he checked my throat there'd be a clue down there! And if he didn't find some spot, some anomaly, some aberration with his silver instruments, little light and probing fingers, he'd note how cowardly I was when I had to get a shot. That cringing, that weakness, was a dead giveaway!

But, of exactly what? At that time, my image of the inside me was confused, blurred. The feeling went beyond the notion many children have that they are out of sync with their families or peers. I sensed deep in my marrow that I was wrong in some serious way, that it was only a matter of time before my vileness was uncovered. What it was I couldn't yet say, but in some inner secret sanctuary I seemed to have amorphous feelings that were not only different but heinous.

I loved kindergarten from the first day. Miss Gilmore always wore bright colors and exuded a good-natured, accepting aura. I suppose I've always preferred a structured environment, felt comfortable with rules and regulations, and this was structured *fun*. If I liked setting tables or refused to play with trucks, I have no memory of it. I remember the clay that came in different colors, out of which I recreated the family cat. There was a phonograph in the corner, cookies and juice breaks, sun streaming in through the large windows and generally carefree hours in the playground. It was a good way to dip toes into the waters of school, and I suppose it left me with the feeling that school was easy, simple and safe.

It was, but not for long. By first grade, definable shadows appeared. It seems that half the world's humans, including heterosexuals, complain of feeling isolated, disliked or out of step at some time during childhood or adolescence. Feeling that you don't fit in comes in many shapes and sizes — being part of an ethnic minority, economically disadvantaged or too small for your age — but waking up one morning having the wrong sexual orientation has to be among the worst. The sense of having a tainted soul, of being in some way sordid, deviant and dirty, is the deepest and most tearing shame possible. Now, the earlier vague sensibilities slowly began to crystallize. I felt for boys what I should have been feeling for girls: the flutter in the stomach, the tension, the urge and the pull. For me, it was a war I waged against myself for most of my life, a war I now know I was destined to lose.

Conscience or not, during those years my friend and I continued playing tum-tums when the weather was bad or when our mothers arranged play dates, but otherwise, Ted was veering into the neverland of baseball bats, hockey sticks and soccer balls, while I, already feeling the misfit, retreated into solitude or the company of girls.

Summers were the worst. All my grade school, and subsequently my early teen, summers went something like this: I was sent to a local camp, where the day began with baseball, followed by swimming lessons and then archery, where we shot arrows at bull's-eyes until lunch. Hating every minute of every activity, I despaired of being compared with natural athletes Tommy, Jimmy, Brad and Kip, whose arrows always came closer to the bull's-eye, who were stars in the water and on dry land, who were big shots at age six and seven and eight. By summer's end, my parents had to start talking about what camp to try next year, since Chris was so unhappy at this one. All the while I felt not only deficient but guilty. I was letting them down. Getting my father upset. I wanted to like camp and not trouble my parents. My brother took to it all like an Italian to pasta; why couldn't I? As always, I felt there was this terrible something, nameless and mysterious, wrong with me.

One day, the yellow camp bus picked me up at our old house and that afternoon dropped me off at a new one. I knew nothing of the large social and financial step my parents had made. All I knew was that our new house had a bigger and more beautiful room for me, and I would probably never see my old school friends, specifically Ted, again. If I had any pangs, they were short-lived. I was just beginning to feel like a persona non grata with the boys in the old neighborhood, and at my new school I would be given a fresh start.

If playing tum-tums was my first clear-cut homosexual memory, my amorous history did not actually begin in quite that focused a way. In my new neighborhood, I had crushes on girls beginning in second grade, tried to plant a kiss on Angela's cheek, kept calling Bethie on the telephone, walked home with Meggie, played with Deedee. I also liked boys and wanted to be with them, but the *feelings* I developed later that year for a boy named Sam were altogether different. Just as using words to describe the color blue or the taste of garlic is impossible, so is using language to describe a seven-year-old's sexless but sexual interest in another boy. Something pinged in my heart for Sam. Something stirred me. Something heated my little boy's blood when my mother, who was trying to interest me in same-sex playmates, asked me why I didn't invite a boy from my second-grade class to my house to play. Wasn't there anyone at all I liked well enough?

She called Sam's mother and Sam came over. We sat together at the kitchen table and drank our milk and ate our brownies. He had very dark hair and the sort of beige skin that looks year-round like a summer tan. He lived in a grand house a few blocks from ours, a gray, castle-like place surrounded by rolling lawns and boxy hedges. Like me, he had an older brother. Unlike me, he was athletic, sinewy, already muscular. I was in awe of Sam, more timid than ever in his company.

Sam wanted to go outside to play. When I was with other boys, even those much less dazzling than this neighborhood king, there was no question of who would take the lead. I shrank into compliance; it was never me.

The moment we got outside, Sam headed for the nearest tree. He wanted to climb right to the top. "C'mon, Chris!"

Not for me climbing, or taking physical risks. Not for me tearing my clothes, wobbling on branches that might break and send me hurtling to the ground. Heights, among a whole slew of other daring activities, were to be avoided at all costs. I made some excuse about not being allowed, the possibility of doing damage to the foliage or whatever, and so, determined to ascend something, he settled on climbing the pole that held the street sign on the corner. I stayed at the foot of the pole and watched while Sam began his climb.

And now, as he rose, I peeked at the skin under his shirt. The shirt had pulled out of his jeans, exposing a few inches of taut, second-grade flesh. What did it elicit in me? I don't know. I did not touch or make any move toward him, but my eyes must have burned too brightly; Sam became aware of my not-kosher interest. He felt it and now played on it, seemed to enjoy being the focus of my strange attention. Not inadvertently, he managed to raise his shirt higher, giving me more of a show. Not by accident did his body move in such a way as to allow my eyes a very brief picnic.

Until he turned on me. His dark eyes seemed to glow darker, and his face turned cold. It's as if he drew a line, sensing danger ahead. Nothing was said, but I could read the thought: What do you think you're looking at? A scrim went down. Sam tried, without success, to unlatch the street sign from the pole, and then he scrambled down. I felt he'd suddenly gotten afraid that things could go further. A look passed between us, still no words, but I read disdain and mockery, maybe even a tinge of disgust. The afternoon, and our relationship, soured.

I had just turned eight years old.

Things got better — until they turned worse. I found a new friend, Kevin Spencer. Kevin was not much of a student and about as reliable as a cocker spaniel. He was also not at all athletic, which is probably why we hit it off. I buried my secret deeper. Having a buddy gave me a shot of confidence, and lo and behold, I became outgoing, a bit of a fourth-grade clown. The teacher loved me (all my teachers loved me), my grades were good, as always, and I found myself in the heady situation of having classmates who actually thought well of me. We had an election and — whoopee and hoopla! — I was voted class president. My father congratulated me, my mother was proud. I had been hoisted into a zippy new life where I was respected by my contemporaries, lionized in my classroom and, for the first time, riddled with self-respect.

The joy was temporary. At what I now know was at the request of my mother, my father (not much of a football fan himself) began taking my brother and me to Jets games. It was a big deal. It's not that I liked the cold, the stadium or even football. I hardly even cared what was happening on the field. Tickets to Jets games were impossible to come by, therefore more precious than oil gushers, and gave me more status than being CEO of fourth grade. My father did not have just any old seats, either. We sat practically on the field in a special box, our spectacular corner of privilege. And Dad was magnanimous too, with extra programs, all the hot dogs, ice cream and sodas we could get down, and on this occasion a special souvenir.

It was a pencil sharpener shaped like a Jets helmet, all smooth and gorgeous green and white plastic, a showoff item of the highest caliber. I took this grandiose acquisition to school the very next day and displayed it on my desk for my peers to see. And there it sat in all its sportsman's eminence, tempting envy and, unfortunately, theft.

Sure enough, when I came back from lunch, it was gone.

"Has anyone seen Chris's pencil sharpener?" the teacher asked. I had reported the theft immediately, of course.

No one spoke up.

It was a day or two later that someone whispered in my ear, "Jeremy stole it. I saw it in his desk." Jeremy was a tough kid who lived in my neighborhood, a sneaky, beady-eyed guy with three older, even tougher brothers.

That's when I made the biggest mistake of my school career. I told the teacher.

She confronted Jeremy. "Do you have Chris's pencil sharpener, Jeremy?"

Jeremy said he did not. The teacher got up from her chair. I see her before me, walking down the aisle, moving in on Jeremy's desk with a stern face. She lifted his desktop and pulled out the pencil sharpener.

"Whose is this?" she asked him.

"Mine," he said without blinking. His face looked frostbitten, without so much as a twitch of revealing guilt.

I felt myself go from a pink blush to red-faced frustration. "It's mine. My father bought it for me last Sunday!"

"It is not! My father gave it to *me*."

The teacher wavered. She looked from Jeremy to me and back to Jeremy. "I'm going to put it on my desk until I decide what action to take," she said.

And there it sat, until one day it disappeared, stolen again.

The injustice made my mother angry. She called the teacher, with fuzzy results. The teacher summoned Jeremy and me up to the tribunal of her desk. She chastised Jeremy, but only slightly. The tantalizing pencil sharpener was never seen again.

Now Jeremy's three older brothers taunted and threatened me on my way home from school. "Baby had to tell the teacher, call his *mother!* We're going to get you! You're going to get paid back, tattletale!"

Our front doorbell rang repeatedly, but no one was on the doorstep when we went to answer it. A few days later our living room windows were pelted with raw eggs. I became afraid of walking to school or playing outside. My brother, not much of a fighter himself, wasn't interested in vanquishing my enemies, so I began to feel even more defenseless, scared and isolated.

But much worse than eggs and threats was my sudden fall from grace and popularity. Beating Jeremy bloody would have marked me as a man. Seeking justice from a higher authority, teacher and — worse — my *mother,* flagged me as a wimp. My status collapsed, my friends in class turned against me, I was washed up.

My life as the all-American elementary school scapegoat had its enduring aftermath. This experience and the many others that followed it produced in me a defensive layer of protection, turning me into a perpetual diplomat in my personal life and, later, in business. The accumulation of these demeaning incidents gave me, and probably other gay men who knew of their "irregularity" early on, a total immersion in straight-kid psychology, the tough-guy-don't-mess-with-me mentality. I learned to work around the potential physical responses of my childhood tormenters by often giving in when I shouldn't have, avoiding confrontation at all costs, holding back my own anger for the sake of peace.

Now it seems almost like a part of my DNA: it instinctively feels better not to alienate the adversary, whether he is stealing a pencil sharpener or a business idea. On the other hand, although I tend to fall into the habit of swallowing the vindictive juices and letting the problem play itself out at its own rate, these days I often have to take forceful action. Life and business have taught me that I occasionally need to adopt a tougher style. It sometimes even takes straight-kid psychology.

3

IN THOSE DAYS, I told my husband everything. There were no secrets between us then. If someone crossed me, he was right in there on my side, pitching hard. "Tell them to go to hell. If you don't, I will!" His eyes gleamed, his nervous tic ticced. He loved to throw verbal punches. Nothing increased his energy more than rising to the occasion of justified anger. "Get off my lawn, you damn kids!" "I made a reservation and I'm not waiting on any fucking line!" "You're in the wrong lane, jerk!"

Bob was as scrappy as an old pensioner under the best of circumstances, but when I began articulating my worries about Chris, his response varied from irritation to fury. At me. In his defense, most heterosexual men, then and now, don't want to hear that a son of theirs might be headed for the lavender world. And so the bull began to rage. "You're *wrong!*" he said. "I think you're dead wrong!" In one sense, his adamant denial was comforting. Since he was right about so many things, I assumed that maybe his was the voice of reason after all and that Chris was "normal." But later, Bob would turn on me. "If you keep saying it, you're going to make him that way!" The message I got was that somehow my words had the power of creating a catastrophe even if they were never overheard. Leaps of logic did not deter my husband from repeating this caveat many, many times over the next decade. It seemed to underscore the universal opinion that mothers had magic energy, a great capability for shameful mischief. One way or another, they had it in their power to be four-star mothers who could make their sons go sexually in the right direction, or washouts who could, by taking a misstep or two, cause their boys to turn out "that way." It's no wonder that during all those years I felt my responsibility like a little black dog that kept nipping at my heels, following me wherever I went.

In the climate of the sixties, when every TV comic made fag jokes, when the echoes of Joe McCarthy investigations of "links between homosexuals and communists" were still being heard, my general paranoia about having a homosexual boy was definitely in keeping with the Zeitgeist. Not that we needed a McCarthy to vilify "homos." My husband did a nice imitation of a limp wrist when he was describing a man who preferred men. So did most of his red-blooded, square-shouldered contemporaries. The term "gay" had not come into common usage, and "queers," "pansies," "faggots" and "queens" were the terms we used, without a twinge of conscience. "Very light on his feet," "from the Swish Alps," "fruitcakes with nuts" — we were all guilty.

Chris was born at the start of a chaotic decade during which a president was assassinated, the iconoclastic Beatles bulldozed into the culture, desegregated schools in the South created the catchword "white backlash," Martin Luther King led a Poor People's March on Washington, heroin became a middle-class problem and the Vietnam War killed off a generation of young men and the American taste for war. In this decade of sit-ins, peace marches, militant demonstrations, flag burning and riots, our suburb of Larchmont, New York, was an untouched freeze-frame.

Our male neighbors commuted to the city in uniform — gray or blue suits, white shirts, striped ties — discussed the Super Bowl and fought school busing, trimmed their hedges and, more assiduously, their hair, resisting the hirsute counterculture and its look, and took up a wholesome sport — golf, tennis or sailing — on weekends. Wives were at home not only to bake cookies and pay the repairmen, but to be benevolent watchdogs of their children and their neighborhood. I talk of neighbors, but we were them. We read what was happening in the world around us as if it were happening behind glass.

On the domestic front, there were no Oprahs then to expose what we now know was going on behind some neatly painted doors. Improbabilities such as incest, alcoholism and physical abuse existed then as they exist today, only these secrets were not out, so they did not exist as part of our landscape. The watchword was wholesomeness, and the local image homogeneity. In our suburb one did not see handicaps, obesity, faces that were not Caucasian or any deviation from an *Ozzie and Harriet* script. The unwritten rule everyone obeyed was: Keep in step, follow convention, conform.

Here things stayed pretty on the surface, with ethical standards set by the presidents of the garden club and the admissions committee of the country club. At a party I remember a neighbor saying, "I don't care what church anyone goes to, as long as they go." No one challenged the statement — even grammatically. We cruised along, served mint jelly with lamb, never wore white after Labor Day and kept unpopular religious and political beliefs chained in our attics. Tradition ruled with an iron fist, whether or not it was logical. What had been had to continue to be.

This was the atmosphere in which our family lived, what our son Chris was born into and was what was then considered an enlightened society. It goes without saying that I was not going around the neighborhood dropping any hints. On the contrary, I buried my worry so deep that it was years before I breathed the suspicion even to my open-minded mother.

But I spilled over to my Bob, and pretty often. Our boy was not playing baseball. Well, so what? Many boys don't play baseball. Still, when Chris passed boys playing ball in the street — any boys, any ball — he showed not even the slightest flicker of interest. Walked right by without so much as turning his head. I began to note how different his taste in television shows was from his brother's. No team sports, no *Star Trek,* no shoot-'em-ups, no blood, no gore. Chris was enamored of *I Dream of Jeannie,* and during play he imitated the genie. The genie was a *lady.* Why wasn't he pretending to be Captain Nelson? Why not Captain Kangaroo?

Every summer, after the boys spent a month at camp, we went to the country. The year that Chris was six years old, we went to

Wilmington, Vermont. The place was an inn, a farm and a cottage colony combined. We rented an A-frame cottage on the premises, took our meals family style at the main house with the other young couples staying there while our children ate separately. Teenage counselors took the kids off our hands during lunch, dinner and part of the day, leading them on hikes, hayrides and little farm excursions. It was paradise to have a family vacation and yet be free of responsibilities for hours at a time.

But it was not quite paradise. Christopher didn't like the kids' group. He didn't spark to the camaraderie of the boys his age, to the rough give-and-take, to the "in" bunch on the hay wagon or pickup truck. Forget playing group games, sleeping in a tent, playing tag or pinning tails on donkeys. He found a soul mate, a quiet, offbeat girl a year younger, named Laura. Laura and Chris, Chris and Laura. Everywhere I looked, there they were — always together and apart from the group, suspiciously weird. They didn't want to go anywhere. They'd rather pick berries or just sit around near the grownups. Our son — the son of two regular, with-it parents — was turning irregular and eccentric. In full view of the whole vacation crowd, he and Laura were the oddballs of summer.

It happened so many years ago, but I still remember when the resort's owner, a sharp young entrepreneur named Ralph, took Bob and me aside. Right away, I knew something awful was coming.

"Chris has some kind of a problem," Ralph said, and for me the sky went dark. No matter what he said, it would be something condemning. He wasn't unkind, just frustrated by this recalcitrant camper. His two little boys were gung ho to do everything, great at sports and self-confident as rock stars. His two boys would never in this life be caught talking to a girl, let alone one who was a year younger. "There's something wrong. When you get back to the city, you ought to go take him to somebody." Ralph was the first outsider to see what I'd been seeing most of my son's life, and those well-meaning, terrible words might have come direct from a blowgun, they stung so deep.

I remember how mortified and insecure a young mother I was.

Bob told him about Chris's eye — Chris was born with a strabismus that had been cosmetically corrected, but he had (and has) limited vision in his left eye — as if that explained his departure from normal-kid behavior. We both always ascribed Chris's lack of athletic skill to this disability, although Bob's brother is totally blind in one eye and has been a talented athlete all his life. Nevertheless, it seemed a credible alibi for the crimes of maladroit pitching and general indifference to sports. We defended Chris to Ralph and tried again and again to push our son into any kind of group activities, but it was no go. A chill crept into my heart every time I looked at my son. What was obvious to us and obvious to Ralph must be clearly visible to the world! At every turn, I saw Chris standing apart, head to head with the quirky Laura, not fitting in, the square peg in the round hole of our vacation and, in all probability, the square peg in the round hole of his life, and ours.

Having been confronted with Chris's persistent nonconformity, Bob reluctantly agreed to "go see someone." I made an appointment with the highly recommended, well-credentialed Dr. Rachel Stadler. She was fiftyish and the sort of psychologist my snobby young heart cottoned to. She spoke warmly with a hint of London, dressed like Greenwich and lived in Scarsdale. The lower level of her sprawling house was her office and waiting room, and a calm, noncombatant Bob and I proceeded downstairs for our consultation.

I did most of the talking. Bob fidgeted. His nervous tic in those days gave eloquent testimony to major league stress. Never mind what had happened in front of his eyes all summer and all the other cracks in his son's all-boy façade; he calmly expressed the opinion that I was "all wet." Nothing pre-homosexual about Chris. It was all in my head. Based on this, and on the opinion that I was the cause of whatever the problem was, if there even was one, Dr. Stadler and Bob heartily agreed.

Kind, well meaning but certainly not cuddly, Dr. Stadler guessed that given my lively pessimist's imagination, I was creating a situation that might turn a normal boy into a sexual deviate. I was doing things wrong, "overmothering." "You are feminizing your boy." Her words.

I was anguished. No, worse; I felt shot down. All the efforts to hold Chris at arm's length, to keep him nowhere near the temptation of my earrings and high heels — he never did parade in mother's finery as many little boys do — to banish him from the kitchen, to encourage my friends to bring their boys over for play dates, all my unkinking endeavors were thrown out with the bath water.

"What am I doing wrong?"

From our interview, when she'd dug and delved into the minutiae of our daily life, she now pulled rabbits out of her shrink's hat. Mostly, I wasn't to overprotect! Big dangers lurked there:

"Stop bathing him."

"I don't bathe him. I only shampoo his hair when he's in the tub."

"Let him shampoo his own hair."

"He's six years old!"

"He can shampoo his own hair."

To this day, I sting and smart at the next restriction she placed on me. "You must stop picking Chris up in your car after school."

"I only do it when the weather is bad!"

"Don't do it. He can walk home perfectly well on his own."

We lived almost a mile from the elementary school, and that mile was mostly uphill. There was no lunch program, so it meant a four-times-a-day trek in any weather. Thinking back now on all the times I let my six- and then seven-year-old walk or try to beg rides when it was really pitiless out there, when I stood at the window watching and listening to the rain and snow pelt the glass and waited for him to appear at the corner, it is all I can do not to wish the well-meaning Dr. Stadler just one uphill struggle in wind and snow and sleet and rain, to experience once what I see as a metaphor for my son's early life.

* * *

I've checked back to some studies published then, those guides put out by responsible publishers to which I turned for help in the absence of an oracle. Dr. Stadler had strongly admonished us to keep all of our suspicions private, and this turned out to be the wheat in the chaff of her therapeutic advice. We never breathed a word of any of this to a soul. Of course, letting Chris walk in terrible weather changed nothing, and letting him wash his own hair only meant his scalp was itchy from soap residue. As for the other stuff — fewer hugs and kisses lest they bond him perversely to Mom, as well as constant distancing for the same reason — only the couch knows what damage I did on a daily basis during those years.

From a study of 106 subjects conducted by Dr. Irving Bieber and his wife, Dr. Toby Bieber, in the early sixties, I discovered that the child who becomes a homosexual is usually overprotected and *preferred* by his mother. Uh-oh. That applied to my husband, whose mother had tried to conceive a child for eight years until he, often referred to as her little Jesus, was born. He was asthmatic in the bargain, and no more nourishing soil could have been found anywhere than in this household for developing one of *them,* but Bob certainly turned into a full-blooded, non-table-setting hetero.

Conversely, according to the study, the subject may be underprotected and *rejected.* Hmm. That applied to half the people I knew, men and women. Oh, those evil mothers: 81 were dominating and 67 were overprotective, 66 made that child their favorite, 64 made him excessively dependent, 62 tried to make an alliance with their favorite son against their own husbands, 62 were considered puritanical, 61 babied their favorite sons, 61 demanded to be made the center of the favorite son's attentions, 58 actually behaved in a seductive way.

A messy bunch of mamas; my head was spinning. Which of the above was I guilty of? Could somebody objective please stop me before I committed one of the iniquitous "deeds without a name"? And what did it mean to be seductive with a six-year-old?

It was the stuff of O'Neill plays; I wouldn't have known even how to begin.

If there had been support groups then, I would have looked for one that helped mothers walk lines thinner than a human hair. We would have requested equal time, asked for a control group of 106 heterosexuals. Sixty-six of us would have called our mothers strong, puritanical or just a generic pain in the butt. As it happened, there were no such groups and not much guidance, and despite studying the literature and pushing Chris into living the rugged life of a pioneer instead of a middle-class kid like every other child in his peer group, it was a downhill struggle all the way up.

When the neighborhood girls were a little older, no longer playing in the back yard after school, I remember my ongoing, endless search to find playmates for my son, who was caught in unwanted solitude. It was painful to see him at the window looking out at nothing at all, or in the doorway of the kitchen watching me prepare dinner. I had to hide my heartache when he wandered aimlessly through the living room or sat in front of the television in the den with only the cat on his lap for company. I see myself at the telephone talking to my friend Brenda, whose boy was a year older than Chris, trying to keep it light, trying to promote camaraderie between her son and mine. In those days, her boy was so popular, in such demand! And Brenda was ever complaining. "The kids march in here, they camp out in the playroom, I can't keep them out of the refrigerator, they're noisy, they're messy, oh, you should be grateful to have it so quiet!"

I never told her I would have given a year of my life to have the mess and the noise of a stampede of boys through my kitchen.

We've talked on the telephone lately, Brenda and I, and it's only now that we're willing to really come clean. All the time I envied her boy stampede, her homey madhouse, her husband's good-natured *fatherliness*, she was envying me for my husband's being such a good husband.

It's ironic that something went wrong later in Brenda's boy's life: he dropped out of school and turned against both his parents, became acid with bitterness and ended up very much alone. And it's also ironic that my husband's good-mate behavior turned out to have an expiration date, but that a fatherly seed in him began to grow little green shoots long after the children were grown.

It is twenty-five years later and I'm still struggling to discover the mystery of the cause and effect of parenting. Perhaps the answer is buried behind a star in some other universe, because it's clear that a quarter of a century later, it still eludes not only me but everyone else who has raised more than one perfect child.

4

- - - - - - - - - -

DURING MY EARLY school days, it is not exaggerating to say that I never felt altogether safe except at home, indoors. No bullets were flying in those days, but I imagined bullies were lying in wait behind every tree. It wasn't literally true, but they were the ubiquitous predators of the neighborhood, and if they saw me, most times they harassed me. My fear exceeded the reality, but if there was snow, I invariably became the target of snowballs. There were catcalls, shoves and sprays from water pistols. These were actually only occasional events, but I learned to take circuitous routes to school and back, just in case. And all the while I tried to look and act exactly like the tough kids who were tormenting me.

What was it about me? Whatever the boys in school saw was not readily visible to the naked eye. I was exempt from teasing and harassment in the Unitarian church Sunday school, where I made good friends of both sexes over the years. During vacations, too, I made short-term bosom buddies and fit in with whatever ad hoc crowd had gathered at the slope or on the beach. So what was this mysterious radar that seemed to be picked up only in the local precincts? Nothing shows in my face in the color photographs in our family albums; nothing strange about me in the home movies I watched years later, trying to pick up a raised eyebrow or giveaway sway. Yet there seemed to be signals I couldn't help giving off. I wonder if this invisible aura is the burden of all gay people, like those hand stamps that can be seen only under ultraviolet light. When I was growing up, I thought it was a bad joke of God's to turn me visible, like the time in Saint Croix when I wore an off-white short-sleeve shirt into the ocean as protection against the dangerous rays of the tropical sun. My mother had insisted I put on the shirt and by God, as soon as it got wet, it perversely turned a bright, incriminating pink. Me in pink on the beach! Had God Himself found me all the way down here in the islands, only to point an accusing finger at me from His seat in the sky?

It wasn't always athletics that separated me from the other boys. I look at old pictures and see that my classmates and I were dressed alike, pretty much an interchangeable bunch. I didn't lisp, walk funny, had no other affectations. What was it then? Did too lingering a gaze at Tim, John or Hank get them nervous? And while my contemporaries were developing that quirky boy-girl thing, self-consciously pummeling, pushing, teasing the object of their affections, I eased into relationships with the most "desirable" grade school princesses. We hung around together; they liked me. This of course was reason enough for the boys to set me apart, disentangle themselves from me. I look back on my social development as a day-in-day-out defensive battle, in school and out. And these days, when I talk to my gay brothers, I find that early adolescence was a universal peak time for pain and self-hatred.

I was in my own back yard one fall afternoon, sitting on the rocks that separated our property from our neighbor's. I was enjoying my favorite delicacy, those chocolate snowball cupcakes covered with coconut flakes and filled with cream. From out of the blue came Walt, one of the three children who lived diagonally behind us. He was a big-brother specimen, not one of the bullies I feared at school. A year or two older, an inch or two taller, with the confidence that comes with muscles and a marginal IQ, he swaggered toward me.

"You're on my rocks," said Walt.

As much as I feared these hard-boiled types, I could be simultaneously attracted to them. Sometimes, to my deepest shame, I developed crushes on them. Walt was a shadowy idol with broad shoulders and an attitude, whom I observed always from a respectful and reverential distance. Secretly, I had a minor thing for him. Though I can't describe this "thing" as specifically sexual, it clearly differed from a crush I had on my female first-grade teacher. That was a look-up-to-her kind of affection, which was different again from my feelings for certain female classmates, for whom I felt an I-want-to-play-with-her sort of puppy love. Watching Walt swashbuckle provoked an altogether different tension.

"Those are our rocks," I protested.

"The hell they are. They're our rocks."

And so on. I had recently been warned by my mother that I was to be courageous. "Stand up to them!" I took the advice to heart and stood my ground. It escalated. "*Our* rocks!"

"I'm gonna have to punch your fucking face in!"

There was a shove, I shoved back, and here was another thing: I didn't know how to fight. I didn't know how to put up my fists and swing or slug or plant one. I just flailed my arms in self-defense, a little grade school windmill. He swung at me and landed one to my chest, knocking the breath out of me. Predictably, I ran away, raced to the back door and pounded on it until it opened and my mother let me in.

"Whose rocks are those?" I panted.

"Our rocks. Now go back there and for God's sake stand up to him!" she said.

"I can't! He's bigger!"

"If you don't, he'll never leave you alone. You have to fight your own battles!" These clichés were the wisdom of the day, and probably still are. The reality is that fighting one's own battles is a waste of time. Knockouts and brawling are no-winners, whether done with fists or missiles, and a boy getting beaten up by someone older, tougher and taller is going nowhere at all.

My mother wouldn't let me in; I suppose she meant well. "He's probably a coward. Don't *you* be one!"

I pleaded, but she was unyielding. She wasn't going to overprotect me; she wasn't even going to protect me. She forced me to turn around and go out there and "let him have it."

So Walt and I faced off on the rocks, and the fight spilled over onto our lawn. If he so much as suffered a scratch, I don't remember it. I wound up with torn pants, a sprained finger, pain in my stomach and bruises from my temple to my jaw, not to speak of the bruises inside. He pummeled the hell out of me and told me if I ever stepped on his rocks again there was more where this came from. I bled a little from my ear, and nothing whatsoever was gained or resolved. Resounding defeat came from standing up for myself; I stayed off our own rocks for the year before Walt and company moved away, unless I was sure he was nowhere around. I never passed his house when I could help it, and when the other kids in his family passed ours, I looked the other way.

Certainly my parents' intentions were good. I knew that then and I know it now, but they both also managed to have human bugs. Many times they hit me psychologically where I live: I didn't understand my mother's reaction, nor her logic. At the time, though, I took it to mean that she, too, had a problem with my lack of square-shoulderedness. This began a long history of my trying to be what she, and more so my father, wanted me to be. I was very upset in this case, clearly losing my rightful defender, but converted my anger into concern over my mother's view of me. Despite what she perceives as her "withholding of affection," I never saw it in that light. It may be that in contrast to my father's limited show of feeling for me, my mother was at least emotionally available, if not overly demonstrative.

Now, I would hate to think any parent would expect his or her child to go into back-yard combat just to improve his "character." Combat at home, in the form of loud browbeating, took its toll too. It came from my father, who I greatly feared when I was very young. His destructive temper was tornado-like, striking without warning and often out of proportion to the cause. Perhaps it was my bike left in the driveway. Or I forgot to turn on the lawn sprinkler. Maybe I jostled him — my father hates to be jostled! — knocking something out of his hand. Once I drew an ink stripe across the rug in my room. My father's eyes would glow with fury, his voice would rise, he would be born again into a shaking column of rage. While it lasted, the eaves and the roof shook, the floor under his feet trembled. My mother's disapproving comments were not easy to take either, but there seemed a more rational and predictable pattern of cause and effect, punishments that fit the crime. My brother's sins, greater, more frequent and almost always school related, caused my father's anger to shake the sky. I cowered during these scenes, determined to toe the mark, to do better and never to break a single rule that could bring down this sort of wrath on myself. In the father-son tradition of the day, there was never, not once, a hug for either of us. Physical affection was reserved for the much beloved white cat and, in copious measure, our little white dog. (The tender ogre melted at the sight of four legs; we all did.) Dad's embraces for his children came in the form of hard currency or consumer goods, purchased most often in duty-free shops. But also, to be fair, in the form of hand-wringing worry — that we might get an infection, a cut, an allergy attack. It's how he folded us to his heart.

Living with my larger-than-life father, my hero and my nemesis, was like picking petals off a daisy: he loved me, he loved me not, he loved me . . . We were sitting at dinner in the elegant restaurant of the Wychmere Harbor Club on Cape Cod, on vacation, and my father suddenly decided he didn't like the way I pronounced my words. I was probably about ten years old, so happy to be here after doing time at summer camp, when the storm clouds began to gather. All eyes at the table turned to me. "You don't talk right. Your esses. Why do you say your esses that way?" Dad has a nervous tic and I tensed as I saw it come and go.

"What way?" What had I done wrong, said wrong? How was I speaking that was so displeasing to my father?

He had heard something in my pronunciation that sounded effeminate to him, but I didn't get it then. I kept trying to talk in the way he wanted me to, but I couldn't seem to get it right. "Don't pronounce the last letter so hard!" he was saying. He was angry. Getting angrier. The tic. I tried to say nothing, but he asked me a question. When I answered it, I pronounced my s the way he didn't want me to. And then, the t. It was too loud, or too sharp, or too something. He said a sentence the way he wanted me to say it, and when I imitated him, it seemed all right. A minute later I spoke another sentence, and my father threw down his napkin.

"Oh for Christ's sake!" I was all wrong again. He was red in the face, disgusted with me.

At the end of the meal, as we got up to leave, a woman at the next table smiled at us. "My daughter and I have been watching you all through dinner," she said sweetly, "and you know, we were both saying, you look like such a fun family!"

That comment was an intramural joke for years. Once, after packing the car for a family trip to Washington, D.C., my father became so enraged at the traffic on the George Washington Bridge that he turned the car around and took us all right back home, stopping at an amusement park on the way for a few hours, to appease us. Whenever there was strife — my recollection is that we all took a part in creating it, but my father often seemed the catalyst — someone would say, "But we're such a fun family!"

I knew Dad didn't like homosexuals. What father does? When I was twelve, he gave an industry award to Elton John, who was still in the closet but known to be gay. It was an eyeglass promotion, an honor bestowed on the singer because he owned hundreds of pairs of eyeglass frames and had done so much for optical fashion. A week after the ceremony, Dad brought home the publicity photographs. In one of them, the two men's hands were touching. I overheard my father's comment as he showed the photo to a friend. He made a limp-wrist gesture, pretended to wet his fingertip and touched his eyebrow. "I think he *likes* me," my father said with a knowing smirk. This was followed by big laughs all around.

And how did the cowering son of a man who ridiculed homosexuals feel about himself then? By this time, I feared I was destined to be more Elton John than Robert Shyer — and felt that dying in a ditch in Guatemala would be easier than disclosing this abominable secret.

I was missing not only the dignity of allowing myself to be who I was, but even one role model, living or dead, I could relate to. I hungered for ears into which I could whisper my secret, and I covertly sought help in the library, to no avail. No book, pamphlet or magazine to guide me along my isolated path. Were there no me's anywhere? From His and Hers guest towels to every movie and book and even the comic strips — there was for every hero a heroine, a he for every she. Love stories that were not heterosexual did not exist; the two actors who took part in every clinch, hug and kiss I'd ever seen on a screen, a stage or in real life were a man and a woman. The closet door was not only closed, but under lock and key, and still is, to most boys.

Love between members of the same sex? Never spoken of except in language so derisive that it seemed a special vocabulary had been invented just to describe it: degenerate, perverted, depraved. Even the syllables had an evil ring. I didn't learn the words until years after I had my first exposure to sex between grown men.

It happened in the unlikely venue of the Beverly Hills Hotel, where our family was staying under unusual circumstances. My mother was writing a segment for *I Dream of Jeannie*, the television show I adored with all my heart, and we were going to meet *the stars*, actually going to come face to face with the in-the-flesh Jeannie, Barbara Eden, and the true-life Captain Nelson, Larry Hagman. They were coming to the hotel to meet my mother, and my brother and I were permitted to sit in the lobby to witness this moment in history.

We waited in the glitzy lobby, kneeling on the cushions of a sofa to look over the back as patiently as possible, while ordinary mortals passed through and the clock ticked on. We waited what seemed like hours in a sort of bubble of suspense, eyes on the door, itching for a sight of the god and goddess of television. They kept us waiting forever, and during that forever my bladder began to fill. I ached to go to the bathroom, was desperate to relieve myself, but what if I missed the momentous event? Barbara and Larry were not likely to wait for me while I took a pee, were they?

I held it in, and in, and in, and just when it felt like I couldn't go another instant without bursting, the glamorous, magnificent genie swept in. Larry Hagman had been delayed, but here *she* was, a little boy's dream dripping in honest-to-God white fur, a full-length cloud-white movie-star mink. Kirby's flashbulb went off and immortalized this vision. My mother on the left, my idol on the right, toothpaste smiles, the photo shown to every visitor to our house for the next two years. At this pinnacle moment, I managed by some miracle not to wet my pants.

But as soon as my mother, father and the genie had swept off to the Polo Lounge together, I ran to the men's room, which as I remember was located down a carpeted flight of stairs. My brother was sent to accompany me, but waited outside and down the hall, eyeing some merchandise in the window of the drug-store–gift shop on the same level. In the men's room, I passed two men smoking at the sink. Cigarettes or marijuana? I'm not sure, but suddenly both men were in the stall next to mine. At first I thought they were fighting. I watched, frozen with fascination and immobilized with anxiety, while two sets of pants were pud-dled on the floor under the wall dividing our cubicles.

I stood there alert to something that was going on a foot away from me — but what? There was scuffling of sorts and guttural grunting noises, like snoring. I tensed, ready for what I thought would be throwing up, or maybe a fight. Then I heard the name Rex, which I remember because it was also the name of a dog in our neighborhood. "Rex," a sigh, a cry, a swallowed gasp, and then what sounded like sobs, and those hairy calves in socks and black leather shoes — dancing? The image is all mixed up with my reaction to Barbara Eden coming out of a bottle. I left the stall and then, too curious, ran back inside, locked the door, crouched to the floor and took a quick look. One on his knees, the other facing him, two hands clasped on the back of the head of the man kneeling — it was just a glimpse I got, an inchoate im-pression of white sleeves, black pants and bare buttocks covered with black body hair. Perhaps they were waiters or busboys. I knew they were doing something dirty, something wrong, but all in all, I didn't know what to make of it, and ran out of the men's room to find my brother. When he wanted to go back there and see for himself, I got cold feet. I told him we didn't want to miss

Larry Hagman, who was due any time now, and talked him out of it.

I told nobody else what I'd seen and put the episode out of my mind. It was easy to do; Larry Hagman was going to be at the hotel very soon, and sure enough here he came, big as life, with a fancy camera in a leather case around his neck, a Hollywood smile and — shockingly — a conversation peppered with non-prime-time profanity. Altogether, a confusing dazzle.

A bit of heaven, a touch of brimstone; it was a big day for a little kid from the suburbs. The murky exposé, sandwiched between the cloud-nine viewing of two deities, sank into a tunnel in my subconscious and stayed buried there for a decade.

5

- - - - - - - - - -

OUR FORTUNES ROSE. I suppose I was plenty spoiled in those days, used to getting what I wanted. Bob's eyeglass frame business was booming, and when Chris was six and Kirby almost ten, I decided what we needed most was about the only thing we didn't already have — a daughter. Bob, whose love for me was stronger than his antipathy for another bout of parenthood, went along with this heady gamble. We were prospering and could now afford household help, which would make this sort of a no-drudgery bonus baby for me.

Having my wishes granted was easier in those days than keeping the gray out of my hair. Past thirty and feeling very much an old lady, I worried about delivering a healthy child in "middle age" in days when most women had finished childbearing at twenty-five. Alone in the recovery room and coming out of anaesthesia, I examined the plastic bracelet on my wrist and read the verdict, typed black on white: SHYER, GIRL. Another wish granted; a perfect, healthy baby daughter and unparalleled joy on June 17, 1968! Alison appeared a month after Chris's seventh birthday. The sun was shining down on us from every angle, no doubt about it.

At that time, we moved to a larger, marvelous house in Larchmont. It was a stately white Normandy reminiscent of sugar castles, a winding staircase hidden in its turret. With leaded glass windows and surrounded by manicured shrubs, it sat on a street of ancient trees and prosperous neighbors. If there is such a thing as a Utopian suburban life, complete with a new white kitten and one of the best elementary schools in the county three blocks away, we lived it. I am not romanticizing a past, I am back there, remembering days so uncomplicated and untroubled that losing at tennis was as dark a cloud as passed over the rose-covered life we lived.

We had money, health, a live-in Jamaican housekeeper named Mavis, new friends, a busy social life, country club membership, grandparents by the carload. We bought paintings, the latest tennis racquets, a Mercedes. I had my career writing short stories for women's magazines, some television scripts, then novels, the shots of prestige and self-fulfillment that were enough to keep me from feeling like simply a receptacle for the next generation. I loved my husband and he loved me. His hair-trigger temper was an occasional issue, not a daily occurrence, and down deep we all knew he was tender as a peach. His outbursts were followed not only by gifts but by sincere remorse and a spell of exemplary behavior. I never lost sight of the fact that his selflessness and generosity allowed us our extraordinarily luxurious and carefree way of life. And so, in our blue heaven, I clipped recipes, cooked up a storm every night and let someone else clean up the dishes. I had time to be a full-time, hands-on, total mom.

A couple of years after settling into our new house, I remember standing at our front hall mirror and looking at my own image. I was pretty enough, healthy, privileged. You're living an MGM movie, I would think. I had a feeling things were too good. Having grown up as a somewhat lonely only child in much more modest circumstances, I never took anything wonderful for granted. Maybe, deep in some hidden psychological locker, I felt Chris was my comeuppance, the reminder that nothing could be altogether perfect.

He was getting older — almost nine — and his anomalous non-boy behavior was becoming more obvious. Mavis dropped comments, unwittingly putting the dagger into my heart. "He be like a girl, that one." It wasn't that he wasn't interested in ball sports. It wasn't only that he couldn't pitch or catch or play soldier or spaceman. Or that unlike his brother he didn't have buddies who sat around our basement rec room horsing around. Not that he seemed disconsolate or insular. He was in fact a mother's cheerful dream child at home, causing no problems, the best of all listeners and cooperators. Still, I counted these positives as warning signs, worried about the aggregate bunch of symptoms, the most chilling of which was his choice of playmates. Out the door he happily went, straight for the girls in the neighborhood. Of all the intransigent, enduring warning signs, that was the one that glowed bright red.

Courteous, clean, dependable, he was the favorite of the neighborhood mothers. Shunned or shunning the boys, he became a maestro at make-believe and created imaginative games that turned him into the Pied Piper of little girls.

Reading Bruno Bettelheim, the University of Chicago sage and authority on child psychology, I was both encouraged and despairing. In hindsight, I see Dr. Bettelheim's theories as misguided at best, but then, he was yet another of my print-media gurus. "It isn't that a boy at a certain age wouldn't like to be masculine. It isn't that he wouldn't like to be attractive to women and be admired and loved by them. It is that his fear of them is even stronger than the desire because of his earliest impressions . . . As a psychoanalyst I know there is practically only one source of homosexuality both in boys and girls, and that's the fear of the other sex." Score a point here for Chris's not being afraid of girls. And subtract two for his being devoid of even one true buddy of the same sex.

Until Kevin Spencer. At last, a respectable same-sex playmate, real and live, a best friend, came into Chris's life. Kevin was the brother of three sisters, so perhaps this full house of females had smoothed some rough edges, but I saw him as all boy. He and Chris found each other and our troubles seemed to be over. "You see?" Bob and I breathed our unspoken sighs of relief. We were raising a boy of a gentler nature, probably straight after all! The friendship blossomed. Kevin was at our house constantly. The boys went out into the back yard and played with little cars and trucks. We could relax! Now when Chris watched *I Dream of Jeannie*, he had a real boy friend to watch with him. It seemed wholesome, the right direction. His focus changed from Mama to a playmate and now — wonderful! — like my older, socially adjusted son, Chris was engrossed, busy, filled with joie de vivre.

During that school year, there was a respite from the bête noir of my worry. Maybe we'd actually managed to "elevate" Chris's future into the mainstream of normalcy. My little boy seemed happy and well adjusted enough, except for an occasional lapse. One in particular came out of the blue: I went upstairs to tuck him into bed one night, and his eyes welled up with tears.

"What's wrong, Chris?" His tears overflowed. As far as I knew, it had been an uneventful day and a peaceful evening. "What is it, dear?"

"Kevin said all boys have to go into the army."

"Well, not all boys."

"I don't ever want to be in the army!"

This brings a smile these days, when the front pages are filled with news of the pressure homosexual groups are putting on the military to get in, not stay out. Chris didn't want to carry a gun, fight, go into combat. I don't know if a revulsion of battlefields is gender related, but at the time I certainly thought so. If I was looking for signposts, they were still coming.

I told him the poor vision in his left eye would keep him out of the army. He was tremendously relieved and went happily to sleep. I did not of course give gratuitous hugs or comforting kisses he so desperately needed; he was lucky to get a light good-night smack on the cheek these days. The prevailing wisdom was that too much physical affection would induce homosexuality. Yet even this was contradicted in a case study I had recently read in a book by Peter Wyden on growing up straight. He described the case of a homosexual named Mr. Harrison, whose mother "belonged in the . . . fairly common category of mothers who help promote sexual identity problems by being detached from their sons." The comment that struck home was from Mr. Harrison. "One of the things that I missed most was being handled," he said.

To handle, how to handle, how not to handle. These were the moments I now dread to recall. Here was my natural and urgent pull to hold, hug, kiss and comfort my boy, in brutal conflict with the psychological signs of warning that were lowering in my head like gates at a railroad crossing. It was a constant forward and backward spin. Unlike my reflexive mother's affection with my other two children, I had to *think* before being demonstrative with Chris.

Kevin, the new friend, the godsend, was a likable and easygoing child, but scatterbrained and unreliable. Once, Chris was invited to a day in the Wall Street office of Kevin's father. What excitement! Chris, ever punctual, tidy and dependable, eagerly dressed in his Sunday best, sat waiting at the front window for the Spencers to pick him up for the drive to Chase Manhattan in the big city. There sat Chris on the window seat, watching for the familiar station wagon. There I was, looking at the clock. The Spencers never came and no call did, either. "Oh, that boy is off in his own world," his mother, off in hers, later apologized. Kevin had forgotten to notify Chris that the trip had been postponed. So had she.

There are children raised in the country on farms, or in the wilderness or in lighthouses or on mountain peaks, and I'm aware that they survive lonely hours perfectly well. I also know that many children prefer solitude, and that for every lonely homosexual boy there are others who are heterosexual and have felt equally alone. There is also no doubt that in a world that is filled with children who are abused, abandoned, starving and disabled, these disappointments seem trifling, but to a mother, the look of desolation in her child's eyes, that ongoing menu of injury, is a sore and heavy personal heartache.

When Kevin was unavailable, my lonely son would hang around his toddler sister by default. If Alison wasn't old enough to play with, at least he could tease her. If he couldn't throw a ball, he could toss a pillow at her and get her to laugh. Or he could grab a toy and hold it out of her reach until her laughter turned into a howl, then a siren. Making his sister laugh and then cry became a pattern for Chris and the trigger that invariably detonated Bob's anger. In my memory, teasing Alison is not only the biggest but possibly the only misdemeanor of which Chris was ever guilty.

Chris's record in school and at home was always exemplary. He was never fresh or late, sloppy or disobedient. He was loving toward the cat and, unlike his siblings, was quite willing to walk our West Highland terrier. When Charles Lamb wrote, "A sweet child is the sweetest thing in nature," he must have meant a boy who hung up his clothes and kept his desk neat, remembered everyone's birthday and behaved always like a miniature adult. Chris.

Ordinarily, this little epitome of cooperation was guilty of no sin of commission, which is why whenever Alison let out a wail, or even looked as if she might, his father focused his anger on Chris so severely. Over the years, when Alison became older and took a part in encouraging him, Chris played with her until somehow the game turned sour, and she let out her familiar personal shriek, alerting Daddy, who intervened vigorously. Chris took a lot of excess heat from Bob for relatively innocent sibling skirmishes.

From me, too. In research I did for a book I wrote about a mentally retarded girl, I saw that even loving and sensitive parents treat handicapped, "aberrant" children differently. The very human and deeply buried feelings of embarrassment or revulsion come into play, and translate into a sort of "holding back" of affection at best, and overt hostility at worst.

Although this comparison may seem somewhat of a stretch, the undercurrent of tension based on distaste and spiced with frustration is somewhat the same. One adores one's own "different" child, one's heart breaks again and again over others' view and treatment of him, but then, in a moment of stress or fatigue, when he makes his sister cry or knocks over a glass of milk, one makes him the target of overreactive or misplaced wrath. Often followed by cascades of remorse, rivers of guilt and, sometimes, overindulgence. (The children's cupboards were filled with gifts Dad brought home after one of his blowups.)

One day, as I sat in the den hemming a skirt with Chris and Alison on the couch next to me, Chris asked if he could sew. I said, "No, you're a *boy!*" Then, out of boredom, he began the sort of harmless gesticulation that was momentarily about to turn his toddler sister's laughter into a resonant shriek. If there is a scene in everyone's life one would like to rewrite and replay, that three-second interval would be mine: I poked his thigh with the tip of the needle I had in my hand. He let out a scream. "I warned you to stop!" I cried.

I had warned him once, but to this day I hardly understand how I was capable of pricking my son's leg with a needle. This was me acting out, Mommy, a rational grown woman, a mother who adored her child, who had never given any of her three children more than a smack on the behind in days when physical punishment was not as anathematized as it is today. How could I have done such a thing? On that day I would have said Chris drove me to it. I would have called myself tired, or cooped up too long, irritated by something extraneous like menstrual discomfort or car problems. I would have blamed it on all sorts of things but never looked at the real issues: my ever-seething anxiety and a good dose of homosexual antipathy hiding in some dusty psychological secret passage.

Recently I had dinner with a friend. We were discussing a local boy who stands accused of breaking into the home of a couple in town, both physicians, and stabbing them to death in their beds as they slept.

"Well," my friend said, discreetly lowering her voice, "the boy comes from a really screwed-up family."

"How so?" I knew the boy's father was a banker, his grandfather well known in local politics, his mother a former president of the Junior League. These substantial citizens were churchgoing Catholics in the bargain.

My friend's children were well acquainted with the siblings of the accused and she spoke with some authority. "Many problems. One sister had a baby out of wedlock, and at least one of his brothers is gay . . ."

Murderers, unwed mothers, gay men, spoken in the same breath and tarred with the same condemning brush. These words came from the mouth of a sophisticated and educated business-woman in the 1990s, who is neither unkind nor disparaging. And this might have been my voice not so long ago.

We tried another therapist. This time we went to a kingpin in Manhattan, an expert in the field of the development of gender identity. I'd read about him during one of my bouts of research in the local library and wrote a note requesting a consultation. Dr. Isaacs was a psychiatrist with a flourishing practice on the West Side, and I saw him as a potential lifesaver.

What had precipitated this appointment was a late summer event at our country club. I'd taken Chris to the annual kids' barbecue, a low-key party arranged for members' small children every August. When I dropped him off, the beach was already teeming with exuberant kids who would spend the afternoon playing games, swimming and eating hamburgers and hot dogs. Chris, always looking for social interaction, was game to go. I left the club somewhat optimistic; he'd spend a few hours in the sun-shine, maybe meet some new kids, possibly — a long shot? — make a friend.

When I came to pick him up a few hours later, my heart sank. I was greeted with a scene fit for a Fellini movie: children of all ages making merry on the beach while my son, a miniature professo-rial specimen, walked in slow motion alone on the boardwalk, black umbrella raised over his head to ward off an insignificant, slight drizzle that had begun to fall. While his contemporaries cavorted through the mist, my nine-year-old senior citizen had gone to our locker and found his father's spare umbrella. What this eccentric behavior had to do with sexual orientation I had not a clue, but I felt it spoke volumes. At the time, it never occurred to me that Chris was just doing an accurate imitation of his father.

I brought my worries to Dr. Isaacs at his West End Avenue office. It was paneled, dark, impressive. All psychiatrists should have walls of books, windows of leaded glass and little half-glasses over which to look sternly at patients. This marionette of a man had surprised me by greeting us with an effeminate lisp. He was married, however, so in my youthful naiveté, I guessed he must be straight. It passed through my mind that sometime in the past he'd bent himself against the grain into the proper sexual orientation. Perhaps that sort of wisdom was a bonus, since that would give him greater insight, make him more than just an authority on paper.

He listened intently and asked questions that seemed irrelevant. When had Bob and I sexually consummated our relationship? How long was our baby nurse staying with the new baby? What did Bob think of my mother? How did we spend Sundays? The Q and A's lasted for hours. Chris sat quietly in the waiting room. We always told him these conferences had to do with his visual acuity or physical coordination, and taking our explanations at face value, he went obediently along and never asked further questions.

Dr. Isaacs finally called Chris in and incorporated him into our meeting. More questions: Do you like school? What games do you like? Do you have bad dreams? On and on. His feelings about his brother, his sister, his teacher, ad infinitum. I assumed he was moving toward a mysterious goal known only to medical practitioners with very long training in psychiatry. It all sounded so schematic, like a courtroom melodrama. At any moment I was expecting to hear "Aha!" and get a blueprint for future action, right out of some esoteric textbook.

"He's very bright," Dr. Isaacs announced when he'd sent Chris back to the waiting room. "And although I appreciate and understand your concern, I have no guarantee as to what his sexual preference will be when he grows up." Then he advised Bob to be very much a part of Chris's life. Suggested pitching balls to him in the back yard or involving him in some father-son activities, like Boy Scouts. Old news — didn't we know all that? Never mind, it was a relief to hear it verified by this Great One. And he said we were not yet doomed to be parents of a queer. There was hope. Maybe he'd turn out "all right."

Hearing from this lofty shrink that Daddy had to pitch balls to Chris had a greater impact on Bob than my consistent prodding. While both our minds were spinning on the pivot of activities Bob and Chris could possibly enjoy doing together — cutting the grass? washing the car? walking the dog? — Dr. Isaacs suddenly took out his big gun and torpedoed me.

"There's one thing that worries me about you," he said, sitting so small but so regally powerful behind his mammoth desk. He was speaking to me.

I must have frozen in my chair. I'd squeezed every drop out of my heart to put in front of him, given him didactic proof of my best loving intentions toward my child, and here I was, suspect? transgressing? What now, for Christ's sake?

"I think you have a problem with motherhood," Dr. Isaacs intoned.

I knew I had a problem maintaining my weight, a problem with tennis, an occasional problem with Bob's personality, but one thing I'd always felt good about was motherhood. I didn't like Chris's gender problems, but I'd always liked being a *mom*. Until now, I thought I had a talent, enjoyed it most of the time and was really good at it.

What had I said in the last hour and a half that was a sinister tipoff to this sensor of the subconscious? What question had I answered wrong?

Dr. Isaacs continued: "You had a baby nurse. You had her for four months. Why didn't you want to take care of your baby yourself?"

There it was. Mea culpa. We could afford a nurse, who relieved me of feedings every four hours, diaper changing and interrupted family dinner hours. Allowed me to continue writing and guaranteed me eight hours of sleep. I'd hired someone else to assume the grunt work in infant care while I did the fun part — feeding or cuddling the baby when I was rested and unhassled. Singing a lullaby only when I felt like it. I never did enjoy the spitting-up part, the rock-the-carriage-to-get-the baby-to-stop-screaming part, the oil-the-scalp routine. Having gone through it all twice before, it had been sybaritic to mother selectively those first four months.

The real mystery is why we took anything Dr. Isaacs said so seriously. Swallowed every word as if what little information he had conveyed had been divinely inspired by the holy spirit of his hospital residency. In fact, he was not the last member of his profession to take a cockeyed turn with us. Seated in the impressive ambience of leather and mahogany, we were open-minded and ingenuous subjects, easy targets. The word "expert" held hope and magic for us every time.

Then and now, I'd be willing to bet that one can get sagacious advice from half the psychotherapists in America. And half the waiters, hairdressers and bellhops as well — if one picks carefully. It's a question of faith, timing and blind luck.

6

- - - - - - - - - -

MR. PAULSON STOOD in the gym, the whistle gleaming silver
on a string around his neck, the volleyball, soccer ball or softball
gripped in both his hands. The distinctly simian phys ed teacher
with black hair cut butch, a heavy horizontal eyebrow stripe and
long, powerful man's-man arms was our machismo role model
and perfect enough to be bronzed. This muscle of a man was an
excellent specimen except for one thing: he was missing a part, a
small chunk of the brain, the feeling depot. An automaton moving gracefully across the gloss of the shellacked gym floor, he was
so at home here he might have been born in a locker, conceived in
a place where there were basketball hoops and climbing bars. He
thought of nothing except catching, throwing, running, scoring.
For him, life began and ended on a clipboard. Not intentionally
vicious or malevolent, he was the curse of my sixth-grade life.

Here in the gym is where our athletic skill, aka manhood, was
tested. This cavernous, high-ceilinged purgatory is where, already
on the threshold of self-doubt, I was humiliated week in and week
out. Here I was pummeled and battered psychologically, embarrassed and ridiculed, because here is where Mr. Paulson, with his
tacit mark of disapproval, tagged me as a useless clunk for all my
world to see.

They don't do it anymore, but it was standard procedure then
— two sixth-grade boys, the captains, the stars, were asked to
pick their teams. The captains picked boys in order of their prowess on baseball or football fields or on basketball courts. Guess
who was always picked last? Guess who cringed, turned inside
out with humiliation, always to be singled out as the lowest of the
low-rungers?

Worse was the measurement of our ball-throwing ability. This
was a nationwide test, in which the distance one could hurl the

ball was recorded in some serious hardcover work of phys ed reference. The procedure was to have each boy throw the ball, while a few other boys stood eighty or ninety or one hundred feet away, depending on the thrower's prowess, ready to catch the throw.

When it was my turn, with Mr. Paulson watching, the boys circled within ten feet of me, doubling over with mirth as they urged me to try to get it all the way to their feet or their baseball mitts. Burning with the red fever of despair, more than desperate to get the ball into the arena of a decent throw, I tried too hard, flailed my arm and repeatedly reinforced everyone's image of me as klutz/wimp/girl. And Mr. Paulson stood by and not only allowed them to publicly humble and disgrace me, but sometimes smiled his humorless hangman's smile at my classmates' jeers.

Later, when the derision continued in the locker room, when Bill or Gil or Phil razzed and bullied me, when it became hip to push me into a locker, make fun of my throwing or catching score, or whap me with a towel, Mr. Paulson made not a move to save me or stop them. For reasons that burned and baffled me, Mr. Paulson always managed to look the other way.

If my mother tried hard to point me subtly in the direction of heterosexuality, Mr. Paulson could not have been more overt. His message was loud and clear, but hating him could only be internalized, because any sort of open confrontation would have been too hazardous. My fear of intensified cruelties from my classmates also overrode any inclination to appeal to his human side and beg for a change of procedure. His response would have been to single me out, and to be treated differently than the others in public would certainly have led to even more egregious roasting.

What happened in gym washed over into the classroom. It became unfashionable to be seen in my company. It became fashionable to ridicule and make fun of me, trip me in the aisles, knock books out of my hands. Oddly enough, I was not even a very effeminate boy. I was neither overweight nor underweight, and looking at old photographs now, I see a perfectly attractive boyish image. I dressed exactly like my contemporaries with the exception of sneakers. Why did I prefer leather shoes always? Sneakers on my feet remained pristine and clean, while the other boys' were scuffed and worn from the sandlot or playground. Sneakers were a symbol, a constant reminder of what I wasn't but aspired to be. And so all through my school days and to this day, I prefer unobtrusive dark leather on my feet.

So what was it about that eleven-year-old me, anyway? I wasn't a lisping caricature of limp-wristed foppishness. I copied all the male paraphernalia in vogue at that time, walked with shoulders erect and hips steady, like a little man. I admit I did care more than my contemporaries that my shirts were clean and my pants pressed, and I didn't much cotton to the blue jeans that were becoming ubiquitous. I took an interest in sartorial correctness then, and I suppose I do now. If that is a clue to my bent gender, let's put it into the medical literature. Let's change the old saying from "Clothes make the man" to "Too much interest in clothes makes the man suspect."

Never much of an actor, I was given the smallest possible part in the sixth-grade production of *Hamlet*. Another "soft boy," Tim Strauss, was chosen to play a leading role. We were two of a kind and could have been friends, but he was clearly afraid to be tainted by association with me. He escaped becoming a scapegoat for mysterious reasons, but was just as isolated and friendless. He later signed my sixth-grade graduation program "To the fairy," and is now out of the closet himself. I played the silent part of a palace guard, and although I would have given anything for a major role, was grateful not to have to memorize dialogue and risk possible further disgrace. Of course, I was happy to be part of the excitement of the production. The ham part of me loved being on stage, and the costume — puffed sleeves, tights, a wide belt and magnificent cardboard sword — was terrific.

There was high-pitched excitement and a pulling together on the big night as we peeped out of the curtain at the packed house. I spotted my parents in the audience. My father, often away in Europe and the Far East on business these days, was in town and attending this milestone event. That alone was good enough reason for my wanting it to be a stellar show.

We did our eleven-year-old best with the Bard, no one forgot lines or knocked over the cardboard trees, and the curtain went down to prolonged applause. Within minutes, my mother was backstage singing the praises of the production, the scenery and the actors. My father, right behind her, was characteristically more interested in the logistics of getting us home, pushing me along to go change so we could beat the traffic tie-up in front of the school. It seemed to me even then that my father never touched the base of here and now, but lived in some outfield of the near or far future, always coordinating forthcoming operations.

"Go change, hurry up, go change," he urged. My father had, and has, a way of saying everything more than once. It's as if he doesn't trust the first delivery to be heard, obeyed or believed. And again, more insistently, "Go change!"

I hurried to the classroom that had been designated as the boys' dressing room. There I took off my sword, my tights, my puffed-sleeve shirt. There were temporary clothes racks that had held our costumes and on which our street clothes now hung, and I went to the section of the rack on which I remembered putting my clothes on a hanger. At first I thought I'd misplaced them, confused the spot. Maybe I'd put them closer to the rear of the rack? Or maybe someone had thrown his coat over my shirt and pants? Where were my things? Some boys hadn't hung their clothes up at all, but had thrown them across desks or on a bench in the back of the room. With my mind on my father waiting in the hall outside, I scurried about the classroom in my underwear, going through piles of clothes, pulling at the hangers on the rack, becoming more and more anxious. No sign of my pants, my shirt, my down jacket.

I became aware of four of my classmates, Jeremy included, who were tittering together in a suspicious huddle near the teacher's desk. They were watching me and filling the air with the usual mocking ridicule.

"Can't find his clothes!"

"Hey, I wonder what happened to his stuff!"

"Did someone make his pants disappear?"

They laughed, taking time to make a ball out of a pair of socks and throw it at me.

My father's patience could be stretched only so far. His face appeared in the glass window of the door, looking for me.

"What'd you guys do with my clothes?"

Now other boys, in various stages of undress, noticed me scurrying around in underpants and T-shirt, shivering, nervous and worried. Tonight I was less afraid of my classmates than that my father would burst into the room and make a scene. That would mean humiliation today and living hell tomorrow.

"Where are they?" I asked of no one in particular.

The boys-will-be-boys boys leaned against one another for support and hilarity. "Where are they?" they mimicked.

"My father's waiting!"

"Ooooh! Daddy's waiting!"

Sixth-grade harassment was contagious. Parts of the Elizabethan wardrobe came flying at me from every direction. Someone had grabbed my cardboard sword and was coming at me.

My fidgeting father had spotted me through the window and was gesticulating. He wanted to know what was taking so long. Finally, Hamlet himself took pity on me. He whispered, "Your stuff is in the boys' bathroom."

In order to get there, I had to retrieve my costume, while socks and gloves flew, put it back on as my classmates howled, borrowing from Shakespeare — "So much for him!" "He is pigeon-livered!" "Get him to a nunnery!" "Methinks it is like a weasel!" The laughter followed me as I ran out of the changing room.

I had to pass my father, whose familiar anger was about to bubble up in the school corridor. Other boys and girls were ready and leaving. Why weren't we? What was taking so long? Why the hell was I back in my costume? My mother was standing nearby, trying to tranquilize my father and looking at me with her antennae up. "Where are your clothes?"

I didn't want to answer.

"Where are your clothes?"

I headed for the boys' bathroom.

My father had turned up the volume. "Where are they? Answer your mother!"

It turned out they'd stuffed them into the bathroom wastebasket among the used paper towels and pushed down the lid.

"Who did that?" My father was outraged. My mother seemed frazzled with concern. "*Why* did they do that?" she wanted to know. And the unspoken question I read in her eyes: Why you? Why always you?

It was during gym class that year that I first heard myself called "faggot." Although my ball-sports skill was at zero, I could run fairly well. I was a sprinter, and on this testing occasion we were to run the hundred-yard dash while Mr. Paulson, stopwatch in hand, stood ready and alert with his whistle and clipboard.

"Shyer!"

I stood crouched and ready on the starting line.

"Go!"

Off I went, a streak in blue shorts and white shirt, the pristine sneakers galloping forward.

Mr. Paulson announced my running speed to God and my classmates — and whatever it was, it was very low, and it was very good.

But my moment of triumph was short-lived.

"Of course he can run fast," snickered someone to my left or someone to my right. "He's a faggot. He's got to keep running to keep away from us."

Oddly enough, the meaning of the word "faggot" to those boys was not at all what it meant to me. To them it meant I was weak, wimpy, unathletic and not one of them. To me it meant the sky had fallen: by this time I knew what the feelings I had were, by this time I knew what "faggot" really implied, and I thought they were on to me. They knew my disgusting corruption; my secret was out. "Faggot" rang in my ears for weeks and months.

Until I got used to hearing it.

It hadn't come to me in a single moment or epiphany. Little by little, the derisive terms began to ring a disquieting note in my consciousness. By sixth grade I realized I was more aware of the boys in their bathing suits in the school swimming pool than interested in their conversations in the locker room about who was starting to fill out her bikini. And, between Sam in second grade and the time when my voice began to change, I witnessed too many times boys in my class making fun of one another for sitting too close together or inadvertently touching each other in anything other than a backslap or shoulder punch. Words used to describe homosexuals seemed to describe my secret feelings.

It was like that time I had been dreading for weeks in sailing class: capsize practice. Fear of being thrown overboard had haunted me all summer, and now the day was finally here.

It was windy, the water seemed unusually tempestuous, my teeth were chattering. The sailing instructor waited until we were a mile off shore and then sprang it on us. We were going overboard to survive "turtling," and the time was now!

The boat cut through the water at what seemed like race-car speed until the instructor flipped it completely over. I found myself in the shock of glacial water, tangled in a thousand lines and fallen sails. Panicky, desperate, terrified, I struggled not to be pulled down into the death grip of Long Island Sound, which seemed intent on sucking me into its deep.

It's pretty much how I felt about the dangerous grip of my sexual pull.

How did I get past all this? What made me so strong was a combination of things: my vacation friendships that confirmed I was not the pariah my schoolmates considered me; my continuing friendship with Kevin Spencer, who lived across town and saw none of the torment I was living through locally; the fact that I was beloved by six grandparents, that I was the "good" son in my parents' eyes and had a "groupie" who loved me — my sister, Alison. In those days, I never felt lonely. The real meaning of that word would be spelled out, in capital letters, later.

7

- - - - - - - - - -

Recently a friend called to tell me about a party she'd been to. The hostess's husband seemed "faggy," she said, and knowing my son is gay, she quickly corrected herself. "Of course, I don't mean that in a way that — well, you know what I mean," she said, embarrassed.

I'm not sure now about what adjectives are simply demeaning and which are clearly prejudiced, and if I police my friends' casual comments I won't have a single friend left, but I know that "faggy" is not a flattering description of anyone. The innuendo, to my sensitive ear, describes all sorts of troublesome human behavior — visible frailty, personal weakness, sexual aberration. I know what it feels like to hear the word applied to one of my children, whether it is the intention of the user of the word to be derogatory or is merely a thoughtless slip of the tongue.

About a month after the Shakespeare episode was the day I first heard the word "fag" used in reference to my son. He walked into the kitchen, threw down his books, put his head on the table, circling it with his arms. His shoulders shook. I hadn't seen tears in years. "What is it! What?"

"They threw me against the fence after school. Everybody started calling me 'fag.'"

I was having a cup of coffee, and I remember going to the sink to pour out what was left in my cup. I couldn't get another drop down.

He looked like any other boy. Where was the mark, the emblem, the insignia? I couldn't see it. He went to school dressed the same way as his classmates (this year the rage was bell bottoms and circle zippers), for all practical purposes a clone of every white, upper-middle-class sixth-grade boy in Larchmont, New

York. He came home distressed, despondent and, now, in tears. He hadn't cried since I don't know when, and in those days of gender-related rules of behavior, tears were generally not a standard boys' response to anything short of a death in the family. I was beside myself. If they were labeling him, what choice would he have except to think of himself as a fairy?

Within a week, I was in conference with his teacher. I could not speak the word "fag." Mr. Lucardi hadn't known about the episode in the playground or the one the night of the play, but he knew full well that Chris was currently the target of a great deal of "teasing." If I spoke the word "fag," I thought the very echo of that syllable would bounce off the classroom walls, reverberate through all the cells in the teacher's brain. He must not associate the two words "Chris" and "fag." Surely if I put them into the same sentence, I would damn my child with that label and all it signified. The teacher said he would make every effort to stop the teasing. I thanked him and said I hoped I wasn't overreacting, but shouldn't school be a pleasant experience? How would Chris learn anything if he was always under fire? Mr. Lucardi, young and inexperienced, said he'd try to correct the other boys' behavior.

It didn't let up. Some weeks later, I found myself sitting in the principal's office. Mr. Coates was an affable man who had taken a Dale Carnegie course, which he said had enormously improved his ability to deal with people. He had many children of his own and was more than understanding, extraordinarily empathic and eager to help. He said that there was a scapegoat-designate each year in sixth grade. It was sort of a tradition, seemed to come with the onset of puberty. "It's just the way it goes. I see it every year. There seems to be no reason for it, and there is definitely no correlation between the boy chosen and any imperfection in that child." He smiled warmly, said he knew that Chris was an exemplary student and promised to see what he could do. I never used the condemning F word in his office, either. I know now what I didn't know then: "fag" as an epithet was not invariably meant to describe sexual behavior by sixth-grade boys. The kids weren't necessarily pointing a finger at him as someone whose erotic life was destined to be different from theirs. Only, I was absolutely sure they were. "Fag" was a term in general use, thrown about indiscriminately, sometimes even among friends, if not affectionately, at least harmlessly. It was only I, who suspected Chris's predilection, to whom it was a crucifixion.

It also turned out that trying to restore the good standing of a boy with his peers is like climbing a glass mountain, even for a popular teacher or a school principal who's taken a Dale Carnegie personality course. Their intervention counted for nothing, and the harassing continued.

At that time, it was hard to tell which of us — Chris or Mom — the almost daily Sturm und Drang was making more unhappy. Yes, he was living through hell at school, but I was locked into very dark depths of my own. Oh, the ceaseless bite of worry! In those days, Chris's misery dug into the young me with a terrible ferocity. If he was being scalded like this in school, what was to come in life? My young-mother self was locked into the constant struggle of trying to help, in some way to strong-arm the world around my son. Let his peers please respect him if they couldn't learn to like him. Or at least make them back off, for God's sake. It was all I could do to keep my own in check when my son's tears fell.

School hurt; home hurt less. My impression was that Chris was spending too much time in the house with the feminine trio of mother, sister and housekeeper. It was the way we were thinking then, when we were also frying chicken in butter and sunbathing all summer because we thought suntans were glamorous and healthy. Kirby had gone off to prep school and Daddy was traveling constantly. I asked Bob to take Chris with him on one of his business trips. A few days together with his father, man to man, is what Chris desperately needed. It was seventies logic and I really pleaded; a school holiday loomed. Bob refused. "You're exaggerating," my husband said. "There's nothing wrong with Chris. Get off it." Less than six months after our visit to the auspicious

Dr. Isaacs, all ball throwing and trips to the hardware store had ceased by father and son's mutual consent. Now, two years later, even the echo of the doctor's words of advice had faded from Bob's memory, or, it seemed to me, his sphere of interest.

On the other hand, his interest in travel grew. My husband took me on spectacular trips — that winter to Acapulco, or was it Antigua? I see myself packing and worrying, always eager to go, be free, and then not wanting to leave. There was the push and pull between Bob and my children as we ran off to Europe, to Asia, to Hawaii, to the Caribbean, my heart in my throat every time our plane left a runway. And every year, because an industry trade show took place that week in May in Milan, Mommy and Daddy were not at home on Chris's birthday. Of course, we had a celebration at home before we left and called Chris on his day, and it goes without saying that there were always mountains of gifts, a party, a cake with candles, but Chris still reminds me that we were there for Kirby, there for Alison, but never home, even once, on *his* birthday. For him, our absence every year on his day was a significantly bigger deal than I thought. It was the annual, unavoidable circumstance, but for me, twenty-five years later the guilt, too, is deeper than I thought.

When Bob turned me down about taking Chris on a trip, I called his brother, Henry. Again, it was my back-then view of the necessity for one-on-one interaction with either a father or a father figure, and this was an unprecedented move into last-resort territory. Although he was also Bob's business partner and they saw each other every day, our families were not close, and Uncle Henry was not really a prominent figure in the lives of our children. He had his own son and daughter and was an involved and praiseworthy father under his own roof. He was also the far side of the moon as far as a choice for a role model: a good-natured, backslapping, joke-telling, big bear of a stereotypical salesman, a middle-aged teenager who loved to spend every dime he had and then some. I guess I would have preferred sagacity, depth and intellect, but a good man was a good man, and Uncle Henry had a very big heart.

"Henry, I'd like to ask you a favor." He must have had a jolt to hear my voice on the telephone, since I don't think I'd ever in my life called him, and certainly never to ask for a bizarre favor. "Would you consider taking Chris with you on your next business trip?"

I owe Uncle Henry respect, gratitude and a winning lottery ticket for his immediate reply. "Sure." That was all. No questions, no hesitation, no probing for motives, just a warm and soft-hearted promise to include his nephew in his next itinerary.

Bob had not much of a comment on this development. "I have no problem with it." I felt he was relieved to be off the hook. I was steamed to think that he loved his son but not enough to put himself out, certainly not enough to want to be in his company, but in those days I was used to weighing our domestic situation on a rigged scale. I gave extra weight to the good half, added some denial, made some hefty excuses, and the good half always outweighed the bad.

Uncle Henry called from Florida. "My nephew is great company. I took him on a couple of calls and he wrote up twenty-five orders. I'm putting him on the payroll. Then I took him to my in-laws' for a couple of hours and boy, he won't have to eat again until the first of the month!"

I am an only child, and this conversation only confirmed my belief that siblings are the life preservers I've always felt cheated out of. Henry put Chris on.

"Uncle Henry took me to jai alai. It was exciting! He won sixty-five dollars! Tonight we're going to play miniature golf. The motel swimming pool has a slide . . ." and so on. I suppose these days it's called male bonding. Then it was called having an uncle who comes through. Then I thought it was wonderful, second best to a caring dad, but it made my heart ache because possibly it was too late. My son might already have reached the sexual point of no return. I am ashamed to admit that it crossed my mind that if Uncle Henry had been on hand on a regular basis from Chris's infancy on, there was no way my son could wind up anything but heterosexual. With someone like Uncle Henry as a father, Chris would surely have been one of the baseball-mitt and Band-Aid boys and no one would ever have called him a faggot. It's what I thought then, when I also thought women couldn't be dentists and unmarried couples who lived together were iniquitous.

At the end of that sixth-grade year, Chris was besieged on the school bus, which led to another appointment with yet another psychologist.

Here was Dr. Greene, a sort of beardless Santa Claus, an expert on child psychology in White Plains, well known and highly regarded. He was a five-star shrink with an office set up like a playroom and a lovable and pleasant manner reminiscent of chimneys and reindeer. We told Chris he would be seeing Dr. Greene to determine his aptitude in certain subjects, or some story like that; in any event, the consultation went smoothly, the familiar questions put kindly. When Chris left the room, Dr. Greene told us not to worry. He would give Chris a comprehensive battery of tests lasting from nine in the morning until five in the afternoon that would determine definitively whether or not he was leaning in the wrong sexual direction.

"I don't want you to worry. I've been seeing a family with a boy who insisted on dressing in his mother's clothes all through elementary school. He went through her closets and put on her gowns and you should see that boy now! He's in college, playing on the football team! A quarterback!" In those days being on a football field guaranteed virility, and Dr. Greene guaranteed comfort. He pulled these anecdotes out one after another like goodies out of a sack.

We made an appointment to bring Chris back for The Test, and I dropped him off at the office a few days later. At the end of the day, I picked him up. "What was the test like?" I asked him.

"Okay."

"What sorts of questions?"

"All kinds."

"Hard?"

"No. Fun. I had to draw a star."

It's all I ever learned about that mysterious exam. A week later, we had our appointment at Dr. Greene's office to hear him evaluate the results. It was not without trepidation that I drove to White Plains and waited in the outer office. Bob was out of town and I had to face the crystal ball myself. Was Chris or wasn't he?

Dr. Greene sat across the desk from me, his rosy cheeks and white hair exuding avuncular confidence. The examination results were in his chunky hands, and he looked at me over his glasses. I felt defenseless and vulnerable as he tapped his Cross pen on his chin.

"This test is perfectly conclusive. It's just as I suspected: it indicates without any doubt that your son is perfectly normal, and will grow up to be totally heterosexual."

I sailed, wafted, skipped, whistled and sang my way out of that office. The lottery win, pennies from heaven, the ultimate happy ending! Dr. Greene was Santa Claus and God all rolled into one. He had restored our son to normalcy with one wave of his pen, given us a reprieve from the unnatural, the unsavory and the unthinkable. We were suddenly the parents of Chris, straight as an arrow, straight as Dr. Greene's quarterback, a hetero!

I rushed home to call my husband in France.

8

- - - - - - - - - -

HERE'S A PERVERSE little joke nature has played on me: it seems as if in the New York heterosexual singles arena, I'm considered by some (of course, among those who don't know of my sexual orientation) a catch. At business gatherings, alumni meetings, parties and weddings, women approach me, flirt, make eye contact. I've had phone calls, notes, invitations. Not long ago, I was standing on the Larchmont station platform waiting for a commuter train when I was greeted by one of my sixth-grade tormentors, who had clearly forgotten what I never could, and engaged in a neighborly-friendly conversation. For him, time had obliterated whatever I'd been stained with at age twelve, and I now heard him inviting me to a mixer, a singles party at some club in the city. I told him I was unavailable on that date, and to my amazement he called a week or so later, wanting to fix me up with a woman friend. Time certainly does change some things.

But not others. If there was a respite to being a homosexual *in vacuo*, it came for me when I turned twelve and I tried to bend myself into brief bouts of heterosexuality by having girlfriends. I was trying to convince myself — and more to the point, the world — that I was straight. I'd look at this girl or that one and wonder if my attraction to boys could be permanently converted into the acceptable, desirable and correct interest in the opposite sex. So, during the summer preceding junior high school, in sleep-away camp (which was even more hateful when I was sent far upstate for six or eight long weeks), I latched on to Patty. Patty, chunky and pretty despite a mouth zigzagged with braces, held my hand during the campfire and seemed to like me. "Will you be my girlfriend?" I asked her.

She agreed to be my girlfriend; it was that easy. A week later, at another campfire, we segued into a dark corner behind the boathouse, where she let me pull up her shirt to feel first one budding breast, then the other. There was no kiss, no touch of moon-June romance. It was sort of a business deal — she got to be my steady, and I got to squeeze something I'd never squeezed before. It was during this summer that I was privy to my cabin mates' late night conversations about make-out baseball, in which first base was getting a kiss, "hitting double" meant a feel, and the rest of the bases were even more interesting. In that dark bunk, it was easy to talk myself into it: getting to second base with a well-endowed twelve-year-old girl would cure me for good and ultimately get me to a home run.

Sure enough, hitting the double was nice, but I did not feel the blood rush to the right places, nor did I see fireworks. And it didn't stop me from admiring our handsome counselor. Patty's and my relationship ended a week or two later, when she was stolen away from me by another camper, probably more adroit in the mechanics of heterosexual love.

So I approached Vera. Red cheeks, one pigtail, a chain with a cross around her neck is how she looks in the one photograph I have of her. She liked me, or seemed to. She was from some country in middle Europe and spoke with a bit of an accent. She kept sitting next to me in the dining room and throwing looks my way at the lake beach. I asked Vera to be my girlfriend at a square dance, and she agreed immediately. When we managed to find a few minutes in the woods alone at last, when she put her arms around my neck, I suppose my heart wasn't in the kiss, the sigh, the squeeze. For me, kissing a girl was strictly a no-chimes, no-sparks event. The relationship ended very quickly.

There may have been one or two other attempts to find a girl at camp that summer, but I don't remember them. Almost every other boy had accumulated at least one or two girls to talk about, if not to have actual sexual activities with; it was as much part of camp equipment as a canteen and bedroll. The possibility that I would be unable to have a future man-woman liaison began to seep unpleasantly into my thoughts, and chiseled away whatever small gains I might have made in my feelings of self-worth. It was always and forever, "What will they think of me?" and the question invariably had a toxic answer.

Junior high was a breath of fresh air compared to the torments of sixth grade. At first, anyway. New school and schoolmates, a fresh start, and a reunion with Kevin Spencer, whose move across town still allowed him to be in my junior high district. I was actually feeling comfortable in my classes, and through Kevin I met a new crowd of boys who accepted me, knowing nothing of my born-loser reputation.

I am now told that over the years I was taken to several psychologists, of which I have no recollection whatsoever. I do know there was some pressure to get me to join the Boy Scouts, which I reluctantly did. It wasn't all bad; outfitted head to toe in our pressed olive-green regalia, mostly we sat around in the basement of the Episcopalian church eating chocolate chip cookies and planning camping weekends. These weekends in the country were staffed by scout leaders and volunteer dads. My father agreed to accompany thirty boys on such a trip.

Never the roughing-it type, Dad was still great at kidding, drove a few of us up to the campground, and I felt proud to have him along. I felt my friends thought he was a real regular guy, unlike me. There was some ambivalence, though. Was he going to get tense in traffic? His loud stream-of-consciousness profanity in the car was legendary. Would he complain about the food or the tents or the bugs or the outhouses? Would he say everything four times? Would he get angry at me?

But he was on his best behavior — until the Saturday night movie. It had started to rain, and we were herded into the scout clubhouse for a viewing of *The Lady Vanishes*. The lights were dimmed, the projector went on, the audience hushed, and suddenly there was a thunderous fart from the back of the room. It was my uninhibited father, and he was not embarrassed in the slightest. In fact, he took full credit for bringing the house down. I cringed in my seat, wanting to go through the floor. "Boy, that felt good," my father said. "Boy, that felt very good!" He blamed the beans at last night's barbecue. The kids roared for five minutes. I began to feel better. They thought my father was funny. They thought he was great. And then, so did I.

The following summer, with the pleasures of scouting already fading, Kevin and his gang abandoned camp and experimented with a more adult activity. They began sleeping outside in tents set up in various back yards, and soon I was invited on one of these sleepovers. There was Kevin and the O'Brien brothers and a new kid, Lonny, and there were mosquitoes, blankets and sleeping bags.

Then, there was sex. It was never spoken of during daylight hours, but as night fell, the stars and the flashlights came out, and we stripped naked in our summer sleeping bags and took turns. It was manual, it was mutual masturbation, partners were interchangeable, and the events amounted to meaningless, mindless rounds of primitive gratification. It seemed almost an out-of-body experience, ephemeral as a mirage, when recollected the next morning in full daylight. I often ask myself which came first, the tendencies to desire homoerotic activities or the seduction of one uncommitted boy by another? For me, the egg of desire for the same sex came first, but for the others it's hard to tell. Two of these boys are now practicing homosexuals. One is heterosexual. I have lost touch with the others.

I can pinpoint this as the time I knew and felt I was destined for a life of homosexuality. It was Kevin Spencer's saying, "When we're fourteen, this has to stop." He meant, This is when life must begin seriously, when we have to give up this childish activity. I was devastated as much by the thought of stopping as by the possibility that he could instantly channel this sexual interest toward women, whereas I thought I never could. All at once, I felt condemned: I would be left behind, and I began to envision an adulthood without a wife, without a family. What would become of me? Would my parents and siblings want me in their lives? I saw my future in terms of a single-occupancy room somewhere. I always imagined myself alone.

Now I see more possibilities, but even today mental doors are creaking open much too slowly, and on all sides there are still so many limitations. This morning on TV, a talk-show host interviewed a female impersonator whose house was burned to the ground in Las Vegas by a homophobic arsonist. Last month's news was full of reports of attacks on gays in Greenwich Village. Last week a lesbian, the natural mother of a baby, was denied custody of her own child because she and her sweetheart kissed in front of the child. It is unbecoming to be bitter, but I sometimes allow myself to be unbecoming.

If there is a leitmotif throughout my growing-up years, it is the ongoing effort I made, day in day out, year after year, to score points with my peers. God, how I wanted to be liked! If not liked, at least accepted. Just to be "in" for once, privy to inside jokes, part of a collection of guys. The recipient of telephone messages, someone who had weekend plans and a place to go other than my room; with Kevin Spencer and his crowd, I actually began to belong. Sitting with a bunch of guys at lunch, having somewhere to hang out on the weekends — it was heaven. It was heaven, that is, until it spun out of control into hell — in a totally unpredictable way.

A new girl in school, Carla, began to insinuate herself into our group. Dark hair, dark eyes, intense and pushy, she turned up in the cafeteria at our table, most often at my side. Suddenly I found her walking next to me in the school corridors, sitting near me on the school bus. She was lively, she was fun, and having a girl infatuated with me was a new and not unpleasant experience. For a time, I wallowed in her attention. Her affection for me did not turn sour all at once, but by degrees, in direct proportion to her disappointments at my not returning her interest. I began ducking her barrage of telephone calls and her invitations to do homework together in her dim-lit family room when her family wasn't in it, and little by little, giving her a wide berth in school. Hell had no fury compared to Carla when she saw that I was not going to be her boyfriend.

She took her revenge by befriending a girl from my old school, someone well aware of my scapegoat history, someone who promoted my status as grade school whipping boy and major outcast. Carla dug out this old news, embellished it, created new tales to make me look more despicable than any law-abiding thirteen-year-old could ever aspire to. She started rumors and expedited their spread. Exactly what they were I don't know to this day. The whispers began, the glances, the teasing and the predictable fall-out. My new friends looked at me with suspicion, derision, and in time they hardly looked at me at all. Having herself been accepted by my little junior high crowd, Carla turned on me and finally drove me out of it.

These eighth-grade politics had a serious effect on my personality, much more long-ranging effects than seem plausible. What the boys thought of me, and therefore what I thought of myself, drove me into a mobilization of self-defensive posturing. In junior high school, after Carla, after I'd become a social leper again, I turned myself into a new person. I became sort of a caricature. I became the Rich Kid.

It began mildly enough with a silver bracelet. My father had brought this splendid, massive, masculine item back from a business trip. He wore it once or twice, decided he wasn't interested in wearing jewelry after all and presented it to my older brother.

In those days, I tried to copy Kirby. When he began collecting miniature bottles of liquor, I began collecting miniature bottles that were empty. When he became a big fan of Buster Keaton, I got on a Charlie Chaplin tack. When he took up photography, I had to have a camera. My brother skied, and then so did I. When my father presented Kirby with the magnificent bracelet, I was more than a little envious. How I coveted that heavy-linked trophy that shone on his wrist like a polished handcuff!

The day after someone made fun of Kirby's new acquisition, he took it off his wrist and gave it to me. "I'm never wearing this again," he said, and threw it on my bed. Hallelujah, now it was mine! It became a symbol for me, an emblem of my affluence — my one and only possible outlet for one-upmanship. I had things everyone coveted but hardly anyone else could afford.

The showing off was a rhinestone triumph. I had not a real friend in school, but I had a real zillion-dollar bracelet. I parlayed this into more glamor. I lived in a splendid house, my father had a dashing BMW, and during winter holidays, while most other kids stayed home or visited relatives in Florida, I sent postcards from Puerto Rico or Saint Martin or Barbados. Next year, maybe a ski holiday, maybe Cortina, maybe Gstaad. My ski equipment, camera, clothes, everything I owned was top of the line, imprinted with the trendiest and best designer logos. Dad, not often in town these days, substituted overabundance for his presence. I was now a somebody to be envied, rather than a nobody to be scorned.

Materialism was paying off; at least I was noticed. This new showoff had the means to invite "friends" to ball games, dinners at the country club and visits to my father's eyeglass factory, where we were treated like VIPs. Tours, free samples, splendid lunches at nearby restaurants, courtesy of Dad's credit cards, turned me into a walking cornucopia of freebies. I began to have a sort of network of ambivalent followers. In this new guise I became marginally accepted again, but the fallout was a lasting reputation for snobbishness, very well deserved. For years I walked in my own golden aura of what money could buy. It was my adolescent hiding place.

I cringe a bit as I look at myself then, forever putting on the ritz. I know this easy-to-hate me turned off many potential friends and gave my father a valid reason to target his anger at me. ("Who cares if you show up in your mother's Oldsmobile instead of my BMW? Don't be such a snob!") I'm more tolerant of showoffs now, and understand that not all conspicuous consumers are hiding their homosexual orientation, but are likely to be covering up some insecurity. There is a Russian proverb: If money speaks, truth is silent. I wish I'd known it then.

Being a Rich Kid was of course no real insurance against my being a continuing target of scorn. It happened in school and outside, and once, when I was almost fourteen and feeling somewhat grown up, on the bus coming home from school. I was well on my way to a thicker skin in those days, if not confident, at least unshrinking. Or so I thought.

Why do I perspire as I write this twenty years later? It is history, after all, dead as winter leaves. I got on the bus feeling relatively at peace with the world, my secret still buried in my soul's deep freeze, and I boarded in a spirit of calm, if not quite contentment. I had to run for the bus with my arms full of books, and was last to make it aboard; it was still cold outside, which meant few would be walking, so the bus was packed with the usual raucous kids bursting out of the confinement of school. The bus was full of noise, push and crush.

The aisles were jammed and the bus driver, whose face I still see clearly before me, was one of those redheads with pale pink skin. Now he was turning increasingly rosy around his aviator sunglasses. (Then and now, I notice eyeglasses. The family business was always my business.) "C'mon, move it!" he commanded. He said this a couple of times, turning in his seat to give his voice more authority. Kids continued to weave through the aisle, to jostle each other and make noise. "Everybody siddown!" yelled the bus driver. He became even more agitated. "I said, siddown!"

There was some scrambling to obey, and soon most everyone found a seat.

"Okay. I ain't moving this bus until you're all sitting on your asses!" Somehow, last aboard also meant I was out of luck. There seemed to be no more empty seats anywhere.

There I stood, the lone passenger still upright while everyone else was seated. There I stood, looking in vain for a seat that wasn't occupied. "Siddown, willya?" the bus driver yelled.

"Siddown Chris!" echoed what sounded like half the bus.

I tried to find a patch of room on the aisle, next to a kid named Torrey, who looked for the moment as if he might move over and give me an inch or two. He was another former tormentor from my sixth-grade class, but I was pretty much assured we were both older now, and both finally ready to let bygones be bygones. The seat turned out to be the wrong choice.

"Siddown!" The bus driver was glaring, the kids were yelling and I, the cooperative obeyer of all orders, quickly plopped myself down. I landed on what seemed like the width of a small lunchbox at the edge of the seat next to Torrey, but I wasn't there long.

"Faggot," he said, and he gave me a full-strength push, knocking me down into the aisle.

I went flying, so did my books, ditto my notebook, out of which a thousand assorted papers sailed in every direction, spewing into the aisle. The kids went wild and the bus driver's complexion grew redder as he swiveled around in his seat and glowered at me.

"What's your name?" he asked me, as I was trying to get myself up off the floor, simultaneously grabbing loose-leaf papers from under my knees, my feet, and those that had slid under others' seats. If anyone was helping me, I don't remember it.

"Chris," I said. I had the wild momentary notion that it was all my fault somehow, that now I was in for it.

"Okay, Chris," said the driver. "Who pushed ya?"

Call it anger, wish for revenge or my humiliation, but accusing my tormentor was a knee-jerk response, possibly another one of my terrible and quick decisions that have had unpredictably miserable consequences. It didn't occur to me not to name the perp. It didn't occur to me to let him off the hook. I was sprawled on the floor, kicked in the psyche, once again the powerless goat. Once more I didn't want crime to pay. At that moment I wanted Torrey hung by the neck or put to death in the electric chair, preferably in full view of the student body of The Hommocks Junior High School.

Mechanically my thumb left my fist to point at the culprit.

"Okay, you," said the glowering bus driver. His big man's finger pointed at Torrey and he spoke with heavy authority. "Get off the bus. Right now."

The front doors whined as he opened them with the hidden lever under his seat, and for one short and sweet instant, I thought I'd won some kind of justice. How wrong I was. As Torrey got up and wove his way down the aisle, there was an immediate uproar.

It was so loud it might have come out of a football stadium instead of a bus filled with no more than forty twelve-, thirteen- and fourteen-year-olds. It was thunderous, it was cataclysmic.

As Torrey, muttering curses and threats under his breath, stumbled off the bus, his one book under his arm, the cries of "Chris, you faggot!" accelerated to a fever pitch around me.

The bus driver ordered everyone to be quiet ("Okay, everybody, shut the fuck up!"), and while I was still retrieving lost pages from my notebook, he put his foot on the gas and the bus lurched forward.

With most of my papers retrieved, I sat undisturbed in Torrey's vacated seat until we got to my stop. The driver pulled up to the corner of my street and the back doors opened. As I stepped off the bus, my heart sank. Three boys — my old nemesis Jeremy, one of his brothers and a friend of Torrey's — followed me down the bus steps, spitting epithets at the back of my head. As soon as the bus had rolled away from the curb, they knocked me down and fell on top of me — all three — and using fists, elbows and what seemed like extra body parts grown just for combat, began punching until somehow, crying and trying not to, I broke free and ran like the god of wind and found my way safely to the front door of my house.

They ran off and my mother answered the fervent pounding of the door knocker. Bruised and sore, I flew past her into the front hall and up the stairs, my shoulders heaving, a fourteen-year-old crybaby, still getting it wrong, tattling, still hearing the world's chorus resonate loud and louder, "Fag! Faggot!"

Again, sealed tight in my Rich Boy's clothes, sitting on my Rich Boy's bed, I felt I needed just one person to whisper my secret to. I needed one set of understanding, sympathetic ears. It couldn't be my mother. My fear of alienating/disappointing/hurting/shocking/traumatizing her was in full force. I couldn't risk losing the one solid relationship of my life. Never my father. My shame was my shame. And so, with my true spirit in solitary confinement, my school days limped forward.

9

- - - - - - - - - -

TODAY, MY EX-HUSBAND and I live in peace some ten city blocks apart, the tug of married war behind us. Back then, there was another sort of calm, with the rumbles of conflict muffled and distant. I always knew Bob loved us. We were family, we came first. We flourished through many seasons of upper-middle-class equilibrium — three generations on a continuum of harmony — but, to quote John Kennedy, "The mere absence of war is not peace."

The memories now erupt like blisters.

Or like blossoms.

When Bob turned forty, I threw a party. As I've said, I am an only child, and striving seems to be the name of my game. Maybe that is a reason for my having to be more excellent than everyone else in order to feel reasonably adequate. Why does everything in my line of vision always have to be so snazzy? Is this fear of imperfection inborn or self-inflicted? I'm not sure, but I am capable of changing outfits three times before going to lunch, spending weeks picking out bathroom wallpaper, and reading a stack of cookbooks before selecting a party dinner menu.

In those days I was also capable of recording the food served and guest list of every party I ever gave, in order not to duplicate dishes guests had eaten before at our house. Which is how I happen to have a record of the menu served on October 16, 1971, and the list of the ten couples who were our guests. Chris notwithstanding, there are times in our lives when everything is in sync, and this was one of them. The war in Vietnam was a million miles away, a serious California earthquake happened three thousand miles across the continent, and Charles Manson was put safely behind bars somewhere on the other side of the moon. It was a good year for Bobby Fischer and the heavyweight Joe Frazier.

It was also a good year for on-the-rise optical heavyweight Bob Shyer, who had introduced the first nylon eyeglass frames into the American market some years before. They were lightweight and indestructible — instant bestsellers; his company could hardly keep up with the orders. We would sit together in front of the television set and Bob would point to newscasters, comedians, interviewees and miscellaneous sitcom figures. "He's wearing the Invincible," he would say. Those innovative frames could be dropped, bent and twisted, but never broken. They were invincible all right, and we felt as if we were too.

Being the suburban Madame Perfecto in those days meant cooking every last thing myself, and in retrospect, probably becoming a tough showoff act to follow. (The main course at this party, following an awesome assortment of hors d'oeuvres, comprised boeuf bourgignon, smoked turkey, toasted barley, ratatouille and garlic bread.) It was all sit-down, round tables with matching cloths and candlelight in our red-papered dining room, on the walls of which recently completed Bob-and-Marlene-in-their-prime oil portraits hung under picture lights. The children, all gussied up and slicked down, had their jobs — Kirby photographed the guests as they entered, and Chris and Alison were official greeters and took the guests' jackets.

This is a good time to rip off my own halo: my perfectionism must have created intermittent stress through the years, never as obvious as at those times I was giving a party. Nervous, mean-tempered, threatening and hateful, that was Mom before guests arrived.

Charming, hostessy and lovable, that was Mom as soon as the first guest stepped over the threshold.

As tense as I could be about the quality of the food, silver service and wine, what always added an edge was my worry that Bob would misbehave. Social savoir-faire was not his strong suit. Incessantly interrupting whoever was speaking, cutting him off or worse, cutting him down, was upsetting, but more annoying was his prodigal use of obscenities, which were much less acceptable in those days than they are now. Of course, he wasn't always boorish any more than I was always nasty. It didn't happen every time. And it is undoubtably true that over the years, party guests I imagined he'd offended never even noted his quirks or fallibilities, and that my own insecurity magnified what were minor misdemeanors. I wanted him to become the epitome of Amy Vanderbilt decorum, and often I was motivated not only by a desire to be part of a perfect pair but by affection. I didn't want people not to like him. I wanted everyone to see what I saw — a really good soul underneath all that belligerence and mouth. I used to kid, "You don't have a bad streak. You are bad with a good streak." He loved that, and quoted me often.

Recently, in cleaning out some bookshelves, I came across Bob's old high school yearbook. He'd left it behind when he moved out, and during an idle moment I flipped through its pages. Over his own picture, the student council president had written: "To Shyer — I don't know how well you play ball. Maby good, maby not so good. But I know you'll be a success as you're the kind of guy everyone likes." This fellow was a bit more accurate in his life's predictions than in his spelling. Bob was a success and he was basically well liked. With a touch of maby. Like a spoonful of sugar that makes the medicine go down, Bob's wit sweetened the bluster. His bon mots are not very bon, and never since I've known him has he told a bona fide joke, but although not everyone finds him as amusing as I did, Bob had me on the floor with his rat-tat-tat retorts all through the years. His wit added an enormous dimension to our rapport, to family life, and when he wanted to use it, it was the vigor of the laugh that got us through the bad moments.

At his birthday party, what I remember is not the menu, and not the scatological language, but Bob's outrageous and wonderful talent as a natural comic, his self-deprecating one-liners, his rubber face as he pulled this and that little gift out of its box, his spontaneity, his creative ideas: "Oh, yeah, sure, I can use this. I always needed a lard scoop! Hold it — is it a *designer* lard scoop? You mean it's an ice scraper? Oh, *very nice*. Wait, will it scoop lard?"

To me, he was hilarious. I thought so from the moment we met. He came to my freshman college dormitory to pick up a date, and began kibitzing as I sat in the lounge playing cards. While his date took her time getting ready upstairs, I was rocking in my bridge chair over his throwaway lines downstairs. Naturally, every comedian loves an appreciative straight man, and so we were instantly endeared to each other. He was less than twenty then, and although in time I perceived the tough hombre through the fun and the laughs, I didn't project us into maturity, back problems or the treadmill of parenthood. Not that it would have mattered if I had. Call it destiny, circumstance or heavenly deployment, call it love or codependency, we immediately became a monogamous couple, probably at too tender an age. Parenthood was foisted on us too quickly as well, cutting short our carefree years, as was the universal style in those days.

Later, I occasionally let my imagination turn things around to change the equations, rewrite my autobiography. What if I'd married someone else? What sort of children would I have had? And if lightning strikes me dead I well deserve it, for in some of my gloomiest moments of worry, the wistful notion crossed my mind that if someone else's sperm had impregnated my Chris egg, perhaps my son might be someone else, different in one way or another, maybe even a girl, and I would not have to be confronting the problems we were having with him.

Now I turn cold at the thought that I could have wished Chris to be anyone other than who he is. I've done a heart-twisting full turn, and oh, how my perception has changed! I see my son as the special bequest the gods had up their sleeves for me, a gift so generous I sometimes think I don't deserve my luck. It is not that I'm privileged to have a child who is gay; I am privileged to have a gay son who is Chris.

Someone once said the world's brightest lights are the taillights of the last guest's car leaving your party. How applicable on this occasion. In the afterglow of the evening's success, as we emptied ashtrays and carried glasses into the kitchen, Bob and I did our usual postmortems, comparing notes, agreeing on our opinions of our guests, their eccentricities, *their* behavior. The party and its aftermath has a particularly bright halo in retrospect, because it was a marker of a nearly perfect time in our lives and because it seemed to keynote our dream life — health, prosperity, the sacred circle of family. This celebration was a pinnacle moment in our history, illuminated not only by those retreating taillights but by our own perpetual flame of mutual affection. Like those Ira Gershwin lyrics, there wasn't a doubt about our love being here to stay.

Two years later, another birthday. Same leading players, same set, a darker experience. The scene was the front hall. Bob came downstairs for his birthday breakfast and was greeted first by his older son, Kirby, who, having just turned sixteen, was home for the weekend from Westminster School. He was interested in photography in those days, was considered respectably good with a camera at his prep school, already competent enough to be the semiofficial photographer at school functions. He had prepared a special birthday gift for his father.

The odds of getting Kirby at age sixteen to get a sheet of wrapping paper and tape it around a gift had about the same odds as a game of solitaire. Sometimes there was success! (Chris would never have presented a present without wrap, tape and card.) On this occasion Kirby's gift was proferred wrapped — not tied with ribbons, not exactly crisp and fresh, not a theatrical job, but wrapped. Inside was an eight-by-ten black-and-white photograph he'd taken of his father at the tennis courts the summer before. He had developed the photo in the darkroom at school, cropped and enlarged it, put it in a frame from the five-and-ten and presented it as a festive tribute. Voilà!

The younger two stood by with their presents in hand, watching while Daddy picked up Kirby's. The usual breathless moment of anticipation as Daddy slowly tore the paper off and looked at the gift. The moment came and went.

There is a Chinese proverb: Govern a family as you would cook a small fish — very gently.

Bob didn't, or couldn't.

He held up his birthday present, examined it at arm's length, squinting. "This is the worst picture of me I've ever seen," he said, and he slammed the frame down on the hall shelf with such force that it blew the torn paper wrap to the floor and cracked a sunburst in the corner of the glass.

I looked at Kirby's face. It was totally without expression. No flicker of the eyes, no muscle moving anywhere. A blank screen. He doesn't remember this episode, but for twenty years I've carried the image of this tableau in my heart. I imagined my son's disappointment like an explosion behind his mute blue eyes. This was not the first put-down, but for me, one of the most poignant. Kirby then was shy and quiet. His legs of self-confidence were wobbly, and his identity was currently pretty much wrapped up in his ability as a photographer. He had tried so hard to please his father. "Oh, but it's a good picture!" I protested. "I think it's wonderful!" Kirby's expression did not change. At one point, I think he shrugged. An inferno raged in me. *How could Bob?* How could a decent human being be so callous and insensitive? I looked at Alison, not yet six, and Chris, twelve. I felt they were like little gold miners with pickaxes, chipping away at hard rock, never finding so much as a nugget. And no matter how I tried, I couldn't seem to make that rock less unyielding.

Chris, as ever the good, good boy, picked up the gift wrapping that had fluttered to the floor and went to put it into the trash bin, without being asked.

I waited until my anger subsided. It might have been later that day, that week, that month. I sat down with Bob and explained he had to give praise, compliments, strokes. It was his duty, *please.* They needed the gold once in a while. He seemed incapable of expressing emotion unless it was negative. At the back of my mind was my own father, a mild and easy daddy who never raised his voice, who showed disappointment — and so very rarely! — by turning quiet or leaving the room.

"I'll try." Bob was a reasonable man, after all, who loved his children. "Remind me," he said, and although I often tried to, he couldn't seem to congratulate, flatter or commend anyone — unless I practically held up cue cards. The compliments he paid his children were, and are to this day, usually spoken behind their backs.

Only intermittently did I guess that it was some macho conditioning not to applaud your children with willing enthusiasm. Instead, he threatened and bullied them, insulted and bellowed at them. Sometimes when the walls shook with his anger, I thought it wasn't conditioning but chemistry; surely, not all men of his generation were so fond of saber rattling. At other times he simply ignored the children. "I'll try," he said, but when they spoke to him, he didn't listen. He wanted to hear about them, but not from them. It was this way: he cared for his children, but it was in the abstract. He loved them profoundly and always, but more when they were in bed sick with fever than when they were in the same room with him.

10

- - - - - - - - - -

IT WASN'T UNTIL two or three years after my father's birthday party that one of the black-and-white photographs my brother took of the guests as they arrived surfaced as a prominent memento of that evening. I have no recollection of the party, but one particular photograph remains fresh and green in my memory. It was of my father greeting a male guest at the door, and the camera caught them making a big, outrageous joke — pretending to kiss each other, making sure there were many inches between them. One had only to look at my father's face, the stagy puckered lips, the raised eyebrow, to know how absolutely *out of the question* it would be for him to kiss another man, what a completely *off-the-wall* idea that there could ever be more than a shoulder punch or handshake between two men. My father hadn't kissed me since I was very small, had never given me a hug. Certainly he never kissed or hugged his own father. From today's enlightened point of view, I see he was just the Everyman of his time, careful to be "masculine," careless about showing affection. Still, I was always on the lookout for clues about how he would feel about me and my atrocious yearnings if he knew. Since I couldn't ask, I foraged for subtle hints wherever I could. And the message I read in that innocent, party-laughs photo was clear: men could kiss women and dogs, but as for physical affection between two males — well, it was nothing doing.

If the Rich Kid was living in his own psychological isolation, there were at least times of respite. Things began to look up on my fifteenth birthday. The abominable public school specters were soon to be history, because in all likelihood I would be going to private school in the fall, and in a few short weeks I was off to camp in Switzerland for a summer of skiing.

My brother had been on this exhilarating adventure the year before, and here it was my turn to spend my days on Swiss slopes, in the shadow of the Matterhorn with new and interesting people who might actually not find me contemptible. The camp, called Swiss Challenge, was cushy, grown-up, relatively unstructured and wonderfully exotic. Europe, passport, customs, Swiss francs — even the accompanying vocabulary sang with excitement, and of really breaking away. I was determined that this summer would be different. I would, goddamn it, fit in.

My father drove me to the airport in his coffee-brown BMW Bavaria. Not flashy or nouveau riche like a Cadillac or Lincoln, it had marvelous snob appeal. My father, who never cared about impressing anyone, could always be counted on to be instinctively unpretentious and correct. Lacking his supreme self-confidence, I was somewhat nervous, but despite having to endure his usual maniacal outbursts about the heavy traffic en route — this was the Fourth of July — my mood was high. We'd been sent a list of the other campers, and I was dazzled: among them was the daughter of a famous publisher, midwestern kids with famous-sounding family names, landed-gentry-type personages from the South and numerous people with Park Avenue addresses. There was even a real live Kennedy. I was awed by the group even before we walked into the terminal and saw the congregation — knots of apple-cheeked, wholesome-to-die preppies laden with luggage, skis and more status symbols than I could shake a ski pole at.

Obviously, I had concocted my Rich Kid persona to make people like me and to explain away whatever made me seem "different" at home. While it might have created a sort of smoke-screen to hide the real reason I was a square peg there, it backfired among the real rich kids. If I didn't wear jeans at home, the message to my not so financially fortunate peers was that I was not weird, only terribly well-to-do and above it all. Here, I got the comeuppance I deserved. These Switzerland-bound Forbes 400 offspring were going to wear jeans like everyone else. So, here I became a manifest see-through. Clearly, my destiny was that I was never going to fit in with them, either.

I was slightly nervous, slightly exhilarated getting my bearings, when I realized my father had moved a few steps forward, approached a fellow camper waiting to check in and struck up a conversation. Questions like "How long have you been waiting in line?" "Is it moving?" "Is the counselor here?" "Have you spoken to anybody?" turned into "Where are you from?" "Have you skied before?" "This is my son Chris, he's also going on this trip . . ."

My father, undoubtedly well intentioned, possibly reluctant to let me venture unattached into the void of another continent, had inadvertently chosen this nearest body to link me up with. His name was Fields, his nickname Sonny, a combination that initially evoked for me visions of green meadows, sunshine and dandelions, totally incongruous with this oddball, this fish out of water. The irony of it was, in the wall-to-wall sea of high preppiedom, my father had approached the one other square peg. Sonny, heavyset, big and wearing totally God-forbid white overalls, with messy, flyaway dark hair, surrounded by an aggregation of dilapidated luggage, predictably took to me immediately. He had no skis, because he intended renting a pair in Switzerland and his being here at all was sort of a fluke. He lived in modest circumstances with his mother, stepfather and grandmother in Philadelphia, while his rich father lived in Arizona with his second wife. Sonny described his father's "conversion into guilt," to which Sonny attributed the sudden largess that paid for this trip. He glommed on to me, managed to have his seat assignment switched, and off we went, side by side, with fireworks from the bicentennial celebration blasting in the darkening sky around and below us. I thought it was of magnificent consequence to be flying away at that moment, taking to the skies like the red, white and blue rockets bursting in air — even with Sonny Fields next to me.

The Chris vibes, the aura, whatever it was about me that made me a persona non grata with the more desirable part of the human species, appealed to Sonny. In all fairness, I couldn't not like him. He was zany, far out and weird, but he was decent, a good guy through and through. And so, despite my Rich Kid intentions of ditching him in favor of some more right-image friends, Sonny and I became closer to each other than to anyone else in the group. However, we were definitely not inseparable.

Sonny was daring, an *enfant terrible* by that day's standards and the antithesis of go-by-the-rules Shyer. He seemed much older and had no problem passing himself off as sixteen, the legal drinking age in Zermatt that summer. He went out every night with his own clique of Swiss Challenge renegades, was always flirting with and surrounded by the best-looking girls, and turned out to be six months younger than I. At age fourteen and a half, Sonny was worldly, sophisticated and, from my point of view, both embarrassing to be seen with and a compelling draw.

We were sitting in one of the gorgeous mountainside restaurants, eating the usual Zermatt lunch of baguettes and cheese. Bottled water, ubiquitous in the Alps but new to me and unheard of in America, was the exotic beverage in everyone's hand. It was the second week of camp, and Sonny lowered his voice; he had something to tell me. His roommate, Doug Robertson, well, Something Had Happened, and although Sonny felt hesitant about mentioning it to me, he really had to tell *someone*.

Doug, a very handsome American boy from The Hague, a boy I thought glamorous and admirably masculine, had made a move on Sonny. Actually, Sonny said, it was very subtle, but had happened on several occasions. Their twin beds, in the tradition of the Swiss hotels in which we were staying, were pushed together, and although the mattresses and duvets were separate, they shared one box spring.

"For the last several mornings," Sonny confided, making a face, "Doug has been waking up sprawled across my bed." This was no accident, Sonny claimed. "He's coming on to me. It's serious." My ears went up. Doug was an excellent skier and all-around camp star, every inch the dashing hero of summer. *Doug?*

The idea that I could find a special friend, a soul mate, possibly even a liaison, sparked my imagination. Doug Robertson was in fact the slightest bit of a strange weed, because he'd grown up in Europe and was out of it as far as pop culture went. His exotic glamor was very appealing, and catching him alone after lunch a few days later, I took the opportunity to initiate a conversation. Doug was friendly and pleasant, sort of like a new next-door neighbor. I tried again on the ski-lift line, at the ski shed, one evening in front of our chalet. He was chatty but always in a hurry, on his way somewhere. Was he? Wasn't he? I couldn't read him, the way he kept me at arm's length in a warm way — until I visited him in London many years later.

The camp was run in this way: Mornings, when the conditions were good, we all skied with our own ability groups. At about noontime we left the slopes, because the warm sun turned the snow into "peanut butter," took our baguettes and cheese in one or another of the top-of-the-mountain cafés, and then were expected to lock up our skis in sheds and hike down the mountain. As much as I loved skiing, that's how much I hated hiking, and managed always to annex myself to the group with the shortest route back to town.

There was, however, no getting out of an all-day hike, scheduled for the entire camp one Sunday. Sonny went off with his assigned group, I went off with mine. We were all going to converge at the top of a peak six hundred feet above Zermatt. With views of whipped-cream snow and mountain peaks, valleys with tiny smoking chimneys coming out of clusters of cottage rooftops, dark pines and ski lifts, all this under a watercolor blue sky, it is one of the most ravishing places I've ever been in in my life.

But oh my God, my feet hurt. I had not broken in my hiking boots back in Larchmont, as we'd been warned to do, for the same reason I didn't want to wear sneakers: I always felt that being seen in brand-new athlete's footgear, I would underscore the incongruity of my unathletic feet. So, I went whole hog in these killers on an all-day hike, and by the time lunch came, I was in severe pain.

After lunch at our rendezvous at the peak, we resumed hiking down the mountain, each group of eight or ten with our college-boy counselor. Even if it hadn't been for my feet, I couldn't call it fun, what with random collisions with icicles, scratches from frozen leaves and tree branches and occasional spells of high-altitude dizziness. We were to follow a certain route in the direction of the Matterhorn and then head directly into town, but it soon became apparent that we'd taken a wrong turn and were lost.

Now we were clambering through forests trying to find the right path. Impossible to describe the squeezing, burning and awful pain of my toes, the penetrating cold and now the anxiety as the sun began descending in the sky. The forest became gloomier and gloomier, very soon it would be dark, and we were starving. The cheese and baguettes were six hours behind us, and town was nowhere in sight.

We had no idea how far we'd hiked. We were at the base of the Matterhorn, thoroughly lost and turned around, and after another grueling half hour, through some unaccountably lucky turns, finally found ourselves on the right path to town. Suddenly, some distance ahead of us in a clearing, a peasant woman appeared like a transmogrified figure in the dusk, wrapped in what looked like a dark shroud. The figure watched and waited as we approached, then raised an arm in greeting.

Taking a few steps closer, we saw that it was not an eerie peasant at all, but Sonny Fields, who had gotten separated from his group and had wrapped himself in a poncho that almost completely covered his head. We had all mistaken him for a woman, and I joined in making great fun of his outfit and the fact that we'd taken him for female. I kidded and laughed with the rest.

But it was a black moment. What I was thinking was, Here I am, and of all the people here I could have as friends, I am back into my usual groove, associating with this misfit, this odd duck. *And he has the appearance of a woman.* It seemed as if in that forest clearing, on that snowy path, I'd come right up against a vision of my destiny. If I left America behind, it turned out I couldn't leave *me* behind. I may have gotten along well with all my fellow campers, locked steps easily with them this entire summer, might even exchange Christmas cards with them for the rest of our lives, but the only real connection I could make on any continent was with someone who was capable of having the appearance of a woman, someone offbeat, fringy, out of place. Like me.

As we trudged back into town, me limping and exhausted, we made our way to the hotel in which we all gathered for dinner and were greeted by the other campers and counselors. They cheered us loudly, raised glasses of bottled water in welcoming toasts and stayed to celebrate our safe return. And there was Doug Robertson. I tried to negotiate a seat near him, but it was impossible. Sonny was there, right at my side, hanging on, it seemed to me that night, for dear life.

As it happened, his turned out to be very short.

Over the next decade, our friendship solidified. When I went off to prep school the following year, he not only wrote me letters but sent tapes, was like a breath of fresh air during that worst year of my life.

He was bright, different, radical, but not effeminate. I had no clue. During our teenage years, when I was plodding from class to class, at home every night doing homework, doing exactly what was expected of me, Sonny was trying hash and Quaaludes, traveling — really living, as I saw it. He got into college at sixteen and dropped out shortly thereafter. From a letter he wrote me in 1979, when he was seventeen: "Studio [54] was, in a word, an *experience*. My friend Dave and I pushed our way through the crowd, walked up to the rope and Mark the doorman let us right in . . . inside is gorgeous, both the decor and the people. Grace Jones, Bianca Jagger, Robin Williams, Steve Rubell and other celebs were there but they were not the best part of the evening. There was no best part; it was all just really fabulous."

I was, of course, in awe.

A year later, he wrote: "I went up to San Francisco in August for a week . . . It is . . . a romantic place — I had 'mini affairs' in the space of one week!"

I wasn't reading any of that right. All I saw was the glamor, although I was keeping him at arm's length. (He'd shown up at one of my tame Christmas parties — at a time when I was still trying to preserve my precarious image as a regular guy — dressed in women's designer jeans, his hair dyed coal black, his feet in sandals, in midwinter. I explained him as a casual summer acquaintance, felt guilty for distancing myself from this good friend, but when he moved out west I was thoroughly relieved to be rid of him.)

The letters kept arriving though, and finally, when I was in college, one revealed he was coming to New York and that he was gay. By that time, the revelation came as no great surprise.

What is clear now are the disparities in how we handled our homosexual tendencies. While I was exceedingly closeted, Sonny had the drive to be true to himself at the tender age of seventeen. Sadly, with few choices in those days, he could find only the stereotypical homosexual hangouts. We both had no positive role models, but while I hung on to traditional heterosexual ones, Sonny grabbed on to the most accessible group of his time that accepted his orientation. The "free sex" no-commitments atmosphere of gays — and straights — at Studio 54 and in Greenwich Village may have been an extreme way for him to feel comfortable with himself, but it was Sonny's unpropitious choice.

I engineered a dinner in Manhattan so he wouldn't appear in Larchmont. I had never told him a thing about my own sexuality; I was dodging, hedging, hiding as always. In he walked in gray cowboy boots, his hair done in an exotic perm. I looked left and right whenever we were together; who might see me with this togged-up oddball was always the issue.

We did the usual catching up, the normal stuff, and as we were finishing dinner, he said he had "plans" later. I asked what he was doing and he said, "You really don't want me to tell you, do you?" Years later, I deciphered that to mean he was going to a bathhouse or some risky bar. At the time I didn't know such places existed, and it wasn't until after AIDS became a plague that I understood what specifically went on behind those doors. Sonny was promiscuous, but although there are people incapable of intimacy, I don't think he was one of them. I think he, like a lot of gay men of that era, who had no fears of illness and were intent on letting themselves be themselves, felt they immediately had to come across sexually or the new man, this new potential love, wouldn't continue a relationship. It was really not just sex for Sonny but, however short-lived, a need for affection, approval, love and a deep cry for connection.

We lost touch for some years, but once in a while I'd get a postcard from California or a Christmas card from Philadelphia. Now and then I'd send one too. Doug Robertson and I also stayed lightly in touch over the years, and the summer after I graduated from the University of Vermont, I went to Europe on my graduation-present vacation. When I got to London, I called Doug and he invited me to his flat for tea. A big surprise awaited me there: he was living with a beautiful young woman and they were engaged. As we talked about the past, and specifically about Swiss Challenge, Doug lost his charm. He made cutting, cruel and tasteless remarks about Sonny, about homosexuals in general. "I couldn't understand you always hanging around with him," Doug concluded cordially, while Chris, the homo in hiding, took a sip of his host's tea and, cringing inside, kept smiling.

So the irony was not only that Sonny was gay and that Doug had turned out to be heterosexual and homophobic, but that Sonny had read Doug wrong. To this day, I don't doubt that Doug had wound up on the wrong side of the bed, but was it accidental? Or was Doug one of many pubescent boys who experiment with same-sex sex but grow up to be straight, like the boys of my junior high school?

As I look over Sonny's old letters with hindsight, I read more despair than adventure: "I am thinking of splitting on my own to New York or somewhere, to . . . see how I do when I'm faced with a situation like trying to survive."

He always signed his letters "Still here."

* * *

It was several years later that I went to California, and tried to call Sonny. His old telephone number was disconnected, so I called his mother in Philadelphia to try to find him, and Sonny himself answered the telephone. This is a story that is too predictable; it has no surprise ending. He had gone home "for a breather," having tested HIV positive. He sounded upbeat and fine and we agreed to meet sometime soon. We never did. A year or two later his mother left a message on my telephone answering machine telling me Sonny had died. His life ended in Philadelphia on my thirtieth birthday.

And so I am left with my guilt, some old photographs and letters, and Sonny Fields, still here, but only in my memories.

11

- - - - - - - - - -

I THOUGHT OF IT at the time as one of the darkest days of my life. We were among the first to arrive at Kirby's new dormitory, which was still so vacant late on this fall afternoon that one could practically hear voices echo in its halls. We carried luggage, bedding, athletic gear, typewriter, camera, skis — the precious accumulated paraphernalia of a high school sophomore — into an as yet empty building with tile floors, cinderblock walls and all the homey flair of army barracks.

Dreary is how I perceived this perfectly typical boarding school dormitory. Naked striped mattresses on Spartan metal beds evoked penitentiaries and holding cells. Cold light from overhead fixtures, curtainless windows, shadowy hallways and small, empty closets smacked of punishment and deprivation. In this small room there were two beds, two desks, two dressers, two chairs. Kirby chose his bed, his desk, his dresser. While Bob stood in the doorway waiting for the dorm proctor to appear, I sat in Kirby's orange plastic desk chair and watched him paste up pictures of the Marx Brothers on his portion of cinderblock wall. It came over me unexpectedly. My eyes began to well up, I got that here-comes-the-faucet burning, my throat began to close. For Kirby's sake, I must give no sign of psychic misery; we had an image of this-is-for-the-best to uphold here.

Kirby hadn't chosen to go away to school. We were inflicting this on him, tearing him out of his home, neighborhood, away from his siblings, buddies, grandparents, the cat and my cooking. He'd scored high on IQ tests and not correspondingly high in public school academics. It was in his best interest to send him off, get him into a structured environment of smaller classes and bigger expectations. Or was it?

As he pasted up Harpo and Chico and Groucho, the dorm

proctor's wife appeared. God, she was so young. Her husband was out doing errands, getting things from the store, groceries or pizza or something, so she thought she'd stop by and just say hello, see if we needed anything. She was wearing a perky red beret, on which I complimented her. Small talk couldn't fool her; she saw my face.

"Kirby will be fine," she said warmly, intending to comfort and reassure, and I thought, How the hell does she know? And, What the hell does she care? And as soon as she left, I spilled right over. Poor Kirby. And poor us, a fractured family, without him. My tears wouldn't stop. I sat in that orange plastic chair sobbing like a child while Kirby, embarrassed to death, just went quietly about his business, continuing to paste up black-and-white stills of his comic heroes. Bob paced the room saying Kirby would do fine here, just fine.

As it turned out, Bob and the dorm proctor's wife were absolutely right. Kirby never lost his insouciance. I did miss him, but he loved his prep school, never had a day of homesickness or a disconsolate moment, lived up to his IQ academically and made new friends galore.

Which is why, three years later, we enrolled Chris at Kent School.

Kirby's happy denouement at Westminster had fired Chris's ambition to follow in his brother's footsteps. Chris sent away for catalogues and talked about prep schools and nothing else for months, and ironically, he and his father finally shared an interest. Bob was enthralled by the mystique of New England boarding school life, and in fact so was I. These ivied walls evoked *Goodbye, Mr. Chips* civility, high moral and scholastic standards, seemed a century away from the declining standards of dress, behavior and academic achievement at the local high school. Here we had denim, drugs and disorder, there we would have tweeds, gentility and accountability. Here we had wacky course offerings — "Comedy in Movies" — there we had classics and summer reading lists. And, if one is to be honest, these superlative institutions appealed to the snob in all of us. Perhaps we thought of Connecticut and Massachusetts Waspiness as a paradigm for up-and-down, all-around, through-and-through excellence. Certainly it appeared as if power came to those men who were spliced together for life behind these consecrated school walls.

So although Chris was performing masterfully at the local high school and there was no pressing academic reason to leave public education, we made appointments to visit the offices of admissions at Choate, Hotchkiss and Kent, omitting Westminster, because the little brother did not want to fall into the shadow of the big one.

Yet, I had some serious reservations.

During a dinner party not long before, a friend had made an offhand remark. "Everyone knows the boarding school system causes homosexuality. It's why there's so much of it in Great Britain. It's absolutely rampant there." Since she had lived many years in the U.K., I trusted her opinion.

Despite Dr. Greene's earlier conclusive test results and our previous euphoria at his assurances that Chris was a heterosexual, some uneasiness nipped at the heels of my subconscious: boys' schools did have a reputation for promoting, fostering, encouraging sexual deviation. I was back in the library again: "A very much higher proportion of those educated in single-sex boarding schools reported [homosexual] experiences than did those educated at day schools, either co-educational or single sex" (*Homosexual Behavior: Therapy and Assessment,* Feldman and MacCulloch). This academic tome went on to qualify the statement by declaring that the persistence of the effect of these school experiences was unknown, and that incarcerated men did not necessarily continue homosexual practices that had provided sexual gratification while in prison.

I was swimming through a sea of question marks.

And, I had read a Merle Miller *New York Times* article years before, and remembered an anecdote he attributed to Voltaire. Voltaire was said to have had one homosexual experience, with an Englishman. When the Englishman suggested that they repeat it, Voltaire is alleged to have said, "If you try it once, you are a philosopher. If you try it twice, you are a sodomite." Chris living in boarding school? How much would it take to tip the scale from philosopher to sodomite?

A large part of me wanted Chris under my watchful eye. I still thought more bonding with Daddy was a possibility. Now that Chris was older and Kirby was going to college, couldn't Bob spend more time teaching him tennis? Or driving? In my fantasy, I imagined an epiphany. Bob would wake up one day a revolutionized father, take Chris out in the BMW that the boy adored so, teach him to drive, discuss the stock market with him, show him how big sheets of plastic become eyeglass frames. And Bob would stop walking around the house naked.

I wasn't sure it meant a thing, but we had a prepubescent daughter as well as a pubescent son under our roof. Why couldn't he put on a goddamn pair of shorts? Why was he always marching around like this? If we had a son with a possible sexual-orientation problem, well, who knew what effect this could have on him? And an eight-year-old girl — what about *her* sexual development? Bob insisted it was more comfortable to wear nothing, and the realistic cells of my working brain vetoed the pipe dream that he would change. He did not wear the terry-cloth Wraparong I bought him, and for some time he adamantly resisted when I asked him to please, please wear clothes or a robe at home.

This provocative behavior, which Bob felt was harmless and his inalienable right under his own roof, consistently upset me. At the same time, although I knew it was improper, unsavory and in some hazy way possibly peccant where a little girl was concerned, I also couldn't put a name to what harm could come from the children's seeing Daddy lounging around in the altogether. I was well aware that there are sun worshipers and nudists who go about their family business naked as jaybirds on a regular basis, and to the best of my knowledge cause no discernible sexual harm to their offspring. Nudity is also standard issue in some tropical *National Geographic* locales and, for all I knew, in five, ten, twenty percent of all the world's civilized households.

Since causes and effects were unclear, and since Bob's naked-
ness had no conscious salacious intent on his part, the wind was
pretty much out of my sails as far as my arguments went. Which
meant that just as Bob would not allow any of his children or his
wife to take the wheel while he was in his car, he just as adamantly
held on to his proclivity for remaining in the buff at home.

After a great deal of discussion, however, he did make a con-
cession. Naked, he stayed in the bedroom with the door tightly
shut; his bed, his TV, his comfort were everything to him. Now,
more often than not, we were separated from our children behind
that privacy barrier, and so, it turned out to be a very small and
very hollow victory: that closed door meant that the children had
even less access to their father.

Fully dressed, charming, in high spirits, Bob drove Chris to Connecticut to look at prep schools. Sometimes I tagged along. The
directors of admissions would also be looking us over, asking
Chris the "What do you hope to get out of your experience at
boarding school?" questions, and getting the "I enjoy skiing and
photography; my best subject is math" answers.

Each school had its own spin, but there was a sameness as I
perceived it, an oh-golly wholesome, friendly and civilized atmosphere that gave a parent confidence in the future of her child and
the future of the white Anglo-Saxon world. The directors of admissions told anecdotes and reminisced about their own school
days, had an encyclopedic knowledge of course offerings, sports
and school histories, wore oxford button-down shirts to a man,
ties with school insignia or stripes, herringbone tweed jackets.
Just like the movies. Their secretaries, women of all ages, would
be soft-spoken and uncommonly friendly, offer coffee and apolo-
gize for something or other — the smell of new paint, their head
cold, the weather. The offices, usually on the first floor of the
administration building, were hung with pictures of crew teams
from 1924, past administrators and a dead president or two, a
framed quote, and there, on special glass-enclosed shelves, would
be the proud lineup of sports trophies of interscholastic events.

So much seemed perfect: the small classes, the bonhomie, the spectacular libraries and the dedicated teachers. With golden leaves outside and polished wood inside, I sat in these offices in total awe. I pushed out of my mind that what seemed wonderful and genteel here among oak desks and old photos was actually elitist, unreal, not remotely representative of what life was really all about. In this mainly white, male dominated world (Kent and some other schools did have separate girls' schools), there were black students, Asian students, girls. Some. Just like in the movies. But there were also sub rosa cans of school worms: cliques, scandals, drugs.

For reasons that are unclear to this day, drugs were even more prevalent behind these ivy-covered walls than in our public high school. Pot and hash were almost universal. Stress? Money? Boys and girls whose parents could afford prep school tuition provided man-sized allowances. Chris later told me he was one of only a handful of boys who had never tried marijuana while at Kent. Supervision was tight, but possibly nothing can match a parent's sharp eye, and because peer pressure didn't end at three but continued around the clock, it seemed as if more "nice" boys succumbed. Often alumni returned to supply their little "brothers."

The year that Chris was at Kent, a barn on campus burned down, killing most of the school herd. Some cows burned to death, others froze, some had to be shot because they were in severe pain. Arson was suspected.

A year after Chris left, a famous mayor's troubled son was expelled for cocaine use. Students' mental equilibrium was the double-edged part of prep school life. It became clear to us later that many parents' motivation for sending their offspring away from home had nothing to do with scholarship. Too great a proportion were troubled adolescents from recently broken families, the foundering, unhappy children of traveling or uninterested parents. A secret gathering in a dormitory or out of it was less likely to be for the purpose of reading dead poets than for smoking, snorting or swallowing something illicit.

And where does one find a school without cliques? At boarding school they seemed even more deep-dyed and impenetrable, possibly because clannishness began at the showers in the morning and ended when the last light was turned off at night. There was no getting away from it, ever.

"Fate . . . is a name for facts not yet passed under the fire of thought." Had I read this line of Ralph Waldo Emerson's on some school building's wall? Found it scribbled at the back of a chapel pew? Or simply remember it from my own school days? We didn't suspect any loaded dice when we dropped Chris off at his dormitory. It was three years after the autumn day I'd cried my heart out at leaving Kirby to his new life, and this time, as I was to discover, it was altogether different. (In an unrelated turn of events, the young proctor's wife whose beret I'd admired at Westminster, who had tried so hard to comfort me, attempted suicide later that very year, left the school and never reappeared.)

It is only lately that I fully understand what a year at a wonderful boarding school could entail for a fifteen-year-old boy who was destined never quite to fit into the old-boy, mainstream, heterosexual world of teams and regular-guy camaraderie.

So it is ironic that I got it all wrong: I cried for no reason whatsoever when I left my older boy to fend for himself, and this time, as we drove over the little bridge that led to the beautiful campus of red brick buildings, the playing fields, the stables, the boathouse bordering the Housatonic River, I was sanguine, filled with high expectations, at peace, when I should have been crying a river for Chris, and all the other undercover boys like him everywhere.

12

- - - - - - - - - - -

I SUPPOSE I liked Kent School for almost the whole first week I was there. Coming off a great summer in Switzerland, I arrived on an Olympian high as we drove over the small bridge that led to the glamorous campus. As my parents helped fill the closet in my assigned dormitory room with my brand-new wardrobe of shirts, shoes, ties, my first three-piece suit and the just-bought and very *au courant* madras jacket, I looked around me with a Rich Kid's eyes and loved everything I saw. The apple-cider air of New England, with autumn leaves falling on the chapel roof, stone walls and playing fields, guys in tweed with last names for first names — Whitcombe, McWilliam, Jarvis — everywhere, tradition you could cut with a knife. It was where and who I thought I wanted to be. I was assigned to one of the best dorms, and my cozy room featured a dormer, built-in desks and bunk beds, bright with sunshine. It looked out onto brick colonial-style buildings; I could even see the river.

My new roommate, Tad Bartholomew, had arrived before me and was there with his father, a schoolteacher. Tad was a team-jacket type of kid, here on some sort of sports scholarship, and it didn't take long for our inherent differences to make us uncomfortable whenever we were in the same room. It seemed an issue with Tad that while my closet was crammed with clothes, his seemed sparsely populated — a jacket or two, a slicker, his father's hand-me-down tweed suit and much sports equipment.

Almost immediately I began to feel his resentment, and soon, too soon, we had words. I believe I symbolized for Tad what he didn't like about Kent — the aura of privilege, the atmosphere of conspicuous consumption — and although a luminous athlete, he felt disadvantaged and uncomfortable about not measuring up financially. He made remarks: "You going out to test drive a

Lamborghini?" "Having your pajamas monogrammed?" He'd taken to borrowing clothes, his attitude being that I had enough to go around, and in my effort to keep the peace, I was relatively mild about it, until one day he wore my madras jacket to class without asking permission.

"You weren't here and I couldn't ask. Anyway, I didn't do a goddamn thing to your jacket!"

He hadn't, but, hey, it was my high-test, all-color, guaranteed-to-bleed jacket, and I finally asserted myself and let him have it. We really soured on each other at that point, but there was worse to come. After that confrontation, the atmosphere cooled radically, but at least Tad stopped borrowing my clothes. For a time things coasted along in sort of a live-and-let-live calm, while we led our different campus lives. We shared no classes, interests or friends and spent little time in our room together.

A month or so into the first trimester, my honeymoon with the school was over. I'd had the bad luck to draw the most despised mealtime task, kitchen crew, as the first of my revolving jobs. I had to eat in the cafeteria half an hour before dinner, serve all through the meal, clean dirty dishes off trays, put them into the dish racks and shove everything onto a conveyor belt that was so hot with steam that I was continually burning my fingers. I was totally unused to kitchen detail and more than a little spoiled, but although it was a hateful beginning, the kitchen work turned out not to be the biggest school headache.

Nor was it that classes were held six days a week. I recognized the profound difference in the caliber of my education and came to terms with the fact that while I was considered an academic virtuoso in public school, I was not part of the elite here. Classes were small, homework responsibilities college-sized, and teachers' demands major league. Still, I appreciated the challenge and struggled my way into my slightly above average academic slot.

I had a harder time accepting the seniors' power. They had the right to discipline the younger students, and ranged in personality anywhere from humane to Wolfman. Chris, the reliable obeyer of rules, was a few minutes late for breakfast once and had to sweep a stairwell for a half hour every day for a week. It was overkill, and pretty typical.

Every trimester we had to participate in a sport, my predictable bête noir, and my way out was to be a manager of the junior-varsity soccer team. (I didn't have to play!) I simply had to do all the warmup exercises with the players and then clean up after the games, put away the equipment, keep a log. On this particular day, I took longer than usual and was late coming back to my dorm. It was twilight and I was hungry. Very, very hungry. My father had recently brought me a huge hexagonal Toblerone chocolate bar from Geneva, and I'd hidden it in the top drawer of my dresser. It was my hedge against starvation, and I saw it in my mind's eye, nestled among my socks and underwear. My mouth could hardly wait.

Tad was sitting on his bed putting new laces in his sneakers when I came in. He hardly looked up, gave me a halfhearted, dim "Hi," the minimalist greeting lately typical of our exchanges.

I threw my books on my bed and, with my mouth watering, headed for the hidden treasure. I opened the top drawer, dug under my socks, underwear, keys, batteries, tissues, a belt or two, the flotsam and jetsam of my accumulated debris, but there was no Toblerone. I'd put it right *there*, I was dead sure, tucked it in the back corner, under stuff that would hide it from others' temptation should anyone accidentally catch sight of this prize. Accelerating my motor, I tried the second drawer, the third, then worked my way up again. My top drawer was a mess and it was hard to tell if anyone had rummaged, but in any case, the chocolate had definitely been swiped. There was no mistake about that.

I turned to Tad. "Did you take my Toblerone?" I asked in a steady voice, trying to keep my cool.

It was like I'd shot off a starting gun. Tad stopped lacing, went rigid and came close to spitting at me. "Are you accusing me of stealing your fucking chocolate bar?" He made "chocolate bar" sound as insignificant as "collar button," but to me the Toblerone was, at this moment, very significant indeed.

My blood sugar was down, I was sure he'd taken it, and I was mad as hell. "I asked if you took it."

He threw down his sneaker, jumped off the bed, and all of a sudden we were face to face, red and battle ready.

"It's missing," I said. I amazed myself, holding my ground, not backing down a hair.

"You're accusing me of being a thief, goddamn it!"

He'd been steaming for weeks, waiting for an opportunity to let me have it, and here was his chance. This was not so much about chocolate as about Armageddon. This was about the haves versus the have-nots, the classes versus the masses, athletes versus aesthetes.

And this was about square shoulders versus limp wrists.

He threw a punch and hit me in the chest. I think I punched back, because the next thing I remember is hitting the ground, the both of us rolling around between bed and desk chair, throwing fists at each other and panting, until we knocked over the chair. When it crashed to the floor, the fight fizzled out. We got up, retreated to our bunk beds in cold silence and that was that.

Tad's response a few minutes later marked the beginning of my undoing at Kent School. I sensed he was telling the truth when he said, "I didn't touch your fucking candy. And if you had half a brain, you'd figure out who did."

Kent School was considered one of the top prep schools in the country, but it was known to be especially regimented and strict, with rules more rigid than those at Choate, Hotchkiss or Exeter. It had an appeal for parents who felt their children needed a firm hand. My perception was that there were many boys from broken families (girls, too) who had a cornucopia of discipline problems. Drug use was even more common here than at the public school I'd left, and petty theft was not unheard of.

When Tad insinuated I could guess who *had* stolen my Toblerone, I immediately thought of Liman, a black boy in our dorm who was already on suspension for "borrowing" a camera from an upperclassman. Liman came from a well-to-do family in

Washington, D.C., was short in stature but big in personality, an outgoing, hearty type, and despite his reputation for being light-fingered, was very well liked.

Sometime within the next twenty-four hours, I found myself alone in Liman's room, rifling through his bureau drawers, desk and finally a metal footlocker by his bed. By this time I was pretty sure I had the right perp, and there, sure enough, was what I'd come looking for: the glimmer of yellow cardboard and what was left of my Toblerone bar. With box and wrappers off, half eaten, and because this particular hexagonal package was not then available in the United States, there was no question that it was *the* Toblerone bar. Mine.

So, Liman was in trouble.

I reported the theft and my finding the stolen goods to the dormitory prefect, a senior who was likely to be fair and even-handed. I expected Liman would get a slap on the wrist in the form of "hours" — the usual leaf raking, sweeping or some extra kitchen duty — but the prefect threw a curve. He said that since Liman was already "campused," he could not discipline him personally but had to report his latest offense to the dean. Had I learned nothing since reporting Jeremy to my teacher for stealing my pencil sharpener in fourth grade? For me, just deserts somehow always boomeranged. If I wanted justice done, it turned around and blindsided me.

And so Liman was expelled for the theft of my chocolate bar, the final felonious straw, and overnight, the boys in the dormitory, blaming me for putting the finger on him, began a minor persecution. My bed was short sheeted, once was filled with autumn-leaf debris, and one day, slipping into the sneakers I hardly ever had on my feet, I felt an unfamiliar and disgusting squish. Some creative Kent boy had squeezed toothpaste into the toes. All these torments may have been the work of only one or two classmates, but to me it seemed as if these anonymous attacks represented the sentiment of the entire dormitory, if not the whole school. I saw myself again as a pariah, a boy without a friend or ally, evicted again from the group to which I would have given all my Rich Kid's property to belong.

Lonely, attacked by spells of homesickness and depression, I shuffled from class to class, to the library, the dining room, the chapel, feeling more cut off and alone than I'd ever felt in my life. I wrote home, begging my parents to come visit, and came to detest the brick school buildings, playing fields and ubiquitous tweed jackets, the very things that had taken my breath away just a few months before. Tad Bartholomew and I both put in a request for a change of roommates, which could not take effect until the second trimester, so we were trapped together in the icy atmosphere of our dorm room night after night.

I began to spend a great deal of time in the library, and it was there I kept running into a boy named Scott Shoreham. We had originally met in the school bookstore while waiting in line to buy the same protractor, had struck up a conversation then and something clicked; now, in the library, we began a tentative friendship. Having started school late, Scott didn't have many friends, also wasn't getting along well with his roommate, and so, although our backgrounds were dissimilar, we hit it off. Scott was from Chicago, the son of the vice president of a huge international paper company, and was the oldest of six or seven children. He was an extremely serious student and, like me, followed school rules to the letter. Fastidious, handsome, religious, with fine dark blond hair and flawless clothes, he was the sort of boy I found appealing. We got along well; he seemed to fit my grandmother's description of a perfect gentleman; my spirits rose. I'd found a friend!

Scott and I decided to room together. At the time it seemed a good idea.

He turned out to have some eccentricities. My new roommate would sit at his desk endlessly with a woman's makeup mirror, squeeze out his blackheads and zits and examine his complexion and body, which was flawless. He bought his own rubbing alcohol, which he massaged into his skin every night. Solitary and elliptical, he continued to be relatively friendless. No typical jock, he was a refined sort of athlete and played tennis, squash, ran track, the sort of prep school sports that reminded me of the old photographs in the administration building. Ultimately he became a big part of the varsity track team and now, whenever I think of Scott Shoreham, I picture him with a white towel around his neck, a shock of blond hair falling across his forehead.

Late in January, after observing him for weeks, I became convinced he was gay. I felt him out during our many conversations, talked myself into thinking I was right, and one night, or more specifically one predawn — it must have been four in the morning — I made a critical mistake. At fifteen I was already a sexual human being and would occasionally go into the bathroom in the middle of the night to masturbate; it was a pretty common activity, and privacy was hard to come by. Students showered jointly in one large tiled area equipped with spray heads, the rows of toilet stalls in the bathrooms were doorless and faced the mirrors over the sinks opposite, allowing full disclosure of all occupants' bodily functions. In other words, there was total scrutiny of everything, at all times.

Except before dawn, when everyone was in bed, dead to the world.

I crept quietly back to my room and stood watching Scott sleep. I suppose I was in a kind of sexual haze, and as I hovered there looking at Scott, I wished he would wake up and — and do what? He was in the top bunk, continuing to sleep, and it threw me back to when I was twelve years old, with Kevin Spencer, when it was all right to do stuff if you never mentioned it, never admitted it, never again referred to it — as if it were an I-don't-know-what's-going-on sort of instinctive, mechanical behavior.

It came over me. An unexpected yearning, a quirky desire, a sudden compulsion I couldn't name. And what I did, or what my hand seemed to do, was to move up and reach under Scott's covers. But before I could decide whether to dare to touch him, he opened his eyes.

"What are you doing?" Scott said. At first he seemed groggy with sleep and somewhat confused.

I said, "Nothing."

Awake and alert, he shot up. "You were too. You were putting your hand under my covers!"

My small voice got even smaller.

"No." I could barely hear it myself.

"And I know *why!*"

I was in a head-to-toe cold sweat. I said, "I wasn't. I wasn't! I slipped! I was just getting in my bed and slipped and grabbed hold of the top bunk." I know now I should have stuck to that story, but I didn't. I have always been a terrible liar.

"You were trying to touch me!" Scott's eyes were blazing with disgust and hatred.

"I was just stopping myself from falling." I actually now did feel the floor was rocking and I might lose my balance.

"No, you weren't, you weren't!" He switched on the light to get a better look at my face.

I got back into my bed and huddled under my covers, but couldn't sleep, and an hour later, still before sunrise, Scott dressed and went out. I was overcome with shame and remorse. While it was still dark outside, I got out of bed and wrote him a letter, and that was about the stupidest thing I ever did in my life. I remember sitting at his desk, grabbing a pencil because that was what was handy. I wrote:

Dear Scott,

Since I was six years old I've had homosexual tendencies and I've been fighting this all my life. I never wanted to hurt you or anything like that. I don't know what came over me, but I didn't intend on doing anything without your consent. I realize now there's something terribly wrong with me and I'm going to stop and nothing will ever happen again, and some day, I hope to get married.

There was more. I wrote this whole long explanation about how I knew this was wrong and would never do such a thing again as long as I lived, and that did turn out to be the truth. I never approached anyone uninvited again. Ever. In fact, this epi-sode had great repercussions, because for years I avoided making even the subtlest overture to anyone, even if I thought — I was sure — the person was gay. I was damaged severely, frozen into a perpetual timidity, much too afraid to risk making another critical mistake. Over the years I certainly lost many opportunities of finding someone to return my affection.

Later that day Scott came back to the room and said, "I took your letter to Reverend Carstairs."

I don't know what I expected, but being reported to a minister wasn't it. I went absolutely rigid with fear. Reverend Carstairs lived across the hall and was an apprentice chaplain. Young, very handsome, he must have been in his middle twenties. Scott, a devout Episcopalian, already had some sort of a relationship with the minister and must have felt a particular affinity for him. Scott, his voice rising, said, "I discussed it with him and we're going to do something about moving me out of this room!"

He went on shouting at me, calling me a pervert, letting go his full-blown, king-size anger, and I stood there in a freeze frame, pleading with him to please, please forgive me and not say any-thing to anyone else.

Scott was cold, derisive. "Reverend Carstairs wants to see you in his apartment at three o'clock." He turned on his heel and walked out of the room.

The hour of three o'clock sticks in my mind, and it will forever.

How did I get through my classes that day? I know only that I didn't speak a word to anyone, and couldn't get a bite of my lunch down. I also know I looked at my watch a hundred thousand times wanting time to stop. I threw random prayers into the sky, dreamed of catastrophes that could call for a cancellation of our meeting forever, tried to make deals with God.

At three o'clock sharp, I stood in front of Reverend Carstairs's door, shaking as if I'd stripped naked in a snowstorm. I remember him sounding kind and saying "Come in" very naturally, as if I'd been invited over for coffee. I walked in on my rickety legs, head down. I had never crossed this threshold before and have a vague memory of the place as being sparsely furnished, almost as if furniture was still to be delivered, as if no one actually lived here. I was beet red and continued quaking. Inside, Reverend Carstairs had me sit on the sofa in his bare-floored, bare-walled living room and asked me if I wanted anything to drink. I said no, and of course he sensed my terror. Gently he said, "You know, Scott showed me this letter you wrote," and that's when I just broke down.

I started crying and I don't think I stopped for twenty minutes. He kept trying to console me, and when I was able to control myself a bit, he told me that the dean had been alerted about this "situation," and I started shaking and weeping all over again. I cried, "What about my parents?" and he said, "We haven't told your parents. Nothing has been decided yet about what to do about your situation." Never has the word "situation" been so packed with oily sordidness.

The dean of Kent School was effectively the headmaster, and having the dean know was like an earth-splitting cataclysm. He was the hands-on principal of the school, and his sphere was so broad that it included all parts of a boy's existence. It was much more than just what you did in school; this jurisdiction affected *everything* in my life. It seemed to me then that the dean was an omnipotent figure one step down from the Holy Ghost.

I careened into a panic, started thinking, My parents are going to find out, I'm going to be kicked out of school, my future will be ruined, what will my family think of me? I imagined scenarios beyond torture: I would be thrown out of the house at home because of this unspeakable horror of a thing I'd done. Where would I go? What could I do?

Reverend Carstairs, seeing my reaction, continued kindly to explain that he'd discussed the situation with the head reverend of the school and that things could be done to help me. He meant psychiatry, I suppose, but I was basically inconsolable, kept breaking down into tears, and asked, "What about Scott? Please, please tell him not to mention this to anyone!" I knew if this got out, it would ruin me here. Everyone would know. I wouldn't be able to lift my head on this campus and, for all I knew, anywhere, ever again.

Reverend Carstairs realized then that to save my reputation, he should have told Scott not to discuss this, and I do think that he did warn Scott later, but it was too late to close the barn door; the horses were out. Scott had already spread the word.

As I've learned over the years, when boys call someone "faggot," it's a catchall epithet and doesn't necessarily mean "homosexual." Occasionally, over the years, I took it the bad way, felt they were on to me, could look directly into my soul, were perceiving the truth and judging me, but most of the time I understood that they meant, "You're a wimp" or "You're a weakling." Homosexuality, unless there is some hard anecdotal evidence about a certain boy, is usually not a fixed reality in their thoughts. Sometimes "you faggot" is meant lightly, as a joke. Sometimes, among friends, it's almost an endearment.

Unless, of course, boys are told point blank, and with explicit detail, that "Chris tried doing this or that to me." In that case, they know what they know, they hold it in their hearts, and they never forget it.

And so, later that year, when I approached a boy from my English class, a nice kid, someone I liked and tried to befriend, he took it the wrong way. He'd heard the news. I had no idea, was hanging around him, trying to be friendly, asking him, "What are you doing tomorrow night?" that kind of thing, and one day, on the steps of the library, when he was with a bunch of other guys, he turned on me. "Shyer, you gay blade!" he said, to impress the crowd. I'd never heard the term, and shriveled in my tracks as everyone laughed. It was seventeen years ago and I can still see the face of that boy. It was twilight, there was snow on the ground, I remember it all. And I can still hear the laughter.

After my meeting with Reverend Carstairs I had the feeling that doomsday was going to come at any moment. Scott and I were still in a room together until the end of that trimester, and he just didn't talk to me. He made all efforts never to be in the same room, and while he was avoiding me, I was slinking around buildings to avoid the minister, walking head down to every class and sending SOS messages to God. I was tormented day and night with the thoughts of what was still ahead, and for the next three weeks I'd go into the Episcopal chapel and sit there in a pew alone and cry. Then I'd pray: I didn't mean to do it. It won't happen again, I swear it. Please God, let this pass.

I suppose, since there were no letters or calls to my parents, no further meetings with clergy or the dean, and no tangible aftermath, one could say my prayers had been answered. The episode passed, but the experience left a profound and indelible mark on me, and if I had one more pleasant or relaxed moment at Kent School the rest of that year, I have no recollection of it at all.

13

- - - - - - - - - -

Dear Mom and Dad,

I have been here for almost a month now and have decided that I am going to write to you my feeling-s about Kent. Every time you leave after you come up, I get horibly homesick. The only thing that keeps me from going crazy is that I will see you every 2 or 3 weeks.

I don't think I could take another year of being away from family, friends and especially Larchmont.

As for now, I need visitors. Send up Uncle Henry and his family, send up anyone.

The thing that I will miss from here if I stay home next year is the fantastic teaching, that is the ONLY thing that I really like about this place.

I don't want you to think that I cry every day, because I don't, it is just that the idea of living here more than my HOME makes me want to stay home. What made me come to the conclusion of staying home next year was that when I asked a kid where he lived, he said, "I live here. I live here more than at home." That statement absolutely killed me.

Today I started to learn to post on a horse. It is impossible! Write me a letter every day!!!!!

Love,
Chris

I'm not sure why I saved this letter for so many years, although it certainly cut deep at the time. I suppose I thought it terribly poignant, and an echo of a letter I sent to my own parents when I was thirteen, desperately unhappy and homesick at summer camp. The difference between the two letters was that mine got results. My parents came flying up immediately to save me, packed my bags and took me home. In the case of Chris, Bob and I agreed wholeheartedly that Chris would have to finish out every day of the school year. He'd made the choice to go away; he'd picked the school. We were teaching him a lesson: If you make your bed, you lie in it.

Of course, although he reported the episode of the Toblerone chocolate bar to us in elaborate detail, we were in the dark about anything else that was happening to our boy at Kent. The academic school reports were not as stellar as those we'd been used to, so there were little clues: "Chris is not using his ability." "His assignments have been irregular." "It is quite apparent that Chris has lost his interest and drive in the Spanish language this term." These were a far cry from the 90s and 95s we had come to expect on his public school report cards. Still, Kent School was a hard pull, the competition was formidable, and since Chris spilled out his unhappiness but was no longer crying to Mommy, made no mention of the daily reality of tormentors and loneliness, we kept steadfast our determination to keep him there. We even hoped he'd come around by the end of the year and grow to love the school.

But then there were the telephone calls. They stabbed at the heart. Was this child of ours ever going to feel comfortable anywhere? Quite often we drove up on a Sunday — it was a ninety-minute drive — to visit. We took him to the Fife and Drum for lunch, and all I remember now were the positives: a country inn restaurant filled with other prep school families, a walk around the campus, an occasional sports event we'd stay to watch, and everywhere those wholesome, freckled boys in their jackets and ties, calling Bob "sir." If, at our departure, there came a misty moment for Chris, it seemed transient and not too consequential. Until later, when another letter or telephone call came, or until I thought it over, perhaps at night when Bob was asleep and I lay awake, sifting what I'd seen at Kent through the sieve of logic. There were no new buddies, no hint of the sort of hey-you-guys chumminess I'd seen when we'd visited Kirby at Westminster. Different. Chris was forever and always . . . off to the side.

Of course, it wasn't all black clouds, and Bob was so often wonderful. There was much of the auspicious side of family life, and especially of Daddy. During Chris's spring break that year, Bob flew us all to Puerto Rico. The year before we'd gone to Saint Croix, the year after — was it to Saint Martin, Nassau, Bermuda? Daddy not only had deep pockets but a magnanimous spirit, and off we went that year to the Dorado Beach Hotel, then a glamorous resort well outside San Juan, famous for its golf, casino and lush vegetation.

Once the hassle of airport and luggage were behind us, the tension came out of Bob like air out of a balloon. Daddy on vacation was a new and improved version of Daddy at home, and in fact, during vacations he and I took alone together, Bob was even more devoted and noble than on these family junkets. I sometimes felt that if I could keep him forever to myself in four-star hotel rooms, the honeymoon sun would perpetually shine.

Now, at Dorado Beach, relaxed in his chair or on a blanket, a cold drink in his hand and the sun on his face, he was capable of enjoying life and being the true sweetheart I always thought was his real nature. He took photographs, splashed with his daughter in the surf and became relatively mellow when it came to the boys.

At some point he spotted two teenage girls, who seemed to have taken note of Kirby and Chris and were making a not too subtle point of walking back and forth along our stretch of beach in order to Be Observed. Bob became very animated, took a great interest in this nubile twosome and kept prodding the boys to gear up for action. He couldn't, was absolutely incapable of understanding why Kirby and Chris weren't jumping to the bait. "What's wrong with those kids? Those girls are *cute!*" If Bob was indulging in a bit of a fantasy about these bikinied nymphets, living a little vicarious beach adventure, who could blame him?

"The boys are shy, and we're sitting here watching every move they make," I pointed out, and after a while the girls gave up and moved off.

There weren't many teenagers at the resort, and at the very least, these two bathing beauties would have meant company for the boys for the rest of the vacation. Bob shook his head in exasperation; his disappointment was palpable. I actually thought the boys were a bit let down too.

But that night they got another chance. It was after dinner, and we were all sitting together in the piano lounge, getting acquainted with a couple Bob's and my age sitting next to us. They were from Virginia, and this was their second visit to Puerto Rico. We talked about whatever vacationers talk about in the first five minutes after meeting — the food, the golf, the flight down and how long we'd all be staying. And then their daughters appeared, *the* beach girls, now glowing pink with fresh sunburns, wearing pretty backless sundresses.

These two southern charmers were a far cry from the stereotypical retiring belles I always imagined sitting under Spanish moss on a veranda. After a quick introduction, they took matters into their own hands. Flirtatious, outgoing and determined in a rambunctiously charming way, one practically grabbed Kirby, the younger one Chris. "C'mon, you guys. You're not going to sit here with your mom and dad all night, are you?" and off they went for a walk on the beach. I thought, This will develop into a foursome for the rest of our stay, the boys will have a grand time with their new friends, and who knows, a romance — under winter stars over a tropical beach — could erupt by the end of our vacation. Just suppose the synergy of Dorado Beach and beautiful girls could tip the scales for Chris forever? Hadn't I read that positive heterosexual experiences were used as therapy in cases of sexual deviation? There I was, still at it, trying to kick the poor kid into the right circuit.

Within an hour the boys were back. The girls had wanted to go dancing, but our sons were not interested. "Touch dancing —" Kirby made a face, letting us know what he thought of that idea. Chris echoed his brother's sentiments, at least he pretended to. For the rest of our stay, Chris chose to be in the company of his eight-year-old sister, and Kirby found some kindred (boy) souls in the hotel game room. Both boys loved the resort and later said it was a marvelous vacation. In our family photograph album, the children are seated together at the swimming pool of the Dorado Beach Hotel, all smiling lighthearted smiles.

If I seem too focused here on Chris's ongoing resistance to play a heterosexual role, it was only an intermittent anxiety. Other elements of our family interactions, and in particular this vacation, were sunny, literally and figuratively; when my children were enjoying life, I enjoyed life. In fact, my two sons, divided by three and a half years in age and altogether birds of a different feather, hardly noticed each other at home, but for a brief spell here, I was delighted to see the boys meshing, bonding, being brotherly.

I don't know why I knew that Kirby's lack of interest in those two girls had nothing to do with his sexual orientation. He wasn't secure enough to be ready for dancing with a girl he'd met fifteen minutes ago who seemed a decade more mature and confident than he was. At eighteen he was still into pinball machines and the Marx Brothers, and these girls for him were less interesting than, say, being old enough to be allowed to play a few games of roulette in the casino. I also don't know whether I felt, sensed, saw, surmised or guessed that Chris was relieved to be rid of this high-voltage wench pair. All of a sudden I knew that he was threatened by the possibility that this situation would create some sexual pressure, that there might be the necessity to become heterosexual, even if it was just for the rest of this vacation week.

Then again, I might have imagined all of this. Two boys and two girls who just didn't hit it off is what anybody else would have called it. But anyone else wasn't keeping company with my little set of demons. They invariably packed their bags and joined the family — everywhere we went.

My mother was now living in South Carolina and we talked frequently, but I was selective in what I told her. I basically tried to share only our life's good tidings. In those days that was pretty easy, since most of our news, barring an occasional bout of tonsillitis or a crushed auto fender, was good. She baffled me by picking up a minor chord on her mother's radar. Amazing the way she caught vibrations, as if she had a staff of psychics whispering in her ear. Then too, of all my children, I think she liked Chris best. (So did Bob's mother, I believe; he was, and is, any grandmother's dream.) And so one day, not long after this vacation, my mother asked what was worrying me. She could tell something was troubling me. Out with it?

"I'm afraid Chris may grow up to be a homosexual." I could almost strangle on that sentence, it was that knotted and stiff. This was more than two years after the erosion of my firm faith in the test results of Dr. Greene's magic psychological profile.

Her response was unexpected. She was, after all, an older woman, the product of another culture and of an even more repressive age. Moreover, she and my father had divorced and she had remarried, to a most conservative conservative. He later became a supporter of Jerry Falwell's Moral Majority, and my mother always fell into step right behind him. So her comeback was a kicker. "So what do you care?" she said. "Why are you so worried? What's so wrong with being a homosexual?"

What indeed? What picture of Chris as a gay man did I have in my crystal ball that I feared so much? Perhaps there was no one fixed or solid image, just a composite, an amorphous sludge pile of adjectives that had blossomed into a full-blown, full-grown homosexual in my imagination: some flamboyant southern gent, renting an attic room in a relative's house; or my high school drama teacher, high strung and temperamental, suspected of "carrying on" with one of his students; maybe my first literary agent's fussy friend, given to wearing a wild red wig and often hospitalized for depression. Possibly I perceived the generic gay man as a security risk, denied government jobs, decent housing or any prestigious career outside window-dressing or theater. In my mind's eye I saw mincing steps and lisps, funny clothes and men who were everywhere excluded, ostracized and derided. I heard the echoes of all my teenage boyfriends' put-downs of "fags" and "pansies"; I saw the homosexual's life's road as rutted with humiliation in society, imagined sex in alleys and doorways, membership in sordid secret clubs, and promiscuity. And I predicted for men who were not heterosexual, therefore without a family, a lonely old age, and a death somewhere seamy, dark and solitary.

With the help of society, stereotypes and my protective maternal imagination, I conjured up a vision that now seems age-encrusted and mythological, but the conception was not altogether unique at that time. It was the specter a good part of mankind superimposed over the word "homosexual," which I saw as a manifest obstruction to the dignity and decent quality of life I desperately wanted for Chris. I wanted him to have precisely what I wished for my other two children: access to those three magic components of a fulfilled life — health, satisfaction in work and monogamous love, as well as entrée to any professional doors he might want to open, whether to an executive suite, a flight deck or the Oval Office.

I don't know why I didn't listen harder to my mother, but clearly her open-minded sentiments were neither ours nor the world's, then. We were living in the days of Anita Bryant, whose crusade against homosexuals had heavy support; we joined the crowd in snickering when the flamboyant piano artiste Liberace denied he was gay, raised eyebrows at Truman Capote's in-your-face homosexuality and thought nothing much of President Carter's mother's saying, "In my part of the country, we don't have 'em." Even the most enlightened of us were calling homosexuals "creative" and "charming." It was the "some of my best friends" syndrome, and it exists to this day. They were, and continued to be, a "they" and a "them."

I was particularly wrought up by the words of another writer, Laura Z. Hobson, whose book about her gay son, *Consenting Adults,* had lately come to national attention: "For twelve years his secret, of course, had been my secret . . . In public I had laughed at jokes about homosexuals, fearful that angry protest might 'give something away.' When somebody would ask, 'And your other son — is he married?' I would offhandedly say, 'Still playing the field, I guess.'"

I read the reviews avidly and digested every word. Would that be me, the next Laura Hobson, speaking in a few years?

There were more personal touches: a friend from New Jersey casually mentioned that his plans to attend a local dinner-theater performance of *The Boys in the Band* — a contemporary play about gay men — had been canceled, because the owner of the restaurant did not feel it was proper family entertainment. I heard "not proper family entertainment" as a euphemism for vile and dirty, and a random remark like that could ruin my day.

There was nothing equivocal about the messages the world was sending us. And nothing equivocal about my husband's and my polarization. When I expressed my worry about Chris, it invariably ignited Bob's temper.

"You're way off base. Will you get off it!"

Not the first time I'd heard those words. Not the last.

"You're dead wrong. And I'm telling you, it's you! If you keep saying it, you're going to turn him into one!"

There were moments when I actually believed him. Why not? Freud was always in the woodwork, and who knew but my suspicions were emanating from my soul, like some kind of insidious mist? If my mother was catching my vibrations, was Chris?

From my husband I wanted comfort, a dialogue, a bit of hand-holding. I wanted some intelligent dissent, a shoulder to lean on. I needed a friend who would listen without condemning. But Bob turned his back, muttered angrily, left the room, snapped off the light. "I don't want to discuss it. I don't even want to hear about it. For Christ's sake, drop it, will you!"

It never occurred to me then that my mother was right, that we were wrong, and so was the rest of the unenlightened, condemning universe.

When Bob and I traveled the globe, we visited museums, ruins, and of course cathedrals, churches and chapels. Now and then,

I paid a peseta, groschen, lira, franc or drachma in a flickering nave to light a candle. For a nonbeliever, this was tantamount to throwing money into fountains in piazzas, blowing out birthday candles or wishing on a star. The wish was always the same. It was never for a long life, a bestseller or good health. For many years and to my dying shame, I wished that my middle child would straighten out, grow up to marry and replicate the gray-flannel life of his father, grandfather and every heterosexual ancestor in his family tree.

In a dream I could go back, shake some sense into the young me, retrieve those coins and bills and do it again. I would light candles as far as the eye could see to send forth apologies, and a new request. I'd wish for the world to acquire twenty-twenty vision when it came to human individuality, and forever stop condemning men who did not wear gray flannel, who did not lust to shoot their sperm into members of the opposite sex.

Better yet, I would light candles to illuminate the godly spirit in some of those who preach from the pulpits that stand in the light of very stained glass. Universal tolerance under a crucifix or the *ner tamid* would be a good beginning.

14

- - - - - - - - - -

THE DORADO BEACH girls' names were Patty and Leigh, and the younger one, Patty, obviously designated for me, looked like Jaclyn Smith of the big hit TV show *Charlie's Angels,* of which she was very much aware. Patty would shake out her long hair as if she were advertising shampoo, and her fifteen-year-old's self-confidence was something to see. Off came both girls' shoes, they seemed to bound forward rather than take steps, they giggled, they flirted. They developed a routine of running into the cold surf, then shrieking with the excuse of icy toes or a wrong step onto a jellyfish, came running back to us, leaning on our arms or brushing our chests. If my mother figured I was afraid things would get out of hand sexually, she was not far from wrong.

As we moved off down the beach together, urged by both girls to take off our shoes and get our feet wet, what might have been harmless flirting began to make me increasingly nervous. Patty and the dark beach, with my brother as witness, was hazardous territory. One of the straps of her dress kept falling, and she was in no hurry to get it back up. I plotted to take off my own shoes, "accidentally" step on a broken shell and limp back to the hotel, pleading injury. I am not a good faker and hate skulduggery; luckily I was saved.

The hotel had a dance lounge, the girls had a passion for the then hot Chicago, and they wanted to dance. We were two awkward adolescent boys without much teenage-hero status, and I guessed that dancing had been their motivation and interest in us in the first place. My brother was not enamored of his presumed partner, Leigh, for reasons that were unclear but greatly appreciated by me. He kept yawning and saying he was tired and his back hurt from sunburn, so I was spared from having to plead a disabling injury. Kirby was designated the "party pooper" and inadvertently rescued me.

This ducking of sexual responsibility was unique only because it was my first really close-shave hetero episode, and potentially a most embarrassing scene for me, but over the years, experiences like this were part and parcel of closet gaydom. Having been rejected more than once, I always had a pang when I was the one pulling away. I only hope that some of the women who have come forward during the last decade or two with the hopes of getting my attention will read this and forgive my inevitable withdrawal.

The misery of life at Kent continued with a new spin. Nothing much more came of Scott Shoreham's disclosure to the minister, neither the dean nor the headmaster ever had words with me, and although my fear of repercussion never entirely left me, it did abate with time. The one positive result of the episode was that I was allowed to move into the only dormitory on campus where the students had single rooms.

It had the usual lower floors, but a group of cubicles had also been built into its attic, cells that were windowless and monk-like except that they had high, pitched ceilings. These private rooms were a catchall for boys who for one reason or another weren't fitting in with roommates. That included me, a few other offbeats, some privileged seniors who wanted to be alone and got the few single cells with windows, and a boy named Marc Schreuder, who subsequently became infamous, inspiring at least two books and two television miniseries.

I got along with most of these characters — odd birds of a feather did flock together — although none became a friend. Marc, a study in eccentricity, with dust-mop hair, sloppy personal habits and too much flesh, came close. Unkempt even by teenage standards, he was an amusing dissembler who irritated everyone by keeping a high-wattage lamp on in his room all night. Since the partitions did not go to the ceiling, the lights of Marc's lamp kept the dormitory bright as the noon sky long after lights out, at eleven. At midnight you'd hear the voices of protest resound left and right: "Turn off that light! Fuck you, Schreuder, turn off that goddamn light!" Everyone hated Marc, and once he found a shoebox in his room filled with human excrement.

He told me stories I didn't quite believe but were certainly interesting, about his super-rich grandfather, worth millions, and his mother and grandmother, who would sneak money away from the old man to pay rent and Marc's tuition.

I had a vested interest in the outcome of Marc's inheritance. He and I had a joint fantasy about his coming into big money: he promised me one or two million dollars if he got one hundred. (What are friends for, anyway?) I fantasized not about fast cars or stereo equipment, but about my future security in case I was expelled — my sin and true nature uncovered — and I was disowned by my family. With no clue about the bloody hands to come, I saw Marc's grandfather's money as my personal disaster insurance.

His grandfather, one of the wealthiest men in Utah, with money pouring in from his auto-parts business and from investments in land and gas and mineral rights, lived the modest life of a workingman, on a middle-class street in Salt Lake City. Marc's mother cooked up a murder scheme, bought a plane ticket for Marc under his older brother Larry's name and sent him to Utah. There Marc went into his grandfather's auto-parts warehouse on a Sunday, when Grandfather, who worked seven days a week, would be in the plant alone. They had a conversation (it was assumed about money), and when Grandfather turned his back, Marc shot him point blank with the gun his mother had acquired for him for the purpose. Mom tried to pin the murder on her other son, whom she had somehow exiled from her life and affections, and the crime was not uncovered for four years. Marc and his mother are currently doing prison terms in Utah penitentiaries. They were cooking this all up during the time Marc and I were schoolmates.

A letter I got from him, sent to me from Kent during his senior year, said something like, My grandfather is finally dead and he's worth four hundred forty million dollars. This was a bit of hyperbole, but what was true was that Marc had already murdered him. Sadly, Marc was remarkably intelligent, excellent academically and, I thought, all in all not really a bad sort of kid.

It does strike a profound chord in me to think that during all our neighborly conversations, I was afraid he'd guess *my* secret.

Escape from Kent became my obsession. I lived from vacation to vacation, times at home or away with the family, and yearned for the company of one or all of my "second next of kin." The brightest light of my adolescent life was the wonderful relationship I began with the Dorans, the family of my new friend Russ. I'd met him a few years ago at the bar mitzvah of a classmate, but it wasn't until later that we developed a rapport. We kept running into each other, and little by little the relationship ripened.

My free time was spent with him, partly at our house, very often at his. I was welcome at the Dorans' always, and almost felt adopted by them. Expected to make an appearance not only on birthdays and Christmas Day but at all Doran social functions, I was treated generously by the nuclear family and by assorted Doran aunties and cousins. Their friends became my friends, and life became pleasant and normal, thanks to them.

It is hard to describe the Dorans in any but the kindest terms, for their genuine feelings for me pulled me through the most difficult years of my life. This relationship became more than social; over the years I became locked into their lives through affection and habit. In summer around their large oval swimming pool, in winter in front of their fireplace, my second home was my refuge and my snug harbor. To the Doran sisters I was big brother and possibly potential beau, to Russ I was brother, alter ego, best and only friend. Russ, a somewhat effeminate homebody with a sharp sense of humor and a good heart, whose life was his family, hung out, went to movies, played Hearts with me, gossiped and cut school when I was home on vacation. We were inseparable cronies then.

If it is hard to describe the Dorans without mentioning their kindness, it is also hard to portray them without mentioning liquor. Mrs. Doran, the trim, elegantly dressed matron who played bridge, entertained like a professional caterer, had hair, nails and lawn done every week, seemed to sleep with a copy of Amy Vanderbilt under her pillow and treated me like nobility. Charming and thoughtful, she was impossible not to like.

It was also impossible not to notice how rarely she greeted me at the door without a glass in her hand, how often she had on a bit of a buzz, how much of Doran life had to do with glasses, ice cubes and mixers. It was also difficult not to see, as more and more of what was in her glass entered her bloodstream, that she became increasingly kissy and loving. Except at their parties, no one was ever visibly drunk at their house, but although Mr. Doran — a devout Episcopalian and an unusually loving and involved father — was temperate, sobriety was not the family watchword. It was the Dorans' way of washing away problems, keeping the dark spirits of trouble at bay. Nothing but brightness and 100-proof laughs ever seemed to surface in their carefully decorated colonial house, and sometimes I wished a glass full of something would work that magic for me. Unfortunately, liquor only made me sick and gave me a headache. Or perhaps, looking at the Doran family through the corrected lens of time and maturity, sensing the fragile nature of their domestic happiness, my aversion to alcohol is not such a bad thing.

With a great sense of release, I was honorably discharged from Kent School by my parents and transferred to a local private day school, Hackley. I was enormously grateful to my parents for not requiring me to go back to get my comeuppance at the local high school, where the same old bad relationships would have been replayed. Located in Tarrytown, New York, with a diverse student body that included the children of the Reverend Sun Myung Moon and Malcolm X, Hackley had a high standard of academic excellence, small classes and esprit de corps. But the most valuable thing I got out of those last two high school years was myself.

Astonishing how the misfit began to fit. I made friends, did well academically, looked forward (well, mostly) to going to school, although it meant, during the winter months, getting up before it was light and coming home after dark. I probably had already stopped growing, but felt as if I'd gained a few inches and gotten a bit better looking too. I still contribute money to Hackley and go to school reunions, and will forever feel a debt of gratitude to my teachers, fellow students, the very brick and mortar of its old buildings.

With my new infusion of self-esteem, I ventured again in the direction of heterosexuality. I suppose I felt that I should give "normalcy" another shot, since everything else in my life had smoothed itself over, on the surface at least. Viscerally, my secret continued to tear at the fabric of my patched-up self-respect. My teenage eyes couldn't see that I could live a life with a man that included the values I'd been imbued with. I still held on to the same homophobic prejudices that I'm fighting in others today, and the specter of adulthood drove me to give heterosexuality one more chance.

With the help of a beautiful, popular classmate, Sheila Castleton, couldn't I perhaps expunge the sole obstacle to my dream of normalcy? It was clear then that non-heterosexuals would not likely become class presidents or prom kings, that they were doomed forever to a shadowland of back doors, pink slips, derision and hiding. I felt that if I could make that one adjustment, I would never have to tell a lie again.

Sheila Castleton was thin, tall, bubbly and very "in." She was a class officer, played field hockey with all the popular girls and hung out with the jocks. Like everyone else I liked her, but there was, I admit, another motive in my asking her for a date. It had to do with image, still a heavy part of my new persona. (It took many years not to have to grade my sense of self-worth on the public quality of my companions.) I'd score high getting involved with Sheila, versus Melinda Broome, a Hackley chum and my constant cohort, who occasionally seemed to want more from our relationship. Melinda was intelligent, fun and available, but

Sheila had the sparkle, the high school queen-bee qualities, and was in the ruling circle.

I asked Sheila out on a real American date, the sitcom kind where boy picks up girl, meets her parents, then takes her out on the town. She accepted, and it went like this: Slightly nervous, I put on my best clothes, polished my shoes, brushed my teeth and had my father's car washed. My father, so proud, kicked in dinner and Broadway tickets. I appeared at her house on the dot and was greeted at the door by her mother, who took me into the living room. There they all were, the Castletons — mother, father, Sheila and two sisters and a brother — looking me over. Anyhow, that's how I felt, Looked Over. What I remember about that family was blond hair and blue eyes. Every single one of them, even the father. His blue eyes were behind glasses.

Sheila and I said our goodbyes, made our exit and headed to the train station, where I parked my father's car. We took the commuter train into the city, walked to Broadway and got to the theater in good time for the curtain. We were seeing *A Chorus Line,* that long-running hit in which one of the prominent characters is a young gay dancer. My mother has since told me she did not want me to see this play because she felt that if I identified too closely with a gay good Joe, well, maybe it would tip the scale. We agree now that was absurd, but what she didn't know was that I never identified with anyone who wasn't pretty much my mirror image. Dancers on Broadway and their lives did not speak to me, nor did poets, Europeans, the black-leather guys, anyone who lived in Greenwich Village. I couldn't relate to many things that symbolized being gay because they were always the extreme, the specifically sexual and simply too overt. They lived on the other side of the moon, as far as I was concerned. Only lately have I come to understand that we are all part of the same worldwide fraternity.

The date was pleasant. As we stepped out of the train and into the Tarrytown station on the way home, Sheila took my hand. We walked to the car in silence, and I drove her back to her house. When it came time for the romance, the kiss, the denouement, we stood awkwardly face to face at her door. "I had a wonderful time, but you know, I've decided not to have a boyfriend until I'm in college," she said. It was a little rehearsed speech. It was not a kiss, but a kiss-off.

In a way I had expected it. I had subconsciously chosen the most prudish, pristine woman with whom to make my heterosexual debut, so I somehow knew, not that the relationship would fail, but that it wouldn't go very far. It might even have been that she had picked up the old no-sex-please vibes from me and was giving me the brush, but in any case, it was our first date and our last and I was monumentally relieved. I sometimes think that if the social climate had been different, or I'd been more like Sonny Fields, I would have been able to date someone of my own sex, would have lived a real yearbook romance in the open, and would never have had the guilt of hoodwinking and disappointing the likes of Sheila.

A year or so later I found myself sitting in the same car with Melinda, in front of *her* house. She and I went out together as buddies, often with our friends. It was in the middle of the disco craze, and we'd go to Manhattan hot spots with Russ and his sisters and a Hackley group and dance till four in the morning. If everybody at school thought Melinda and I were an item, it suited me fine. I kind of let it go on — all we ever did was kiss once in a while — but on this night, sitting in the circular drive in front of her house, Melinda let me have it. She said that all my friends were upset with me because I wasn't paying attention to them, seemed distracted, strange, cool, and whatever other adjectives came into her head to signify my weird, unnatural detachment. I didn't get it then but I get it now: she was angry as hell at me for my total lack of mating instinct and increasing lack of interest in her. I'm not sure she knew she was firing ammo in the wrong direction, but no matter how she tried, she couldn't get a speck of amour out of me. What girl wouldn't be furious? I am still embarrassed about this, sorry too. What if I were Melinda?

I wasn't falling in love with her, and couldn't. I had in fact met a boy that summer, and against my will, with my libido performing the usual treachery, was already in up to my emotional neck with feelings for him. How could I then let myself lead Melinda on? I suppose it's not unlike carrying an amulet or a four-leaf clover into surgery. Good sense tells you it's not going to save you, but it's something you can do when things are completely out of your control. So, members of the opposite sex were my rabbit's feet and good-luck charms, but hard as I tried, no woman could stir my blood. It was always *cherchez l'homme.*

It was the way it went again and again. I knew what was best for me; it's just that my heart didn't. It went its own way. And still does.

15

THERE WAS NO question that Bob wanted Chris to stay at Kent, but at first I was both disappointed and relieved to have him return home. Running true to form, Bob was into industrial-strength denial and kept reminding me that I was "all wet." Chris was obviously as male as Sylvester Stallone; he had begun dating, hadn't he?

I knew that one date did not a heterosexual make. Chris had friends now, that part was wonderfully true. The phone rang for him! He was invited to parties, was no longer hanging dolefully around the house, and I became enamored of the Dorans, who had taken our son to their hearts. We invited them to dinner and became neighborhood friends. Their drinking was not an issue, but their son's sexuality was. I saw Russ as too overtly effeminate; might Chris suffer from guilt by association?

People are always incredulous when I say I foresaw Chris's sexual destiny as early as kindergarten. Now, at sixteen, although he was built as well as any male athlete, had a deep voice, walked without a mincing step, even had become a stamp collector like my father (considered a masculine hobby in those days), little clues cropped up like reflective road signs. For one thing, the differences between my two boys were conspicuous and marked, if not to Dr. Greene, at least to me.

Here we had Exhibit A, Kirby, resisting the entire process of civilization. It was a monumental struggle to get past his Tarzan tendencies and teach him gentility — everything from table manners to thanking Grandma for a birthday gift. It was not easy to get him to polish his shoes and pick his clothes up off the floor of his room, which was in such chronic disorder one could not move

from corner to dizzying corner without — as I kept saying —
taking a Dramamine pill. His interest in his mother as a role
model was nil. His interest in her feminine paraphernalia, from
cooking equipment to cologne, was less than nil; his movements
were more lumbering than graceful, his friends in constant motion, pummeling, poking, pushing each other, spilling things, yelling and never, for some reason, able to keep shoelaces tied.

My fellow feminists will undoubtedly come down hard on
what we now call gender stereotyping, but I am talking statistics
here, and there are not that many girls out there playing stick-
ball or sitting at home watching *Monday Night Football* with a
can of beer in their hands. We know that all men don't do these
things either, but this paragraph is about generalizations, averages and statistical means. There are men who knit their own
socks and love shopping at the mall. I know there are red-blooded
fellows who embroider, love writing thank-you notes and spend
hours picking out wallpaper, but this is not about exceptions.
When a mother is talking about her own boys, she is not concerned with abstractions and averages. She is into revelations and
realities.

Chris, Exhibit B, was genteel and polished, the perfect little
gentleman from as far back as he could hold open a door for an
older person, jump ahead to pull a chair out for a grandmother,
arrange his shoes in neat rows at the bottom of his closet and
not object to carrying a white handkerchief in his pocket. Chris
had table manners and enjoyed learning how to tie a necktie
around his own neck. He liked dressing up for Sunday school.
He liked museums and was interested in interior design, sculpture
and painting. He took note of what was hanging on the walls
of the homes he visited and whether the hostess was wearing
diamonds. He did not feel in any way uncomfortable walking
our West Highland terrier even though she was not a mighty Lab-
rador or German shepherd. The adjective to describe this behavior is anachronistic and outmoded: ladylike. It has a strong
pejorative ring when used to describe a man's behavior, although

the reverse, "tomboy," sounds not unfavorable when describing a girl.

Now I ask myself why.

The summer Chris was in Switzerland, I decided to redecorate his room. Although we could not consider ourselves rich, I was writing and selling short stories that added to the household kitty, and Bob's business continued to prosper, thanks in part to Gloria Vanderbilt. He had hired her as his "designer" — a euphemism for the rental of a famous name, to be stamped on a line of eyeglass frames someone else had designed, an arrangement typical of his and other fashion industries — and we had the kind of income that allowed us freedom from worry and some luxuries. A touch of ancient ironic history was a conversation I had with Gloria on a plane trip we took together to an optical convention, in California.

From the time of my children's infancy, when I compared feeding schedules in the playground, I couldn't help measuring the progress of other mothers' offspring against my own. I know now that one of Gloria's sons' lives ended in a tragic suicide, but then we were simply a couple of mothers of adolescent boys, and this was a common denominator. I remember the conversation with Gloria specifically, but these note-comparing encounters were an ongoing part of the interactions I had with other mamas as well. My ears always picked up and amplified the phrases to which I was sensitive: "my son's girlfriend," "the guys are all going together," "Jack won the trophy." So when Gloria told me how well her boys were doing in their prep schools, how much they loved their summers in Southampton, I felt a wistful shot of envy: obviously there was not a cloud in *her* maternal sky.

Being a mother was my primary job, and kids were shop talk. As usual, shop talk put me on my guard, turned me slightly evasive, generally made me uneasy. Other mothers, including Gloria Vanderbilt, who presumably had many other things on her plate, were doing something right, and I wasn't. It never occurred to me that other mothers might, like me, be leaving important things unsaid.

I worked on the redecoration of Chris's room most of the summer. Three years before, when I had done some sprucing up of Kirby's room, I found a dozen or so hoarded back issues of *Playboy* and *Penthouse,* as well as some seamier versions of these magazines, hidden under the cushions of an old couch, all the evidence a mother ever needed to assure her that her boy was all boy.

I half hoped that in redoing Chris's room I would find that sort of indisputable evidence of masculinity, but no luck. On the other hand, the nagging fear that I might find incriminating evidence of cross dressing or some such parents' nightmare of debasement did not materialize. It was a boy's room holding no salacious secrets, and I made it even more boyish: blue-and-green-plaid carpet, tailored bedspreads, no-nonsense window shades, ski posters and a bulletin board.

This redecoration project was to be a big surprise into which I had put great effort and creative energy. I'd had closets built, put in new bookshelves, made a wall hanging out of hotel keys Chris had collected, framed his photographs . . . As the date of his homecoming approached, my suspense built. He *had* to like it! On the day he was due to arrive, I ran from window to window, waiting for the airport limousine, practically rubbing my hands together in anticipation of his reaction. What would he say? Would he be knocked out, overawed, dazzled?

He was home! I waited upstairs, anticipating his step across the threshold. And finally here he came, with his duffel bag, suitcase, satchels, skis. There was the usual welcoming rigmarole downstairs, and I stood at the top of the circular staircase that led to the hall and his room, summoning him here for the big surprise, suggesting he come up full steam ahead and leave his stuff downstairs for the moment, I had something to show him!

"Well, how do you like it?" I stepped aside to let him walk into his room.

Another manifest difference between the boys: a redecorated

bedroom did not register high on Kirby's Richter scale, but for Chris it was a major life's event, a red-letter day. Wide-eyed, thunderstruck, speechless, stunned — I saw in his face all the responses I had happily expected.

"Oh, my God!" he said, many times.

This memory is shaded by my recollection of Bob's response. He was right behind Chris, and I thought he too had come to see his son's big-bang reaction and to bask in the pleasure of Chris's happy surprise.

But Bob stood on the threshold of Chris's room, and I have an indelible vision of him in the doorway, naked except for a towel around his waist, flattened against the doorjamb. "I've taken off ten pounds!" he said, patting his own stomach. "Didn't you notice? Ten pounds!"

In the snap of a finger I went from hooray to frustration. This was the man who contributed to the Foster Parents Plan, took color movies of his children's birthday parties, wrote the checks for camp, tuition, music lessons. Why couldn't he live in the moment, share his son's excitement? I saw it as another of his parental deficits, although in all fairness, it was also my creative effort he was diluting. What I saw as Bob's intrusive self-involvement diminished my own sense of accomplishment, my own self-involvement. If I did it for Chris, I did it for myself too. Yet the overwhelming drive then was for Bob to please be, for just five minutes, Dad.

My first boyfriend, John Rieber, the boy who took me to my eighth-grade prom, turned out to be homosexual. Coincidentally we wound up in college together, became good friends, lost touch, then were reunited twenty years later, in the early eighties, when he was already ill with AIDS. John never discussed his sexual orientation. With childlike naiveté, at our first meeting after many years, he said, "You know, I never married." He died without letting on what it was that was killing him.

He was the son of a widow, and when we were in college together and I had the chance to observe his behavior closely, it seemed logical to assume his femininity was the result of a one-fe-male-parent upbringing. Why else would he be so interested in women's perfumes and the upholstery fabrics in our dormitory?

My continuing fears that Chris might grow up to be a John Rieber instead of the all-American heterosexual boy next door strike me as misguided now, but in my defense, I was not only a product of my time but also a living sponge. I was busy sop-ping up all the current attitudes in print, and was propagandized by every fuzzy psychological "expert" who ever owned a type-writer and got published. I kept ingesting things about Oedi-pal stages and this "illness," "decadence," "deviance," "distur-bance" — case studies reinforcing the wickedness of mothers. "Sexual cripples" is how someone in an article described homo-sexuals. Labels appearing in black and white, and from the pens of Ph.D.s, were not only magisterial but adhesive. They stuck in my memory for life, like old song lyrics.

Covertly, I continued to dig and delve at the library. Stealthily, I scanned the card catalogues under Homosexuality. The dictum spoken by the first of our own psychotherapists, Dr. Stadler, was not to discuss my suspicions about Chris to *anybody*. That finger-wagging warning had been stated severely, like a commandment. With this Thou Shalt Not constantly in my mind, I was not eager to speak up at the reference desk. Some of the books had to be brought to our branch from other libraries, which did necessitate human contact with a local librarian, and there is a touch of gallows humor in my looking back and seeing my furtive self. Here I was, a nervous Larchmont matron, skulking around the checkout desk, pretending to be using these incriminating materi-als for some writing project, feeling as if I were carrying explo-sives sewed into the lining of my coat.

Among the nuggets I uncovered: A psychiatrist at UCLA had developed a point system for recircuiting the behavior of boys who were not assuming traditional male roles in play. The boy was given five points for taking the role of the father when he was playing house, but five points were subtracted if he wore a dress. These scores were tallied by parents on a blackboard, and when a certain positive total was reached, the boy was rewarded with a trip to Disneyland or some other perk. If he accumulated too many demerits, he was to be punished with some loss of privileges. And this was the University of California speaking!

I give myself credit for not succumbing to this sort of loco behavior modification, but less credit for my conviction that the "problem" could be fixed. The origins of homosexuality remain a mystery, but efforts to redirect boys' play activity can only cause psychic pain, if not future psychological disability.

It is only recently that what I saw as "feminine" behavior in boys — embroidering, candle making, getting the draperies to hang just so, what have you — is so defined and imposed by our particular culture. This gender categorization has no meaning in other societies, and is surely open to modification, variation and change. And if branding a boy's behavior as "girlish" is derisive, if boys who are "feminine" are seen as less worthy than boys who will be boys, if sisters can dress like their brothers but not the other way around, what does that say? One does not have to be a politically active feminist to see that it disparages our sex, relegates it to lower status, diminishes and denigrates it. This brings to mind another thought: Is it possible that a subconscious hatred of women underlies some prejudice against gay men?

Gender is not fixed but mixed, they say now. Variation is not illness; Chris's interest in art and culture, his lack of interest in basketball may have been at odds with the culture, but it's the culture that needs a course in behavior modification. His "pain beyond shame" was not his fault — nothing could be clearer. It was ours.

In front of our New
Rochelle house in April
1963, just before my
second birthday.

Big brothers Kirby
(*left*) and Chris with
baby sister, Alison, in
our Larchmont dining
room, 1969.

There was never coal in the stocking of the good, good boy. Christmas, 1970.

All dressed up for
Easter dinner after
church, 1971.

Look who's not wearing sneakers. We three siblings were closer than ever among the lions, cheetahs, and wildebeests, June 1979.

Mom waits patiently while Chris attempts to get a giraffe on camera.

Grandpa Eric Fanta was proud to witness my graduation from the University of Vermont in May 1983.

Proud, accepting, and loving Mom with her gay son, Chris, visiting Martha's Vineyard, 1993.

16

- - - - - - - - - - -

HE WAS OF Armenian descent and not very tall. Clean-cut, with
dark hair and dark eyes, he had the sort of olive skin reminiscent
of tropical drinks and ceiling fans, and was not unlike a grown-up
version of Sam, my second-grade crush. I met Brad Karasian at a
graduation party given by one of my classmates, and right away
something clicked. Of course, my being attracted to Brad was
perilous. After my experience with Scott Shoreham at Kent, I
could not, would not, dared not! make any overtures toward any
member of my own sex, no matter what. This fear was like a
low-grade fever I couldn't shake off. To this day, I always assume
that although I may suspect a man of being gay, I could be wrong.
In those days, even if he was sending torch signals, I didn't trust
them.

There was another issue. I was yearning for acceptance, at
whatever price. At eighteen, I still had not acknowledged that
being gay was my assured destiny. In one of the few books I was
able to ferret out of the depths of the local library, I had read that
one good heterosexual experience might change me and that there
was something wonderful about boy-girl sex I was missing, but I
had performance anxiety as well as a fear of hurting someone's
feelings, of dating a woman under false pretenses. It was always a
tough thing for me to ask a girl out.

And to whom could I say, "I like women, I enjoy being with
them, but what if I can't take it further?" and "I'm ashamed,"
and "I'm afraid!" I dreamed of finding someone to share my secret with, someone who would listen without condemning, who
would like me, maybe even — dared I hope? — want a relationship. I wasn't looking for a fling, but like many eighteen-year-olds
I didn't project myself into the long term, couldn't see myself at
age thirty, forty, fifty. I needed someone who would make me

happy now, be at my side, double my strength, give sturdiness to my soul. If I had that, I told myself, I could better cope with the harmful world outside. That may be everyone's dream, but for a young man who is gay, it has a deeper and more eloquent dimension. It's a buffer, umbrella, helmet, goggles, circuit breaker, bulwark, lightning rod — all that wrapped up in one. It's the human face across the table, and it's the one voice at the other end of the telephone with acceptance behind it.

Because I'd always scored high on standardized math tests, my father, meaning well, tried to push me into engineering. Seeing his own success, I assumed father knew best, but with my aberrant sexual tastes it was too frightening to look ahead; I didn't know what could possibly be in store for me. I often thought about the Hackley boy who committed suicide after he left the school, where he'd been taunted and picked on endlessly. I've since learned that one third of all teenage suicides are gay related, and assume that some part of the will to die has to do with letting the family down. Imagining the anguish of my parents was definitely the rapids of my own darkest thoughts.

Also, I despaired of ever finding that soul mate, that one and only, despite the Dorans and my new social life. Since no one had come my way thus far, I had the thought it would never happen. I was growing older, physically more muscular and male, shaving every day now, and edging toward some sort of personal abyss. Engineering did not seem a way out; channeling all my energy toward a career goal couldn't even temporarily distract me from that yawning void.

For the moment, I tried to get a toehold in the present. With my own image the uppermost worry in my mind, I avoided anyone who might be emanating funny-fellow signs at Hackley, where I was now in my own reasonably decent niche. I knew that people who wore an earring in a certain ear were gay (in the other it meant you were cool — one had to be careful); if a guy had a bandanna and he put it in the left back pocket or the right back pocket of his pants it meant gay/dominant, gay/passive or some such thing; and if you wore purple on Thursday, God forbid, that meant you were queer. No one ever wore *the* color on Thursday except one of my classmates, Minerva, who prided herself on being arty. It was her color, she said, because her parents had conceived her on a purple cushion. Fantasy or not, it seemed wonderfully romantic for her. As for me, it goes without saying that never in a million years would I have been caught dead in any shade of it. On the other hand, without purple, without bandannas, without radar, how would I ever find my counterparts? Anybody who seemed obvious or was actually Out was not appealing to me because I wasn't ready for an Out life, and in any case, there seemed no one at school at the time who was even a remote possibility. There were probably many there like me who were hidden, but to expose oneself in any way was like stepping into quicksand.

At our graduation party, Minerva, wearing her color, brought as her date Brad Karasian. He had been at Hackley some years before but had left the school because his father had fallen on hard times. I had never met Brad, but that evening we immediately took to each other. There was no radar, or was there? I wanted to be near him all evening. Fighting Minerva for his attention, I seemed to be winning. He was veering toward me, no mistake about that. He was outgoing, intellectual, and I wanted to hear what he had to say. He was wearing Polo eyeglasses. What style! And above the glasses, dark eyebrows; I liked them too. We made a special point of agreeing to meet again soon. It was "Let's go see a movie," or "Let's hang out." It was often through the girls that we got to be around each other, but something sub rosa was stirring. My parents were taking the family on an African safari that summer, and I specifically remember Brad saying, "Will you call me as soon as you get back?" There was an unmistakable something eager in his voice. Thrilling.

Unlike me, he had grown up athletic, was into soccer, baseball, tennis and ice hockey. He later said many times he didn't know what it was that made him a homosexual. After all, he could throw a ball, catch or kick one, and he had a great relationship with his father. He had read extensively to try to find out why he didn't fit into the limp-wristed stereotype. And, it turned out, he was fighting it all the way.

That summer he hung out with us at the Dorans' or at our house, at one of the girls' places or at the country club, a very visible part of my social group. Then circumstances added a twist that threw us together more intimately. I got a summer job at a city travel agency that was two blocks away from Brad's father's office, where Brad was doing his school-vacation gig, and we started eating lunch together. It went on all summer, and I noticed that we were both beginning to touch each other at opportune moments, in subtle ways. It was an innocent pat on the back or a light shove to an arm, a little punch in the shoulder or a light grab on the neck — athletic guys' locker room sort of stuff. It happened more and more; we were each waiting for a reaction, I think.

We made a date to see a movie. The summer was about to end and we were both due to leave for college within three days. I had chosen the University of Vermont, for its engineering department, its skiing and because I imagined I'd stand out less in a large school. I kept thinking, seventy-two more hours. Only three more nights and I'd be in Vermont. It was August, the month of shooting stars, and I was aware of the sky, the cicadas, that hot-summer-night smell that steams above suburban lawns. I was drinking it all in because it would soon be over, Brad would be gone, and whatever had developed between us would be put on hold until Thanksgiving, at the very least.

Now here we were, just the two of us side by side, watching *Rocky II,* and throughout that whole long movie, whenever there was anything at all to react to — a good line, a laugh, a special Sly punch — we touched each other. It became ridiculously obvious, and still, I wouldn't say anything. After the movie, walking to the car, driving him home to his parents' house, during all those midsummer-night opportunities, I still couldn't get myself to bring up the thing that was like a hand grenade sitting before us. It was he who finally pulled out the pin.

"I don't know how to say this," he began, and it seemed to take him an hour to get the words out, "but is there a physical attraction between us? Do you sense it?"

What's strange is that at the moment he spoke those words, I was struck simultaneously by a shot of joy/relief and disillusion/disappointment. He had used the word "physical" and not "amorous," and I suppose Cupid's flying arrows were what my soul was really after. For Brad, I meant a first sexual encounter, plenty of heat but no Valentines and no roses, and for me it was a letdown, because I had hoped it was going to be more: a boyfriend, someone to bond with. A meeting of true hearts.

We proceeded to the parking lot of a Scarsdale synagogue, which was totally empty, and we made out in the back seat of my mother's Oldsmobile. Within the next three days we met two more times: once downstairs in the recreation room at my house when no parents were around, and once upstairs in his bedroom, in the shadow of team pennants and athletic trophies.

It wasn't until many years later that I was able to have an orgasm, which for someone of my age, in my fever-pitch mental state, was very unusual; I was so nervous about the whole thing that nothing could get me there. Brad was always worried and kept asking, "What can I do to help you?" but I was happy enough to have found someone, even if it was someone for whom I knew I was just a sexual outlet. We parted reluctantly.

"I'll write three times a week," Brad promised.

At college I got letters that were bright and noncommittal. Brad had become interested in art, architecture and politics. He was looking forward to seeing me, he wrote, but that's as personal as his letters got.

Then, one terrible day in late October, I got a letter telling me he'd done a great deal of thinking and decided that he wasn't gay. I had the feeling our secret meetings had somehow turned a guilt switch on in him, and Brad now wanted no part of me. He wanted a fresh start, aka women. He wanted a "normal" life.

By the time I saw him during the Thanksgiving holiday, he had a girlfriend. Then, during Christmas week, he brought her to my

New Year's Eve party, and there was some sort of joke about her standing under the mistletoe, waiting for her kiss. He finally did so, it seemed to me reluctantly, but still, it cut me deep. She was petite, with a long Italian surname I could never remember. At the same party, Minerva, in a purple blouse with a purple sash, tried to get me under the mistletoe. Without success.

If I'd had a crystal ball, then I would have known that Brad's girl would last until spring. That's when he ended the relationship, decided to hitchhike across the United States and later came back to tell me he'd made many male "friends" over the summer. He had caught gonorrhea, been cured, but no matter what his sexual orientation now, I was no longer interested. He was way ahead of me psychologically and physically. By the time he was in his last year at Tufts, he broke ground by bringing a boy to his senior dance. (Years later he showed me a picture of them in their matching tuxedos.) I was surprised when I heard Brad had died of AIDS at thirty, because except for that summer of sowing his wild oats, he was not at all promiscuous, and by the time he was twenty, he'd settled down with one lover, who was with him to the end.

But that November, I smiled through tears, licked my wounds and limped back to cold storage in Vermont. Brad's shot at heterosexuality was typical, a garden-variety attempt to get it right. At some point most gay males will try what the mainstream culture has mandated. From the time we become aware of our surroundings, we are bombarded with heterosexuality. From Cinderella and the Prince to Mickey and Minnie, from titillating coffee ads to television sitcoms and all the way back to our first personal images of grandma and grandpa, mom and pop, aunt and uncle, the sexual image projected universally is that of a male and a female. From our earliest years it is never Daddy kissing Santa Claus, never girl meets girl, never Jack and Bill going up the hill to fetch a pail of water. Throughout those formative and innocent years, when we are grappling to find role models or at least a clue that we are not mutants who share a bloodline with the devil, there are only he-and-she visual and aural messages reinforcing our freakishness.

Who in his right mind would choose to risk everything by stubbornly plowing ahead against all human traffic?

Homosexuals are the only minority in the world who do not have the unequivocal support of their families. I had no intention of testing my own, and as far as full disclosure to anyone else went, well, it had caused me nothing but wretchedness so far. The pink triangles that Hitler forced homosexuals to wear on their sleeves have now been translated into tie tacks and key chains and sold in catalogues of gay men's accessories, but at that time, I had just heard about those labels in a history course, and it struck me as a particularly potent and chilling symbol. Since Hitler vilified homosexuals in the nineteen thirties and forties, my experience showed me that we hadn't come very far in fifty years at all, and so, like most young gay men, I continued paying the price for what should never be called sexual preference but must always be known as sexual orientation. I felt this penetrating solitude in a new, large school, where again I had defaulted into hateful isolation.

1 7

BEFORE WE HAD any children, I fantasized what it would be like to be surrounded by a brood at a dinner table and hold lofty conversations that dealt with serious issues instead of the quality of the meatloaf. It is no surprise that the reality never did measure up to my idealized fantasy. Life around the hearth did not include sing-alongs or contemplative comparisons of government ideologies. Most of our meal togetherness consisted of "Pass the ketchup" or "Stop kicking the table leg," and too often, tension: "Have you started on your book report? Why haven't you!" The eye of the beholder was mine, of course, and while I was seeing disorder and cultural shortcomings, other eyes, specifically Grandma Rose's, saw beauty, harmony and buoyant happiness under our roof.

My mother-in-law did not look at anything too closely. When she regaled us with the memories of her own boys, unique, handsome and darling in their sailor suits, I wanted to be like her, skimming along the surface of life and seeing and remembering only the gilt edges. When she repeatedly called her grandson "Gentleman Chris" — his inordinate courtesy and gentleness did not go unnoticed! — she meant it as the highest of compliments, but I took it as another shred of evidence that he was headed in the wrong sexual direction. But for some reason, on a safari vacation we took to Africa the summer Chris was eighteen, Alison eleven and Kirby twenty-one, I turned into my indulgent mother-in-law. I began seeing all three children as charming neophyte adults, imbued with the sort of values one would wholeheartedly vote into public office. They were well behaved, smart, responsible and honest, so it seemed the verdict was in: we had managed to raise exemplary offspring. My ongoing now-you-see-it, now-you-don't concern about my middle child was transformed into long-overdue recognition of his real multidimensional self.

Here, in the shadow of Mount Kilimanjaro, I saw Chris in an altogether new light. Where were my brains before Africa got them into working order? In Kenya I was introduced to my middle child's distinct personality as if I were meeting him for the first time. Although we'd always known him as the good boy, Chris was also witty, sharp-eyed, observant, slightly iconoclastic. A less acerbic version of his hilarious father, he was the hit of our show, our family's center of gravity. I was appalled that I had let his sexual orientation overshadow his distinctive essence — his unflappable, congenial, good-natured self.

Kenya is not exactly a perfect place for a holiday. We encountered deformed and diseased beggars on every side, aggressive and frightening native purveyors of beads and leather pounding on the windows of our little van, rutted dirt roads and in some places the most rudimentary of sanitary conditions. And yet we were exhilarated by our adventure, and our family was in total and wonderful accord as we drove off into the bush every day to shoot the animals with our cameras.

Something came over all of us. We became a self-contained, cooperative group with no other agenda than to follow to the letter our daily roster of activities. There were no choices to be made, with no friends or outside business to cause distractions. At this time, I had no inkling of what was happening in Chris's social and school life. He seemed to be happy, to have many new friends. Maybe Bob was right. Perhaps we had prevailed after all, "fixed" the problem.

But if I am nostalgic about that fourteen-day furlough, I also remember our provocative encounter in Nyeri.

We had decided to celebrate Alison's birthday at Treetops, a rustic resort hotel unique in the world at that time. It stood on stilts like a treehouse amid the African ambience of baboons and water buffalo, and here are a few lines from my travel diary of Sunday, June 17, 1979, Alison's eleventh birthday: "Breakfast in our room and a morning of relaxation. Kids happy not to have to get up at five. Played cards together on porch.

"After lunch we watched native dancers and a witch doctor told Alison and Chris's fortunes."

I don't recall Alison's fortune, but I remember Chris's well enough. First, there was a colorful rigmarole of Masai warriors with faces painted chalk white and striped in dark chevrons, drums and bare feet, a little fire, leather loincloths and animal-teeth necklaces, chants and shouts, the whole tableau designed for the tourist trade. It goes without saying that there were many outstretched palms, one of them the friendly neighborhood witch doctor's.

It surprised me that Alison wasn't scared out of her wits, or maybe she was, but after some cajoling she went first. A few feet beyond the dance floor sat the doctor, cross-legged on the ground in front of a hut. He'd spread out the tools of his trade, beads, stones and sticks, and regarded them with great concentration. I assume he told her she'd have a good life and many children or some such; soon she moved off and it was Chris's turn.

Serious and intent, Chris sat opposite the witch doctor, watching the wrinkled brown fingers fiddling with his offerings while Bob, Kirby and I, too old and sophisticated (or uneasy?) to hear about the future, stood to the side, waiting for the revelation. Pretty soon, Chris was back.

"Well, Chris, are you going to grow up to be a billionaire?"

Chris shook his head no.

"Well, what did the witch doctor tell you?"

"He said I would travel the world many times," Chris said.

"Nice. In a caravan, Chris?" Bob kidded. None of us, including Alison, were taking this a bit seriously.

"And I will live in a big house near water," Chris continued. "With a view of great ships."

"So far, so good." Bob made his comedian's face. "You love boats." (Chris had hated sailing since we pushed him into learning the sport when he was ten.)

"He said I will be a happy man," Chris went on. Did he hesitate for an instant before finishing the witch doctor's prediction, or did I imagine it? "And I will never marry."

I suspect that the witch doctor had his repertoire of ten or twelve stock fortunes and that this might be one of them, but it had such a momentary kick that it zapped me to attention. Bob said nothing, and for all I know it didn't register. Witchcraft or no, it was very unlikely the warrior had read eighteen-year-old Chris's predilection in the five minutes they were together.

Or was it?

If I'd written this scene into a play, I would have had intensifying drumbeats in the background and a darkening sky overhead. It was a new setting nearer the equator, there were acacias instead of larch trees, but it was déjà vu for me. On this trip I'd seen my good son as a paragon, my pride and joy, and now, a few hours later, we were back at ground zero. Our rain cloud had caught up to us, as far away as what was once known as the Dark Continent, aptly named from my point of view at this moment. I had taken my anxiety, packed it at the bottom of my bag and out it came: Chris's asterisk, signal, insignia, whatever it was, seemed to be there for everyone — but us — to see. I was sure it would follow him the rest of his life, set him apart, hex him. Equally invisible for me was the possibility that the witch doctor's prognosis was right, but that Chris could nevertheless find genuine contentment. I suppose I'm a late bloomer. It took me too many years to understand that these two elements are not mutually exclusive.

We have endless films and photos of our African safari. In one of them we are all lined up in our matching khaki jackets, wearing our safari hats and smiling at the camera. I am ambivalent about that picture, which we sent out with our Christmas cards that year. It was a beautiful family honeymoon, my heart was full with love for my husband and my children, but I remember something else about that photograph. Our native guide took it, and what I remember about him specifically was that his earlobes had been stretched and wound around his ears like taffy. He was an excellent guide, but that distortion was hard to look at.

Similarly, when I examine my own face in that photo, I see a younger me, a big smile, and perfectly normal earlobes. And still I see a distortion, and sometimes I find myself hard to look at too.

18

- - - - - - - - - -

MY IMPRESSIONS OF Africa, including the predictions of the witch doctor, were filtered through the haze of feelings I then had for Brad Karasian. It meant that as exciting as Kenya was, it was like a backdrop for the emotional twists and turns that constitute a new and possibly soon to be exalted relationship. I loved every moment of the trip, developed a closeness with my siblings that didn't seem quite as easy at home, limited myself to one (don't overdo it!) postcard to Brad and couldn't wait to get back to see him. At one point, Kirby, Alison and I were being served afternoon tea on the veranda at Treetops. Baboons scampered among us like toddlers gone amok. One of them grabbed Kirby's leg, then snatched his bright yellow box of Kodak film and ran off with it. We laughed like fools, and I had such a gush of feeling for my brother and sister that for a nanosecond I was tempted to pour out my love to them. The temptation passed, and Brad, my blinking-green-light focus of attention, was probably one reason the witch doctor's prognosis went in one ear and out the other. The other reason was that in the carnival atmosphere in which it was delivered, no one else seemed to be taking the pronouncement too seriously.

When I got Brad's goodbye letter, I was a freshman at the University of Vermont, just getting my bearings in another new world. Until the kiss-off letter came, I was happy enough with college life, although my first-semester courses were tough going. My father continued to urge me into the College of Engineering, now on the basis of an article he'd read in the *Wall Street Journal* and my strength in math. I have a clear picture of the day I was filling out my college applications, which were spread over the dining room table. I was sitting in his seat at the head of the table, but when he came into the room, we automatically switched seats. He did not request I move into my own chair, but it seemed that in the dining room he always sat in that place, which at every American dining table subtly symbolized power and rank.

When he spoke, I listened. "An engineering degree and then a master's in business is a license to steal," he said, and so I went along. His motives were always that he wanted the best for all his children, so in no way do I blame him for a choice that turned out to be wrong for me. Every course in the College of Engineering was designed for engineers and seemed more abstract, less interesting and harder than anything my friends were taking in the liberal arts. They were taking regular calculus and pulling down A's, while I was struggling and getting C's in the engineering version. My schoolwork was grueling. Between my sexual drama and the frenetic drinking and heterosexual activities in the dormitory, I had too many things going on in my head to concentrate fully. Although I thought myself relatively mature at the time, probably more than most of my dorm mates, the new pressures were wearing me down.

The UVM campus is beautiful and green, with an architectural mix of buildings that overlook Lake Champlain on one side and the Green Mountains on the other. The accessibility of water and slope made for a wholesome and sports-minded undergraduate population. The absence of black inhabitants or other minorities in Vermont (there were only five hundred black families living in the state at that time) precluded the sort of student diversity that might have put me at greater ease later in my college career.

But for now, I did not see myself as belonging to a minority, and arriving in my freshman dorm, the faces around me seemed comfortingly familiar. This was mostly the same white and rosy genus I'd known all my life, and there was even a déjà vu aspect to finding that my new roommate, like Tad Bartholomew at Kent, was a soccer jock. This one left piles of dirty gym clothes lying on the floor in the corner, constantly scenting our room with eau d'armpit. Forgetting the odor, what I loved about our room was that it was on the first floor and opposite the student lounge.

And what I hated about the room was that it was on the first floor and opposite the student lounge. The room had two bunk beds, two desks, two freestanding closets, mine full of clothes, my roommate's pretty bare except for hockey sticks and other sports paraphernalia, all highly repetitive of Kent, except that we were older, more mature, and coexisted amicably — at least until one night when my roommate got drunk and brought a girl into his bed.

It was the middle of the night, and he must have thought I was asleep, which I was, until the sounds of sex woke me. There had been yet another boisterous party across the hall, lasting into the wee hours. Many of the freshmen had reached the legal age of eighteen, and now, on their own and let loose, they were determined to do some unrestrained drinking. There was some sort of bash in the lounge or in one or another of the girls' rooms at least once a week. I partied along with everyone else in order to fit in, and remember getting wildly intoxicated twice that year. The pressure was to connect with girls or be drunk; I'm not a big brew fan, but given the choice, I chose beer.

Now, with my roommate having chosen both alternatives, I was in an awkward predicament. I didn't want to get up and sleep in the lounge across the hall, and I was really pissed off. This was my room, goddamn it! I thought of standing my ground by clearing my throat or something, but I didn't want to embarrass the girl by alerting her to the fact that their noisy lovemaking had a captive audience. He'd known all along I was there, of course, but assumed I'd sleep through the thrashing and the ricocheting sound effects. So I closed my eyes and tried unsuccessfully to fall back to sleep, and remember it as a particularly vociferous and very, very long night.

By morning the girl had disappeared. I discovered who she was later, a plodding home ec major from Vergennes, and it was evident that my roommate wasn't in the least bit interested in her; it was a one-night thing. This was a coed dormitory, so coupling in students' rooms was routine, but ordinarily there was some decorum maintained. I made it clear I never wanted what happened to happen again, and this soured our relationship. Shades of prep school: we switched rooms and roommates the following semester.

No one feels comfortable eavesdropping on someone else's moments of passion, but at the time I couldn't help wondering how outraged my heterosexual roommate would feel if the situation were reversed and he had to be an unwilling voyeur of two men making love in the bunk below his.

Not long afterward, there was another party in the lounge across the hall, and there I was, glass in hand, talking about nothing much — or should I say trying to be heard and trying to hear over the noise — to a sophomore I'll call Wendy. She was taller than me, with a nice figure and a Vermont patois. She was what we called an "organic" type — a no-frills girl who obviously made no attempt at femininity, disdained makeup and possibly cut her own hair. The only thing we had in common was our Czechoslovakian background. She seemed much older and worldly to this unsophisticated freshman. The crowd had thinned and there we were, still talking about Czech tennis players, Czech politics, Czech beer, until we were the last two people in the room. The music was still blasting.

"Let's dance," Wendy said, and now we were together on the makeshift dance floor, and she was beginning to pull me closer, squeeze my hand, and suddenly we were "dancing" toward my room. Her maneuver moved us too quickly past the door, into the empty room, and over to my roommate's lower bunk bed, where she cornered me. We were both somewhat looped, but I was definitely not interested in doing the same thing my roommate had done. I was under adrenaline stress as she began unbuttoning her blouse and I sort of pushed her away. At the time, although I was not convinced that I was heading toward unequivocal homosexuality, I note with corrected-lens hindsight that I acted automatically. I wanted to get her out of my room fast, without embarrassing her. I had a lucky, quick brainstorm. I said, "I'm sorry, Wendy. I'm too drunk to do anything," and, relief and success! It worked. A few weeks later, she switched dormitories and our paths never seemed to cross, and after that semester I never saw her again.

I had chosen to turn down a relatively emotionally detached trial at heterosexual sex. It was instinctive, a clear message from my heart-driven brain. My sexuality was on automatic pilot and knew where it was heading, even if I wasn't sure.

During my first year, I spent most of my time on the girls' floor, in the company of the freshman women, with whom I felt more comfortable than with my male peers. I found female conversations inherently more meaningful and interesting. One of the girls in my dormitory, Megan, and I became close, and there were overtones of more than a friendship between us. I suspected I could have moved in on her had I wanted to, but the relationship remained — as always with a member of the opposite gender — sexless. It developed into a solid, platonic friendship. This is the closest I've ever come to a serious heterosexual connection, but somewhere down the line I suspect she guessed who I really was. We were sitting in her room when out of the blue, and with some guile, she said, "You know, it would really be neat to have a friend who was gay." Way to go! She was a clever girl and waited for my response, probably certain she'd get the information out of me. Later, much later, I let her in on it, but that day in her room I wasn't ready, and said nothing.

When I called my father to tell him I was unhappy in the College of Engineering, that I wanted to switch to the College of Arts and Sciences, he sounded glum and disappointed. I was too — disappointed in myself to think I'd let him down, that I'd fallen short in yet another arena of my life. It was clear I was in some way not holding up my end, and might never be qualified for sitting at the head of any table.

Brad lost, my studies gone awry, my roommate and I in a cold war, snow beginning to fall and, again, no one to confide in — it was in this spirit of heavy weather that I did something I swore I'd never do again. After pouring out my heart on paper in Kent, I'd learned that all around me were closed doors that were dangerous to try to open. I thought I'd learned my lesson, but in a reckless moment of desperation I still dared to reach out again.

I sat at the desk in my room one night and wrote a letter to a man I hardly knew, a former colleague who'd worked in the travel agency at which I'd spent the summer learning how to write airplane tickets and reserve hotel rooms. Bill Van Dyne, as I'll call him, was second in command of corporate finances, extremely handsome and straight-seeming, but what did I know? I had done some flunky things for him — filling out forms, filing records, getting him coffee — but my ears perked up when another man I worked with made comments about him: "You know where he spends weekends? He goes to Fire Island." Though I knew nothing of the gay lifestyle, I had vaguely heard about Fire Island.

Bill had worn no purple, given me no sign, but my college peers were talking sports, beer and girls, and feeling very alone in icy New England, I took the risk. In the letter, I asked him if he was gay and begged him, pleaded, not to tell anyone about me.

I never got an answer to the letter, and again, predictably, like spring floods that follow winter snows, there were consequences.

19

- - - - - - - - - -

I SAW THE TRIP to Africa as a paradigm of what family life should be like for us always. I imagined that behind the clapboard, stucco, brick or fieldstone façades of houses coast to coast, mother/father/offspring dynamics were mostly like ours had been on safari — conversations without arguments, laughs without follow-up tears, and a leitmotif of profound familial affection. Before latter-day talk shows opened our eyes wide to real life, we tended to compare ourselves to our two-dimensional cultural role models, the Nelson family of *Ozzie and Harriet* fame, and others of that sunny fictional species. I thought it sad that we were so off the norm, so far removed from the gentleness of that nuclear foursome, but in Africa we seemed to come close to being like them: laid-back and amusing, forgiving (there was nothing to forgive) and reliably, consistently and wholesomely amicable.

But if Africa was the zenith of what was good about our family life, the nadir came six months later, on the eighth of January, 1980. It was my birthday, that particular day seared forever into my memory.

I woke up in the chilly dark of five on that Tuesday morning, why I don't know. Possibly for a trip to the bathroom, maybe because of a noise outside or simply a sixth sense that something was wrong. I got out of bed and noticed that there was a stripe of light under the bedroom door, which meant the light in the hall was still burning. We always left it on when one of the children went out at night. When they returned they shut it off before going to sleep.

The evening before, Chris, home for a month's college vacation, had left early, about six o'clock, to meet a friend in New York City. He had a social group now, and I was beginning to feel more sanguine about his future. Just over a week ago, this past

New Year's Eve, he'd had a party in our basement playroom, invited twenty or more friends, and it warmed my heart to see this new, gregarious, popular Chris, who was not only making phone calls but actually getting them as well. Since starting Hackley School he was suddenly in demand, part of a crowd, a pack, a bunch, like every other normal teenager of my imagination. These also seemed to be nice kids, polite, well spoken, sensible, who didn't abuse our laissez faire attitude toward alcohol. We tended to demystify it by allowing its consumption on our premises, as long as drivers abstained. We felt that forbidding drinking at home was the surest way to push a child into sneaking it somewhere else. I'm not now sure if this was a wise policy, but it worked well in the case of our children, who nowadays, given a choice of taking it or leaving it, are apt to reach instead for a Diet Coke.

I crept quietly into the hall, going to the light switch Chris had probably forgotten to turn off — although it was rare for dependable Chris to forget a house rule — and saw that the door to his room was wide open. I stood for a moment, my hand on the switch, frozen in place. Chris slept with his door closed, always. From this vantage point, and from the light that was falling into his room, I could look directly inside and see that his bed was made, the bedspread in place. He hadn't slept at home.

My heart was drumming as I flew back into our bedroom and woke Bob. Although there was nothing unusual about Chris meeting his Hackley friends in the city and coming back on a late train, it was unheard of for him to stay out all night. Woody Allen has said of the actions of one of his movie protagonists, "It is not written into his character," and that statement certainly applied to Chris now. He wouldn't not come home without calling. Unless, of course, some unspeakable disaster had befallen him. I suppose it's why I went berserk.

Bob tried to calm me down but, tense and worried himself, could give me little comfort. Still, he was there and we were sharing a panic that was burgeoning minute by minute. During the next few hours, it occurred to me to wonder how I'd have survived the anxiety if, like one or two of my friends, I'd been a single parent facing the probability of horrible news all alone.

We tried calling the offices of the commuter railroad first. We hoped that all train service had broken down and Chris was safely stuck in some car en route to Larchmont. Getting a voice that wasn't recorded was impossible at that hour, so I called the local taxi company; its little dispatch shed faces the railroad station, and its small fleet is lined up near the platform.

"Is something wrong? Are the trains running late?" I asked. It was quite a long shot. A train could not be four hours late for a thirty-two-minute train ride; on the other hand, maybe there was an electrical failure. Possibly train service had been altogether suspended? I'm a nonbeliever who sometimes, in appropriately panicked moments, discards logic and throws in a Hail Mary.

Mary wasn't listening, and the answer wasn't what I was hoping to hear. "Late? The last train in was about five minutes late," a voice told me. It had arrived in Larchmont a little after two A.M.

"Then — when is the next train due?"

"The first morning train arrives at six-eleven."

Nothing will convince me that a minute is always sixty seconds long. We looked at the clock, waited. It dragged its feet, it limped, it dawdled. Bob turned on the television, checking for disasters. A lifetime later, at six-fifteen, I called the taxi company again.

"Did the six-eleven get in?"

It had. I asked if a young man got off. Only one person had disembarked: not Chris.

Bob sat with me while I made more calls. I dialed the local police, and that call was predictably fruitless. No reported accidents, no nothing. Larchmont is a pretty sleepy town.

We sat in the kitchen drinking coffee and looking at each other. We talked about where Chris could be, what could have happened, what we could do next. We looked at the creeping silver hands of the clock over the refrigerator, and waited for the hour after which we could call Ronnie Grad, the friend Chris had told me he was meeting at Grand Central last night.

Kirby, also home from college, was working as an intern at a music magazine, and now we heard him in his room above, stereo on, getting up to go to work. Alison, a student in junior high, was getting up to music too. The allegro beat was reverberating in the walls, as usual. They would both present me with birthday cards and gifts later in the day, but this morning, groggy and hurried, they appeared in the kitchen just long enough to wish me a happy birthday on their way to juice and cereal.

We told them Chris had not returned from the city. We said we were sure he'd call any minute, might have missed the last train and not to worry. They went about their business and didn't, leaving the anxiety and distress to us. "He'll show up," they said, perhaps trying to console, trying to sound as if it were nothing at all. The clock kept standing still.

In Chris's room I found his address book, looked under G for Grad, and there it was: address, zip code, telephone number. I intended to wait until eight, an early but decent hour to call someone at home, but couldn't hold off. At seven I dialed the Grads' number and got the boy's father. I felt I had to explain the reason for the early call.

"Chris never got home last night. Did Ronnie get back from the city?" I asked Mr. Grad.

"The city?"

"He went to the city last night to meet Chris."

Mr. Grad seemed surprised by this, hesitated for what seemed like a long time. "I don't think Ronnie went out at all last night," he said.

"But Chris said —"

"Shall I go wake him?"

"Please!"

A groggy and very confused Ronnie came to the telephone. Bob fidgeted while my head began spinning; Ronnie had had no date with Chris, had stayed home and hadn't a clue as to our son's whereabouts. End of conversation.

Bob challenged, "Are you sure you heard Chris right?" It was a fair question. I have a well-deserved reputation for mental meandering, taking detours while others are giving me advice or information. Maybe it wasn't Ronnie. Who then was it? Chris was in college now, had new friends, new connections.

But I was so sure he'd said Ronnie Grad. Then again, maybe I *was* capable of a lapse. I went back to the address book. Minerva Gold, the girl who always wore purple and lived in Tudor City, was a familiar name. Hadn't she been at Chris's New Year's Eve party? Maybe they'd made a date then. It seemed worth a shot.

Minerva's mother came to the phone and sounded immediately alarmed. So did Minerva, when she took the telephone. She hadn't spoken to Chris since the party and had no idea where he could be. Or with whom. Not a clue.

In the dark sky over our house, the moon was still visible. I think I was surprised it hadn't fallen out of the heavens or simply exploded. And if the moon was going quietly about its business, so were neighbors, who could be seen walking or driving by on their way to work, oblivious of our crisis.

Of course, I called the Dorans and at least three other familiar-sounding names I ferreted out of Chris's neat book. No one had seen or heard from our son. Today was my birthday and there was no possible way Chris had forgotten it; moon or no moon, it seemed a monstrous omen. And every half hour, trains continued to arrive at our station, but Chris was not on any of them.

By seven-thirty I'd called the Missing Persons Bureau.

"We can't report a person missing who's been gone less than twenty-four hours," a detective told me. He seemed kind and relatively lighthearted, considering his job.

"Your son'll be back within twelve hours. With a very red face," he cheerfully assured me. I didn't believe him for a minute. I thought he should put out an all-points bulletin right away. At the same time, a part of what he said comforted us both. "This happens all the time," the detective said. "Kids go AWOL and stay out all night. You're not the first parent to go through it. I hear it all day."

But not our Chris. Impossible. After all, it wasn't written into his character.

The telephone rang at ten to nine. We jumped; I answered it. It was Bob's mother. "Happy birthday, dear!" People — including Bob — always asked how I could stand my mother-in-law calling me at ten to nine every weekday for thirty years. We never did dig very deep, which may be one reason we got along so well. "I got a lovely pair of shoes yesterday." "What did the doctor say about Alison's sore throat?" "Such a wind outside, I didn't go out at all." It was day-to-day minutiae we wallowed in together. Today I had to keep the tremor out of my voice and do a Sarah Bernhardt. I told her Bob was getting a late start and I'd get back to her later. It goes without saying I was not about to tell her that her favorite grandchild was a Missing Person.

Bob called his office and said he'd be coming in late, and we waited some more, drank more coffee, paced from room to room and looked out the windows. At some point we got dressed.

Finally the telephone rang, and it was Chris. "I'm at the train station," he said, just like that.

A reprieve. He was safe. I could breathe again; the moon would not fall! Deliverance from disaster makes for life's most beautiful moments. We had our son back, a most beautiful moment. Followed by a lurch into sobering reality. If Chris was alive and unhurt, the implication of his night out was unavoidable: he was with a man. It had to be.

Bob wanted to drive down to pick him up.

"No, I'll go!" I was adamant. I knew what would happen if I let my husband get in his car and drive to the station. The anger would torpedo out of him, aiming for that fragile target. God knows what sort of damage would result! Bob might even tear the truth out of the boy. If Bob screamed a confession out of Chris, then what? We weren't ready to hear it, were we?

"What happened? Where were you?" I waited until we'd driven out of the station parking lot to ask.

Chris was in the passenger seat, the red face the detective had predicted was more ashen than pink. He was the captured prisoner, subdued and humble. "Happy birthday, Mom."

"Where were you?"

"I went to meet Ronnie Grad."

I looked at him, dumbfounded. Chris, a liar? Not written into his character! "No you didn't. I called Ronnie this morning."

Hesitation. "I went to see Minerva in Tudor City."

"No you didn't. You didn't! *Where were you?*"

There was a silence long as a red traffic light. Of course, I knew, I knew. And didn't want to know.

"I can't tell you, Mom. I just can't tell you," Chris said.

20

IT WAS NO more than twenty degrees outside as I stepped off the train on that January 8 morning, but as soon as I saw my mother's car pull into the station, I began to sweat. All night long I'd imagined that dark beast of consequences, my parents' reaction, and my body was steaming. This was a mess I was going to have to lie my way out of, and when I lie my whole metabolism changes. My heart beats faster, the adrenaline pumps, my voice sounds different, if only to me. I pay physical as well as psychological penalties, so it's easy to see why I'm so bad at it.

Even so, I had a story prepared, created it on the way up from the city: I'd missed the last train and had to spend the night at Ronnie Grad's brother's apartment. And Ronnie's brother's phone had been disconnected, which is why I couldn't call. Was this believable? I hoped to God.

I had two simultaneous terrifying worries. One, the unthinkable worst, was that my parents would find out where I'd been. The other, that what I'd done, staying out all night, not to speak of ruining my mother's birthday, would forever damage the relationship I had with them both. I thought my entire life, including my college tuition, hung in the balance.

"Where were you, Chris?"

"I went to meet Ronnie Grad . . ."

My mother's eyes left the road to shoot sparks at me. "No you didn't. I called Ronnie this morning."

I simultaneously froze and sweated; I should have known! Then again, maybe I'd guessed she might call the Grads, because I had a sort of backup story about Minerva Gold, a tall tale I'd also concocted, much too far-fetched to use except in just such an emergency.

My mother instantly shot me down on Minerva, too.

I threw in the towel on lies. They never have and never will work well for me. "I can't tell you, Mom." My voice still sounded froggy. "I just can't tell you."

I thought it strange that she didn't Carry On. I had expected more upheaval, a greater explosion, fire and fury. This was, however, only my mother. My father was still to come. I was only too familiar with his explosive rages and was terrified that he'd scare my secret out of me. I felt as if I were shrinking bit by bit in my ski jacket, wished I could go back in time and stay home last night. It was so unlike me, my mother kept saying. She told me about calling the police, my friends, the Bureau of Missing Persons, and my guilt almost brought me to my knees. Whenever we stopped at a light, her eyes bored holes into me. Still, I wouldn't tell, I'd never tell, and oddly enough she didn't really pressure me. It was baffling.

My father began to thunder as soon as I walked through the door. He pulled me into the living room, and the language he used I will not repeat here, yet there were other times, other less significant misdemeanors, that had brought out much greater screaming binges. Although he never abused any of us physically, I was used to hearing hair-raising threats about what he'd do to us. Not this time. Relatively speaking, he remained sane. When my mother stepped out of the room, he lowered his voice. "Was it a woman?" he asked.

I said no.

"Was it a *man*?" The look on his face said it all.

"No, it wasn't a man," I lied.

I had waited and waited for a reply to my letter to Bill Van Dyne. We never knew each other well at the travel agency — he worked in a different division — but I admired him, if only from a distance. Bright and in charge, well respected as a "regular guy," he was tall, with fair hair and dark eyebrows, dashing, sort of a cross between an athlete and a romantic, and totally masculine. As each day of postal silence passed, I became more and more panicky. Had he gotten my letter, and if so, why hadn't he answered it, and worse, what had he done with it? I imagined it free-floating dangerously out there in the world somewhere and wanted to kick myself for having written it in the first place.

I began trying to call him after about three weeks of silence, but it was no easy matter. Most pay phones at the University of Vermont were at that time in public hallways, and I had to scour four or five buildings before finding one enclosed in an old booth. Then, because the call must never appear on my parents' credit card bill, I had to prepare myself with a pocketful of change.

Shaking, literally trembling, I dialed that number — and got no answer. I tried again that night and the next, and can't put an exact number on the times I attempted without getting through. For days I was a walking cash register. Finally I succeeded, and a voice — his voice, alive and strong — answered.

"Hello?" There was loud conversation in the background, music too. It sounded like Bill had company, might even be having a party, and I had to speak louder than I wanted to.

"Did you ever get my letter?" My voice was crackling like an old lady's.

"Yes, I got your letter. Didn't you get my card?"

No, no, I hadn't gotten any card.

"But I sent you one!" Then Bill told me it was a funny greeting card he'd mailed to me weeks ago, and began to explain that it was a picture of something or someone, but as he was describing it, I was really just catching my breath, not even listening. I was so relieved that he wasn't saying anything horrible to me on the telephone, that he was actually being nice to me — and all the while I was putting dimes and quarters into those slots, I hardly heard what he was saying.

One thing that did register was that on the inside of the card he'd written, "I'm not that kind of girl," and that was my first exposure to gay "inside" humor. I didn't get it. What did he mean by that? I now know that when gay men get together, they sometimes refer to each other as "she," "her" and "that girl," but at the time it didn't compute. All I cared or was thinking about was my awful secret.

"You didn't tell anyone?"

"Oh, no, don't worry. You have nothing to worry about."

It was all I could do not to kiss the telephone with relief.

Bill told me that I'd be all right, that there was nothing wrong with the way I was, and to call him when I was home for the holidays. He also let me know that he was now in a monogamous relationship. I wasn't clear about what that meant, although it was obvious he wasn't available and didn't sound interested in me. Now I suspect that "not that kind of girl" meant that since he was already seeing someone, he wouldn't cheat. It was a lightweight way of telling me he was taken and unavailable.

"You have nothing to worry about" rang happily in my ears. He had sensed that I was a voice — to him no doubt a baby — crying out in need. I hung up the telephone, the ten-ton gorilla of fear lifted off my shoulders. I could breathe normally again. Bill was not only dashing and urbane, he also had turned out to have a heart.

During Christmas vacation, and after the disappointment of Brad Karasian's not only becoming a turncoat but bringing his girl to my New Year's Eve party, I did call him.

"My friend and I have broken up," Bill told me, and he sounded much more friendly. "Come down and we'll have dinner." We arranged it for January 7, and it definitely had the sound of a date. Now he seemed interested, and here he was, a shocking thirty years old, maybe even thirty-one! I thought, God, this is an old man.

Could I tell my parents I was going into the city to meet an old man? It wouldn't make sense. Until then, I'd gone into town only with school friends, so lie or no lie, it seemed imperative to say that's what I was going to do.

Next came the heavy wardrobe decisions. How dressed up/down should I get? It's not easy to forget that I settled on my Christmas-present Shetland sweater (medium blue) over my staple button-down shirt (light blue) and my standard khakis (khaki), and that I shined my loafers (brown). I took the train and then a bus to Greenwich Village, and it took me twenty minutes of wandering those streets to find the address, which was in a small, nondescript old building one had to enter by going down half a flight of steps into a lobby. I took the elevator to his floor, found his apartment door and, palpitating head to foot, rang his doorbell.

What hit me first was his unexpected transformation. I had seen Bill only in a business suit, shirt, tie and polished shoes, and in that uniform he seemed to fit right into my image of an older me, the direction in which I was hopefully heading. But that night he opened the door wearing jeans, a flannel shirt and funny boots with pointed toes. The outfit threw me off. Those black boots and that unpreppy flannel shirt reminded me of Sonny Fields in his Village period. It was sort of an urban-cowboy look, another world. My friends' leisure clothes would have been oxford button-down shirts like the one I was wearing, and their jeans would not be this well pressed, this carefully faded, this tight. They'd be wearing Frye boots, those ubiquitous symbols of high preppiness, not angel-back heels like the ones on Bill's feet.

Not that his clothes were a turnoff, but they were an unexpected revelation. It was a matter of my being thrown into unexplored, unfamiliar territory, a new place that seemed far from the safe harbor of my psychological home. Exotic. I suppose it added to my already high-wire tension. I was a wreck.

He immediately said, "I'm starving. Let's go out and get something to eat," and we went out and got pizza and brought it back to his apartment. It was a small studio, and in that one room he had a sofa, coffee table, wing chair and a fireplace with a stone façade. There was also a tower of stereo equipment, a full-size bed and a whole wall of windows. I could see a fire escape beyond the glass. This was all very Manhattan, and in retrospect, knowing what sort of rents people pay for cubbyholes not nearly this attractive, I think he had quite a nice setup, but at the time I'd never seen a place like it. My trips to the city were never to anyone's apartment, except to my Hackley friends' ten- or twelve-room places or to the Plaza Hotel suites of my father's foreign suppliers, so by contrast, I thought this place rather humble and couldn't understand why someone like Bill, presumably pretty high up in the travel agency hierarchy, was living so modestly.

I could barely eat my pizza. I was nervous and shaky and very quiet. Bill was doing all the talking. He asked about my life and my experiences and gave me two or three vodka drinks to calm me down. They were strong and unsweetened, unlike the drinks I occasionally had at school, and they tasted horrible. I didn't want to drink them, but as the evening continued, I did sip my way through a few.

It was around eleven-thirty or twelve, and Bill suddenly said, "I don't want you to take this the wrong way, but you can stay if you want."

I had only a little cash in my pocket, and it wasn't like I could just hop a cab to Grand Central. It was getting late. And later. "You're welcome to stay," Bill said. Many times.

I kept saying, "I don't know, I don't know," and I thought: I still have time, there are two more trains, I don't have to decide yet. There was something inside me that was not necessarily enjoying himself, but was somehow afraid to leave. It's as if I'd moved forward, stepped into a new illuminated place, very afraid of it but also scared to go back. I didn't know what to do.

Bill kept trying to calm my nerves. "Don't worry, Chris. You'll be okay." While he fiddled with the stereo, I looked out the window at the fire escape, not at all sure I was going to be okay.

As it became apparent that I was never going to make that critical last train, Bill said, "Do you want to call home?" and I spent about an hour trying to figure out how to make up an excuse as to where I was. I was thinking up one alibi after another, rejecting each one, and finally I decided to postpone doing it. "I'll take care of it in the morning. I'll come up with something."

It was two in the morning before we segued into bed. It just sort of happened, and I never saw him without clothes. Everything came off under the sheets. He held me and said, "We don't have to do anything," while I shook and wished the night to be over. Nothing happened. It didn't work. I was too nervous and the whole episode was a disaster. Eventually Bill fell asleep, and I remained awake all night thinking, What am I going to say when I get home? He's so good-looking, but I'm so uncomfortable here. *What am I doing?*

In the morning I got up, still worrying. I don't think I'd slept five minutes. My head was whirling. How was this going to continue? How could it? The whole liaison was far-fetched to begin with. He wanted me to call him, but how could I? And again, *What will I say when I get home?*

Bill got up and dressed in the dapper suit I was used to seeing him in. He walked me outside and to the corner, waited with me at the bus stop, gave me a token for the bus and put me on it. As it pulled away, I looked through the window and there he was on the sidewalk, and he waved to me. As I went off to Grand Central, back to my conventional suburban world, my sore, eighteen-year-old heart felt packed to the brim with turbulence.

It wasn't until the following summer when I went back to the travel agency that I saw Bill again. "What happened?" he asked. "I haven't heard from you, didn't know if I should call. I knew you were worried about people finding out in college, and your family . . ." He'd already met someone new and everything was fine in his life, and from then on we had a cordial, business-only relationship. After that summer we lost touch, but years later I ran into him on the street, and he was still working at the travel agency, doing well, as handsome as ever. I look back with gratitude and affection; he was a really world-class guy.

My father never got the truth out of me. No one did. My brother and sister never stopped teasing me, and my Hackley friends thought it was a girl thing, assumed it was a fling with an older woman with an apartment, no big deal. I stayed quiet or changed the subject, let them think whatever they wanted to think. I was gaining a certain mastery in subterfuge — it was my whole life, after all.

That night changed the way I was toward my parents. I became even more "good," by which I mean that I was exceptionally cautious. From then on, I became more careful not to cause them worry or raise suspicion of even a minor sort. I turned into kind of a full-time Eagle Scout earning merit badges, and always felt as if binoculars were trained on me.

It also made me take a step back, because I realized how complex this move into accepting my own sexual orientation was. I was not yet capable of combining my collegiate existence with this "alternative" choice, and wasn't about to think of the two as anything but separate lives, each at odds with the other, like a pair of wrangling twin selves.

So I continued making new friends, studying and appeasing my college-boy self, while my other half yearned for the emotional fulfillment that seemed everyone else's birthright.

2 1

- - - - - - - - - -

I WAS IN the bathroom on the second floor of the Museum of Modern Art, and inadvertently I eavesdropped on two women who were standing side by side at the sinks. One, the older of the two, silver-haired and gold-jeweled, was saying, "He is so wonderful. I cannot tell you how good he is to me. He gives me absolutely anything I want. *Anything!*"

My writer's ears went right up. I imagined a gentle sunset-years romance just like those pictured in cruise ship brochures. Oh, how nice. The woman rhapsodized a bit longer, just long enough for me to deflate as I overheard the blighted denouement. It wasn't a new paramour, not an old love. She was talking about her hairdresser, and in a follow-up description she called him "a *faygeleh.*" As I soon discovered, that is the Yiddish term for a homosexual.

"You mean he's a three-letter man?" her companion asked. Giggle, giggle.

"What?"

"A three-letter man — a fag!"

The women, drying hands, applying lipstick, were all hilarity. The older woman added, "But they're so sweet, those pansies. Especially the Italian ones."

Not fifteen minutes later I was sitting in the museum's members' dining room when my friend Jill arrived.

"I'm so sorry I'm late," she said, "but I had a telephone call just as I was leaving the house. Do you remember my friend Flora?"

I hardly knew her friends, and didn't remember Flora.

It turned out Flora had called Jill just this morning with the unnerving news that she'd found pictures of nude men in one of her son's bureau drawers. She'd always suspected, but now she knew. What should she do? She was feeling suicidal. He was a twin. She was sure the other boy was all right, but still: her son, a homosexual! She couldn't tell her husband. He might throw the boy out, how could she face her aging parents and so on . . . For my ears, burning words.

These two conversations, which happened to come back to back, were samples of dialogue the themes of which were not unusual in my life (or anyone else's). Repeatedly and much too often, my sensitive radar picked up some evidence — as if I needed such confirmation — that the world at large, even in the space-age eighties, even among many of those who were presumably open-minded, educated and cosmopolitan, deplored, hated, condescended to and generally bore ill will to men who were not heterosexual. My friends, none of whom knew of our situation with Chris at that time, often hurt me inadvertently with the sort of comments, quotes and jokes that I had also been capable of making at an earlier, less enlightened time.

That is, before Chris stayed out all night, with cover-up stories and no valid explanation. Now homosexuality had a new spin for me. Will Rogers put his finger on it: "Everything is funny as long as it is happening to someone else." And now the someone else was almost surely one of my own. The subject had lost any last shred of neutrality.

Yet I retreated from the evidential probability. I didn't really want to hear Chris's excuse for staying out all night. Although I knew with a near-absolute certainty that it had to do with someone of his own sex, I had enough of a desire for self-preservation to back off. I couldn't picture it and didn't want to. That morning-after homecoming, our few minutes of privacy in the car at the railroad station, was a critical point for me. It's where I scrutinized my own soul and saw myself pulling the shade to stay in the dark. I looked into my son's eyes and saw that I didn't really want to know.

A few minutes after he came home, Chris took his father's car and ran into town, returning a while later with a dozen yellow roses for me. It was clearly Bob's dictum, a little push to get Chris back into his good-boy character (and, of course, out of consideration for me). "Happy birthday, Mom," he said, sheepish, subdued, remorseful, handing them over. Bob and I have always agreed that flowers are an unfortunate choice for a birthday gift, for different reasons. Bob doesn't like them because they make him sneeze. I feel they're here today and dead tomorrow, too close to the story of mortal life, on an occasion that is already symbolic of time passing. It was the first and last time I ever got a bouquet on my birthday, and lovely or not, the flowers did in fact become tatty in a few days and died before the following weekend. Ordinarily I don't like turning good money into mulch, but I was not unhappy to throw these twelve out.

What happened between Bob and me after that night was — nothing. I might have said, "I'm sure it was a man." He might have said, "Let's not get into it." No one suggested a family powwow, counseling or a one-on-one heart-to-heart. The events of that night were the toxic nuclear waste of our family history, too dangerous to be stirred up until now.

"You mean we're finally going to find out where Chris spent that night?" Kirby asked when I told him about this book.

It took almost fifteen years, one hundred eighty new moons and a cultural convulsion. It took courage that comes with maturity, and it took a divorce.

Happy times, good love, laughter and affection do not make interesting copy. If Bob was volatile, hostile, irritable, difficult and overbearing, he was also funny, generous, caring, and most important, he was ours. As someone said of Fiorello La Guardia when he was mayor of New York, "He is a bastard, but he is *our* bastard." Bob, not a villain but a textbook Type A personality with all its dark implications, was our chief and my life. He and I meshed in ways that couples who have grown up together do, interrelating seamlessly. I was secure — so was he — in our good world. The word "dysfunctional" had not come into use. If it had,

I would not have felt it defined us. Ideals, then and now, do not exist except in the minds of televangelists and psychologists. At that time, we survived Bob's outbursts and my reactive silences, his television sitcoms, our dailiness. I look back with laughter, not with anger; we were not an unhappy couple.

What happened the night Chris stayed out until morning was nothing, or almost nothing. I know I internalized what I'd learned, and maybe Bob did too. It wasn't exactly self-delusion, not repression either. Little by little, seeing no further evidence of gay love, I pushed myself into thinking that this may have been an isolated experiment. Didn't all boys . . . ? Then, I continued to read, or should I say pounce upon, any new disclosure about the root causes of homosexuality. Studies came out of Canada or Sweden or Johns Hopkins, and I ingested them as enthusiastically as carbohydrates. Differences in urine samples, brain tissue, the level of testosterone in the blood? It could only be a question of genetics or chemistry.

Or heredity. We visited my first cousin in Canada and met her son for the first time. An Anglican monk, he appeared in a brown robe, a huge Maltese cross hanging around his neck, and he was so clearly and obviously effeminate, there was not a doubt, was there? In her letters my cousin had often written of his difficult adolescence, his occasional "breakdowns." The poor, closeted kid! A light switch went on in my head. Familial anomaly! A surprise, not necessarily pleasant. Somehow, like the blue-green eyes and early-baldness genes my sons got through my chromosomes, Chris's predilection was my fault one way or the other, for sure. Walt Whitman said, "Mothers precede all!" and he meant "cause all"; it's what everybody assumed.

My cousin's son died when he was in his twenties. She wrote a sad letter. It was stomach cancer, she said. This was in the eighties, and until recently I never doubted her word. Now I'm appalled at our mutual shame. I'm embarrassed at the avidity with which I studied all the new "findings." Mulled over articles about revulsion therapy. It might be just around the corner, the new drug that could fix the condition. That thought was back there in my head for many years. Yes, it was the culture, the queer jokes, the off-hand remarks of friends, the raised fist of the church and other miscellaneous propaganda, but I have to take some responsibility for swallowing all of it for so long.

With hindsight, I know now that we left too much unspoken. If only we could have said, "If I'd done what you did last night, you'd be surprised, but would you think me so terrible? Would you forgive me? If so, why wouldn't I forgive you?" Or, "Would you like to talk to us? Would you like to talk to someone else?"

And we could have simply said, "If you spent the night with a man, well, so what? It doesn't change a thing. We loved you from the moment you were born, love you still, and not an iota less."

But we were then still a couple of dominoes resisting the tumbling effect of rapid social change. There were so many of us! We weren't exactly crying, "What is this world coming to?" but growing up in an age known for its rigid rules and regulations, we'd spent Saturday afternoons at movies censored by the Hays Office, were more often than not virgins at the altar and were used to obeying standard canons without questioning their logic. I think that breaking the rules then seemed more tolerable than making the transgressions public. It was shabby to flaunt behavior we'd always considered out of bounds, and maybe worse, a little "ordinaire" — my mother's word for unbecoming conduct. I took that to mean "not respectable," and above all, we always wanted our children to be respectable. And respected! So although we considered ourselves relatively open to "alternative lifestyles" as long as one didn't advertise them, the idea of same-sex coupling was still an uncomfortable concept, and it definitely was unpalatable for one of our own. From Noah until today, a couple meant one of each, and given this mindset, our silence was predictable, if shameful and sad.

After that January 8, life resumed its normal rhythm. Nothing more was ever mentioned about the night again, and for the moment one would have noticed no perceptible change in our family life. Alison was still on the periphery of her adolescent rebellion, and Bob had not yet become afflicted with his case of metaphysical blight. Prosperity still had not revealed its shadowed side, and, as five respectable citizens intermittently under one roof, we mustered in and moved merrily along.

2 2

- - - - - - - - - -

IT'S NOT AS IF I didn't have friends at college. Although the University of Vermont consisted of eight thousand students, I couldn't walk from one class to another, from one building to the next, without being greeted. It was "Hi, Chris, how you doing?" every five minutes. Seeing me move across campus, one would have thought I was Mr. Right Guy, the BMOC. The reality was that I made many friends at school, loved my nonengineering courses and lived an outwardly social collegiate life, but continued a walk-through of my days, my emotional indicator always on Empty.

It was the old story with a new twist. Now I was accepted. Sort of. Surrounded by women, some men, and with at least one straight buddy — a student from my accounting class named Dick Wicker — I was in the swim. I went out every night with one group or another, or at least part of me went. After the fiasco of Bill Van Dyne, there was even more of a feeling of isolation and worthlessness. The repercussions of my night out were another dose of self-hatred. I felt as if I'd committed a felony and would bring down shame on all three generations of my family if it came to light. Chris as evildoer was such a consuming part of me, the nagging thoughts of how my father would be shot to hell and destroyed, how my mother might fall apart, even get physically sick over the idea of a degenerate child — those fears never left me. The anxiety of having a gay skeleton in my closet was there through the raised glasses at parties, the nights at the movies, the French quizzes. It was there first thing in the morning when I got up, and in the dining hall when I stood in line with a tray in my hand. If someone looked at me too long, if a smile lingered, if a sentence was interrupted as I approached, my heart went into a tailspin. I continued to smile through fag jokes, grinned and bore the innuendoes, subtle or socko, and never once considered a confrontation. And all this time, in some deepset part of me, I still thought it wasn't too late. I was like starving Tantalus, neck deep in water, struggling and striving but never quite able to reach the banquet of homosexuality *or* heterosexuality. Perhaps if I tried a bit harder . . . maybe, possibly, what if?

Despite new friends and activities, I was forever hungry and yearning, not so much for sex as for just one person to whom I could pour my heart out. Typical of closet cases of any age, I was living my real life in solitary confinement. It's what caused me to risk seeking out a gay bar in coldest winter, in the unlikely vicinity of the arcadian college town of Burlington, Vermont.

At the university, there was a gay student union listed in the club directory, but for a long time I was too frightened to make contact there. When I had gathered up the courage to call its listed number, I got a recording, hung up, subsequently tried again — and again — until I heard a human voice. It told me there was a gay bar in town called Charlie B Goods, its location, Center Street. Despite its name, the street turned out to be nowhere near any center, and was short and inconsequential enough not to appear on any city map. I set out three times to find it, daring to ask no one for directions, for fear the person would guess where I was headed. I came close once, imagined I'd found the street and bar and found myself instead in the wrong part of Burlington, in front of some modern commercial structure in the suburban part of town. Nowhere.

I was determined, though, and one night set out again on foot. It started snowing soon after I left my dormitory, and by the time I got into town the snow was coming down thick as a blizzard. As I walked alone, a pickup truck pulled up next to me, filled with faces from my dormitory. They began yelling, "Hey, Chris. Where are you going? Do you want a ride? Come on, get in!" I told them I was just walking into town, they pressured some more, finally waved and drove off, while I turned beet red, thinking, They know where I'm headed. I thought they'd spotted me right near the bar, although it turned out to be blocks away, but at that moment my blood was pumping and I kept thinking, They know, they know! Still, I stayed calm, kept walking. And walking.

At last I found the place, slipped in, and was almost immediately crushed with disappointment. After all the searching and struggle, the snow, the cold, the sneaking around, this turned out to be a down-at-the-heels place filled with older locals, not one of student age, and the two or three men who were nearly my contemporaries were not anyone I could see myself connecting with. The front room was brightly lit, the air blue with smoke, the men lined up at the bar all dressed to look like they had stepped out of a Marlboro ad, their steely eyes staring me down. Behind this room was another one, darker, bluer, filled with more flannel shirts, leather jackets, black boots. A DJ played disco, there was a dance floor, and it was the first time I'd ever seen men dancing together. It seemed like a stage set for hell, and I was even afraid of being seen walking out of there. Despite all the grubbiness, I went back two or more times, hoping that maybe, just maybe — with more or less the same disheartening result. I was always miserably uncomfortable there. The place ended up closing the following year, so it annihilated even the dim possibility of finding an intimate during the rest of my college days.

The gay bar experience hit me right where I lived: whereas I would have to sneak around sordid venues, call or write presumed homosexuals at great risk, spend my life deviously trying to seek out just one someone I could relate to, other people around me, the lucky heterosexuals, were meeting each other left and right in natural ways, in classes, the cafeteria, the dormitory, at sports events. On campus, it was Cupid's perpetual spring, and my straight college contemporaries all took this wonderful good fortune of being able to fall in love with someone of the opposite sex completely for granted.

I don't know how my college life would have played itself out if I hadn't met two redeemers. One weekend, I managed to get a ride home with an acquaintance from my dormitory. On the way to

New York from Vermont, his ancient Jeep broke down, stranding us for hours at a thruway rest stop near Kingston, New York, where we waited for a tow truck, mushed through the rain to a Mobil station and sat in an all-night diner over coffee and hamburgers. The second stranded passenger was a fellow sophomore named Julia, a pre-law student from Albany, with whom I fell in platonic love almost at first sight, and with whom I continue to have a close friendship to this day.

Why did we hit it off? Despite our disparate backgrounds, what made Julia an indispensable, irreplaceable commodity in my life? These three criteria, which are probably standard-issue rules for all good relationships, applied to Julia and me: mutual admiration, common interests, common enemies. In our case there were two more that cemented us: we could laugh riotously together, and we knew we were both out of the mainstream and not destined to become members of the college ruling class.

Julia came from a rural background, was bright and, unlike many of my new friends, not superficial. She seemed to have extra ears for hearing what I said, and the sort of down-to-earthness more common in professors than in sophomores. We had the same perspective on people, and we both felt displaced and different. It was long into the friendship before I learned she was a lesbian.

Very slowly, in cautious increments, our defenses went down and our friendship grew. Through Julia I met Pete Lamoureux, who lived two floors below me in our dormitory, and with whom I also struck up a friendship. Now we became a trinity, pretty much inseparable, spending most of our time digging deep into life's meanings and not quite deeply enough into one another's. That is, we skirted the sexuality issue, went round and round it, never peeling it down to the core. We were three non-heterosexuals and never admitted it to each other, until finally we did.

It took a long time. When Pete told me about a homosexual experience he'd had when he was younger, he didn't admit he was gay. My view was that while he'd just had one sneeze, I had the pneumonia, and as usual I was terrified of the repercussions of full disclosure, so for months following that conversation, I kept my mouth shut.

It was around Christmas that Pete came to New York to visit me, and we drove to a small vacation place my family owned in Connecticut. We made a fire in the fireplace, brought in some meatball subs and Greek salads and began one of our deep philosophical conversations. With no one else around, I began to feel safer. This was a controlled environment and I could calm him down if he became, well, upset. Not that I expected him to run screaming out the door, but I'd been burned enough never to know what a man's reaction might be. We began talking about the problems with society, not as if we were gay but as if we were running for office on the Liberal Party ticket, sort of feeling each other out. Then Pete admitted he felt he was gay. The finger was out of the dike! It was like the opening had let in a rushing warm bath on a bitter night; the conversation soothed body and soul; I never wanted it to stop. I told him my life experiences, let autobiography pour out in neat chronological sequence. We talked about what mutual friends might think if they found out, what might happen if certain professors knew, and that ubiquitous subject among young gay men: what our parents would do if they found out. Then it was "What are you going to do?" and we irrevocably affirmed the fact that we were absolutely, unequivocally gay, not a bit heterosexual and not even slightly bisexual.

Bisexualism we took as a joke. Many homosexuals dip their toes into the murky waters of public opinion by claiming to be bi. It sounds less unacceptable, maybe even a bit Noël Cowardish, not as *final*. And less serious. We laughed at Woody Allen, whose quip "It [bisexuality] doubles your chances for a date for Saturday night" had us in stitches, and we laughed about the gays who continued to masquerade as equal-opportunity studs, ready to take on comers of any sex. We said there should be a fraternity on every U.S. campus for them: B.S. for Bisexuals, Beta Sigma and Bullshit.

Back on campus, with our many Beta Sig inside jokes and our

common disdain for my new roommate — who played "Yellow Polka Dot Bikini" on his stereo night and day, who bought a paisley tuxedo, which we considered beyond the pale, and yet who had the secure heterosexual's overdose of self-confidence — our support group of three lumped happily together. We were slightly bitter, slightly angry and, through nights of discussion, dissection and philosophizing, through the unblocked arteries of revealed secrets, we enriched one another and became wonderfully and profoundly enmeshed. For those who haven't lived a secret life, it is hard to imagine the sudden release of finding someone to whom you can reveal that lifelong backlog of black-pit thoughts, someone who will not betray you, not openly or covertly scoff at or pity you, who will comprehend what a closet really means. It allows you at last to know who you really are, because you've been protecting yourself from yourself all your life. For the first time, I felt as if I had friends I could call real friends.

We created a tight social knot, my first comfort zone of human support. If there weren't any positively portrayed gay characters on TV, we would nevertheless allow ourselves to feel positive about our own orientation. It was a new and exhilarating freedom to be able to watch Tom Selleck on *Magnum, P.I.* and verbalize the thought that he was great-looking. For the first time in my life it was not forbidden to admire a man openly for his looks, carriage, intellect (Julia and I each had crushes on same-sex professors) and not be condemned.

It was the exclusive right of heterosexuals, like the most hormone-driven unmuzzled of my dorm mates, to describe new conquests and discuss a woman's body parts in tasteless terms. They skirt chased and talked about it in great detail without restriction, while even my most innocent man-admiring thoughts had to remain behind my tight-sealed lips.

I had not had the sort of young romance experiences every sixteen-year-old heterosexual takes for granted: the flirting, the prom dates, the first kisses, hands held in the park. I still did not have that freedom, but now at least I had a place where I no longer had to keep my mouth shut, and being unrestrained with my friends was a lifesaver. I felt emancipated.

Pete, also gaining strength from our triumvirate, decided to Out himself to someone in my dormitory he was attracted to. The friend took it very badly, told other people, who told other people, until the rumor mill generated enough campus publicity to affect me. I was known as Pete's good friend, and guilt by association began to taint me. Until my accounting-class friend, Dick Wicker, began to keep me at arm's length, I wasn't able to put my finger on the reason, but that big chill hurt. My popularity quotient among many heterosexual dorm mates fell like mercury in a thermometer plunged into snow. On the other hand, if I paid this price for being close to Pete, our three-way friendship lifted me psychologically from adolescence to adulthood. My self-esteem and self-acceptance — and, not coincidentally, my grades — rose like the mercury in the same thermometer in August. Although it took many more years before I was freed of judging myself by the opinions of others, I started being more discriminating, ignored the homophobes and the snobs and began to listen only to people I respected.

It's when I saw clearly that people of worth were not necessarily driving BMWs or wearing brand-name skis, began looking at myself through Julia's eyes, and there I was, just an ordinary guy in ill-fitting Rich Kid's clothing. What had I been thinking to assume that the steps to heaven were carpeted with Aubusson? Thank God I'd found out before I was like the camel who had to go through the eye of a needle, and well before graduation. By the time I got my sheepskin, I knew who the new, no-frills Chris was, and where and with whom I really belonged.

23
- - - - - - - - - -

IT WAS ONE of the worst weekends of my life.

I look at the photograph taken of the five of us at Chris's college graduation and what do I see? Alison, all decked out for the big day but looking grim, the rest of us exemplifying the prosperous American family, two happy parents and their wholesome children, best smile forward for the camera. It seems all bright sun and good cheer, an attractive quintet perfectly centered in this photo my father took right after the diplomas were handed out. It may have been that it was a bad teenage day for Alison, or just that she refused to fake it. She knew it and I knew it: it was a wonderful and momentous occasion, and a rotten day for all of us.

The weekend started with a comfortable and uneventful flight from La Guardia Airport to Burlington, Vermont. Bob hated flying and always had to fortify himself with a rapid succession of bloody marys before he could board the aircraft. That was undoubtedly a contributing factor — his mood was already veering to ominous as we arrived in Vermont. We were flying with Alison and my father and his wife, Helen; Kirby had driven up the day before. The boys were to pick us up at the airport and take us to our hotel.

It is not enough to say that Bob cannot abide hassle. He spins out of control when there are crowds, lines or any possibility of human disorder. When I saw the push and pull of people and luggage at the terminal, I sensed we were in for it. To make matters worse, the boys weren't there as arranged. Bob's familiar twitch began to twitch, his eyes darted left and right, and under his breath he began the four-letter lyrics I knew so well. Five minutes of this relentless score might test the earshot of any good wife, but the pacing and steaming continued for the half hour the boys were late. I felt edgy and apprehensive, knew if they weren't there, there had to be a good reason. So, adding to my embarrassment about my mild-mannered father and his well-mannered wife witnessing this harangue, I was worried that something might have happened to my two sons en route to the airport.

The public dressing down of the boys, who rushed in to explain they couldn't get near the terminal, had been circling the airport looking for a parking space for forty minutes, set the tone for the rest of our stay in Burlington. Although I pleaded with Bob to hear them out before blasting them, there was never an antidote to his fevered turbulence, which had to wind down of its own accord. By the time he'd worked the fire out of his system, humiliated the boys, made a scene and set up my father and his wife for an endless and awkward silence, my own Czechoslovakian Irish was up. To put it mildly, I was ablaze.

The Sheraton was grand, very modern and well appointed, and our rooms all faced majestic Mount Mansfield. Bob, generous as always, had arranged and paid not only for the air tickets but also for a room for my father and Helen. He was also solicitous of their comfort and welfare. Here, then, was the setting for an idyllic family weekend; what more could one ask? I asked for good humor. Patience. A little wit. Wanted for my children a gentle and amiable father, like the one I'd had. Instead, the following day, at graduation and afterward, Daddy's mood veered from tightly wound to mayday, depending on the graduation demons, which conspired to distress him. The ceremony was overlong, the gym hot and stuffy, Chris had forgotten to make lunch reservations, and the new Mercedes required diesel fuel we couldn't immediately find in Burlington.

I don't think I am being too hard on a nervous man with a bad back. My retroactive anger may seem excessive, since Bob wasn't mean or out of sorts every minute, but this was a weekend where his bad behavior was cumulative, where my father and Helen were witnesses, where my level of expectations had precluded Daddy's acting like a pit bull cum laude, and where I found myself forever trying to suppress the beast on what was supposed to be a signal occasion for all of us, and especially for Chris.

On all sides of us I saw the caps and gowns, the kisses, flowers, bonhomie and cheer. Why not us? I was so proud of my son, the B.A. in economics, standing there in his mortarboard. Other graduating seniors were enveloped by familial harmony and love while we were working on just getting through the day. And the night.

Which proved to be yet another disastrous event. Unknown country roads, muddy and rutted, a trip that took us far out of town to some unheard-of place where a dinner dance was to be held, again turned on Daddy's hidden switch. Now it was drizzling in the bargain, and Bob continued as the tight-lipped and glowering navigator. The final scenario had to do with the hustle and bustle of college-help waiters, the confusion and crush of the open seating arrangements and too many insignificant irritating details I have long since forgotten. The dinner was another exercise in Daddy's breathing fire, and my trying to get past it.

And yet, when we'd had our salad, our chicken, our piece of vanilla-frosted cake, the evening took a sunnier turn. Chris brought over his friend Julia, whom we'd first met when he brought her home for a weekend. She seemed to be, according to some wordless messages he was transmitting, a new and special person in his life. He walked this pleasant brunette over to meet Grandpa while I confirmed to myself what I'd picked up the first time we met her: this was a platonic buddy, not a romance. Nevertheless, on this evening and for years afterward, Bob believed what he wanted so much to believe, that Julia was not just a friend but an affair of the heart. I think it cheered him up immeasurably. "I told you so" is the sentiment he expressed or implied, and Julia became every bit as much of a smoke screen for him as she was for Chris.

Sometime later that evening, my husband and I got up to dance, and I suppose that little by little, as Bob cooled off, I simmered down, because the rest of the evening passed rather neutrally. Dancing was always a soothing experience for us. We'd been doing the same steps together since college days and were adept at keeping the beat. I suppose the synchronicity of the fox trots and rhumbas was particularly symbolic that night. Anger dissipated, we were a team and right back in step. As the culmination to the weekend, the following morning we'd all be the recipients of a Sheraton brunch. Bob would treat everyone in sight, including Julia and a bunch of Chris's other college friends; his mood would be up; he'd play to the kids and make us all laugh. Especially me. When he turned on the warmth, the charm and the wit, I'd always find him irresistible. Later, at home, I'd upbraid him for his bad behavior and he'd be full of remorse, tell me again to remind him before we went out anywhere that he was to behave himself. Bob as bad boy was short-lived. The better half emerged good as new and he turned himself inside out to please me. "I know I'm difficult," he'd announce, as if he were saying, "I know I'm an epileptic, please accept the seizures." And for very long, assuming that it would be forever, I forgave him.

24

- - - - - - - - - - -

ALL OF IT comes back to me: the circling of the airport, my father's agitation at lunch because I'd blundered in not making reservations. Although it was not unusual to be chewed out for some small infraction, I felt guilty, embarrassed in front of my grandparents, particularly disappointed at the way things were going this weekend. At the same time, my father's eruptions didn't stand out as any worse than others that took place over the years. It's taken me a long time, but I've gotten to understand that it's not me, it's probably never been me. It's just the way he is.

Although it is true that throughout that weekend I was mostly in the business of getting my father calmed down and everything running smoothly, it was more visceral than that. I was leaving a safe cocoon of friends I might never see again, heading into the big question mark of a future I felt I wasn't prepared for. I was saying goodbye to a life I didn't want to give up and concerned that I was heading for two neatly divided worlds — that of the normal, all-right heterosexuals and of the darker, homosexual system to which I now belonged. Forever after, I was going to have to be with left-field types that had nothing to do with me, aliens. I had convinced myself not only that my homosexuality would decimate my family, but that coming out of the closet would mean losing all the straight friends I had. It meant being kicked out of my safe and solid universe for keeps.

It was hard to move back home again. I'd become enlightened about what I was, and was now no longer capable of living it under this roof. Despite the Dorans, who were still good friends and good fun, I had a lonely summer, missing my college confidantes, especially Julia. Mostly I was feeling at loose ends, hanging around the house or running the thousand and one errands my mother found to keep me busy. I was lucky to find a job the following September, glad to get out of the suspended animation of life under scrutiny at home.

My new boss was a clever entrepreneur. His business was importing Spanish goods, and he hired young college graduates to mentor and direct. It was like being in school again, and happily, although definitely in hiding, I was thrown into a ready-made social group. We co-workers had lunches together, went out to dinner, gave parties. Concurrently, my father and mother bought an apartment on West Fifty-fourth Street, planning to renovate it sooner or later. In the meantime, they allowed me to live in splendor at a tenement's rent. It was wonderful luck and perfect timing. The apartment didn't have a good view or a new kitchen, but it did have three whole rooms, a central location and a fancy address.

So I became a man about town leading a double life. Between my work friends and acquaintances from my university alumni club, there was plenty of night action, if not exactly substance. Late at night, the fancy apartment still seemed cavernously empty.

Today, in the nineties, gay people have many options for meeting each other. There are common-interest groups that mirror those of heterosexuals — a network for gay advertising executives, clubs for hiking, skiing, tennis, you name it — but in the early eighties there were gay bars. Although they did cut across social strata, they seemed seamy and sordid, an urban version of the bar in Burlington, filled with preening hunks, on-the-make older men, frightened husbands hiding behind glasses of Scotch, jaded regulars. There were Wall Street men who went once a week and would take someone home that night and that was it, they'd be straight the rest of the time; the whole assortment ran the gamut of a society I didn't want to be a part of and resulted only in random, short-lived, superficial and, for me, never sexual encounters.

There were also parking lots, rest stops and bathhouses. I didn't even know about those until I ran into a boy with whom I'd gone to the University of Vermont, and he opened my eyes wide to the gay minefields I would avoid at all costs. He was an "obvious" and handsome boy I'd spotted and carefully shunned on campus, but now we struck up a friendship and began to go to the bars together. I wasn't one of the pretty boys, so whenever I went with him, I'd feel even more alone, because he was particularly attractive and would always get the looks and the attention, and I'd feel instantly invisible. He always met someone, went home with him, and that turned me off, but it was apparent even then that I could have friends who had different sexual mores but with whom I'd still have many other things in common. Invariably, in his romantic life and because the attraction was superficial, a hitch would reveal itself that night, the next week or a month later. No matter; he'd meet yet another someone, same place, next time. From a philosophy course I took in my junior year, a Nietzsche quote burned itself into my head: "The lonely one offers his hand too quickly to whomever he encounters." It was a typical gay-bar phenomenon.

Once, just once, I found someone *I* liked — a sort of mirror image of my inner spirit. He worked in the offices of the Park Lane Hotel, had just been transferred from Boston, and it took his move to a new city to get up the nerve to venture into this gay bar. He was mild and shy, just as uncomfortable being there as I was. We took to each other immediately, but after about an hour he abruptly shot up, put the money for his drink on the bar, said he was too frightened and nervous, apologized and practically flew out of the place.

That pretty much dampened my already damp enthusiasm for the gay bars of New York City, and, so, I tried something else.

In the early eighties, there was only one widely circulated gay publication, the now defunct *New York Native*. I eyed this newspaper, passed newsstand after newsstand, afraid and embarrassed to buy it. Soon I began to go to different parts of the city to get a copy, would then wrap it in God knows how many newspapers and skulk into the vestibule of my parents' apartment. Seeing me sneaking into the elevator with my arm around my newspaper bundle, one would have thought I was trying to conceal a severed head. The building was a small co-op in which I knew all the other tenants, and I was terrified that somehow I'd run into a neighbor in the hall and the *Native* would slip out and disgrace me.

The only other reading material available for gay men on the newsstands were porno magazines. Those publications which advertised sex toys and videos didn't interest me; I was looking for personal ads. The *New York Native* was also sexually oriented, but had nothing much to do with gays as a community (the only articles of any interest were the ones describing the new "gay plague," which was just becoming known at that time — another reason for my being too scared to keep going to the bars), though it did run personals. For a long time those ads put me off, because they either tended to be dirty or sounded too lonely and desperate, but finally I found one that attracted me. It had the heading "Two Needles in a Haystack," indicated the man was not out of the closet and was a "serious soul mate seeking a serious soul mate." The ad said more: he was a lawyer, interested in the arts and a recent law school graduate. I rented a post office box under a fake name, paid with a money order signed with a fake signature and answered the ad with my alias and the box number. No FBI mole could have been more careful; I wouldn't even put down my telephone number, let alone a photograph. Against all these odds, the needle in the haystack did write back, giving me his number and the best time to call.

I must have picked up and put down the telephone half a dozen times before dialing. "Hello." "Hi." "I answered your ad." How easy it turned out to be. He sounded marvelous and bright, a lawyer in the entertainment industry, described himself as slim, with brown hair, twenty-six years old. A nice voice. Derek. Twenty-six seemed a bit mature to this nervous twenty-two-year-old, but we set up a meeting at Fifty-second Street and Fifth Avenue, in front of Cartier. Seven o'clock. This address was too uncomfortably near my apartment, and I decided in advance that if I didn't like what I saw, I'd make up some excuse and get out of there grace-fully but fast.

It was dusk, but the lights on Fifth Avenue were bright enough. The moment I spotted him, I decided: no way. He wasn't my type, had bent the truth about his looks, wasn't slim, his hair was getting gray, and he was shorter than he'd said, but after a few minutes it didn't matter. He put me at ease, was especially witty, and at the very least could become a colorful friend. Still, I was anxious to get out of my own neighborhood, and immediately agreed to go to a SoHo restaurant he knew, where we could get good hamburgers. On the subway heading downtown, and with great self-confidence, Derek explained he had three fixed criteria for judging someone new. A romantic prospect had to pass on all three counts: fingernails had to be clipped, teeth had to be white and straight, and shoes had to be a certain type (loafers or bucks), and polished. I suppose I passed the test, because it was obvious Derek was taking to me.

We headed for the Broome Street Bar and Grill, a classic SoHo hangout. I'd never been there, and as we sat at a table talking, I looked left and right like an espionage agent in a spy movie, worried about being overheard, keeping my voice down as I gave him a low-volume earful of family history. He'd gone to Prince-ton, had a law degree from Georgetown and was certainly a bit eccentric. It also seems crazy now, but because he was four years older, and with that touch of silver in his hair, I was afraid I might appear suspicious if I was seen hanging around an "older" guy.

So I was already uncomfortable as we left the restaurant to go somewhere else for coffee, and that's where we were heading on Spring Street when it happened. Derek stopped in front of a brick building with a painted façade, all primary colors done in a geometric design. In the windows, on every one of its four floors, lights were flickering. This arresting oddity captured Derek's attention, and he kept saying, "Look at this. Isn't the city fascinating? Isn't this interesting!" until I got him to move on. When we had walked half a block, I saw a familiar figure moving toward us. The impossible, the inconceivable, the unthinkable had happened: in a city of ten million people, here came my brother.

He was as startled to run into me as I was to bump into him. I didn't realize it at the moment, but it turned out he was as unhappy with his date as I was with mine, although of course I didn't want him to know that Derek was a date. Luckily, I spotted Kirby before he spotted me. "Oh, my God, it's my brother!" I cried, and quickly pleaded with Derek not to give me away.

"Chris, what are you doing here?" Kirby was more amused than curious, but the question put me on such a panicky defensive that a long, dopey excuse came flowing out of my mouth. Instead of simply saying, "This is Derek and we've just had dinner," I found myself concocting an elaborate tale of social connection — "Derek is a friend of Annie's, you remember Annie, I met her during my semester abroad in Switzerland" — and although I am the world's worst liar, my brother took no notice, hardly listening to what I had to say. Not eager to show off his own date, he just wanted to get away from me as fast as possible.

But now, unexpectedly, Derek took Kirby by the elbow. "There's something I want to show you," he said, and began maneuvering my brother down the street, to show him the remarkable painted building we'd passed almost a block away.

I was panic stricken. This Derek was a total stranger and what did I know? Was he going to play some baroque trick on me? Some people have a strange sense of humor; was this his idea of *fun?* Kirby's date was sort of tagging along, while I hung back, certain the jig was up. But Derek was just showing Kirby what he thought was some esoteric New York phenomenon, and having a bit of a laugh with what he imagined was a funny situation. The real rocker phenomenon of this city of ten million was that I ran into my brother again, four months later. This time, much to my great relief, he turned up at a popular disco, dancing a few feet away from me. The gods of the Big Apple were good to me this time: I was dancing with a woman from my office.

* * *

Having struck out answering personal ads, I decided to write my own. I put in my stats, including "straight-acting, masculine, seeks similar for friendship and maybe more," listed my interests and the usual "photo/phone/please." I got an enormous variety of answers. One in particular stands out: it was a Xeroxed photo that accompanied a nice letter. He was way in the closet too, so we agreed to meet at a certain hour on a corner near Gramercy Park. As I stood there looking at my watch — he was a few minutes late — up came a man wearing a ski mask, a jacket zipped up to his neck, with dark hair instead of the light shade in the picture he'd sent. He looked ten years older than his likeness, and when I looked at his shoes I remembered Derek's list of standards: he was wearing multicolored sneakers with unmatched laces.

He came up close, squinted at me and said, "Chris?"

"Yes."

He said, "I don't think this is going to work," and he turned and walked away.

I called another, more impressive letter writer.

This was someone my age who said he'd been to Cornell and had a B.A. in economics, had grown up in a white-picket Boston suburb. He wrote a bright and articulate letter, sounding like something I might have written. Isn't that what I'd been looking for all this time?

When I called, I was even more optimistic. We talked about what we'd studied in school, discussed the Federal Reserve and the state of the economy. I understood his lingo and he understood mine. It felt smooth and easy, with one small hitch: he told me he was bisexual. On the happy side, he wasn't Out at home or on the job. Another me, or almost, no question about it.

After about forty minutes of what seemed like a good combination of both a personal and an intellectual conversation, he practically jolted me out of my chair. "Is your last name Shyer?" he asked.

Had I heard right? I was in my parents' apartment, where I always thought the walls had ears, and in this state of paranoia I thought, Whoever he is, this guy knows my brother or my parents or something. I was really scared. Of course, I asked him his name, but instead of answering, he repeated the question. "Is your name Shyer?"

When I admitted it was, he told me his, and it turned out we'd once met on the station platform in Larchmont when he was doing an office internship in Manhattan and living with an uncle in our town. Oh, relief! What's more, there couldn't have been anyone more Hollywood handsome on that Metro-North train, so naturally I remembered him well.

And he wanted to date me! Instantly, my life turned around. Unprecedented excitement and high anticipation filled the empty corners of my apartment and my heart. Here was the possibility of a love story, sunshine, a happy ending at last. My real-life counterpart had appeared in a most unlikely way, and sure enough we were compatible, saw eye to eye on everything, spent some months going out to clubs, to movies, to parties, and having what I thought was a perfect physical and emotional romance.

Then, one night, sitting in some little West Side Chinese restaurant, he began nervously sipping tea, playing with his chopsticks, seemingly uneasy. Something was on his mind.

Suddenly he came out with it. "You know, being gay for me is something like being Jewish. When I'm in a synagogue, I don't feel Jewish, but when I'm in a church, I do. And when I'm with a woman, I don't feel heterosexual. I feel gay. When I'm with you — I don't feel gay either. I don't feel much of anything." He suggested we stop seeing each other. Stay friends. The usual, kind, awful sounds of a kiss-off.

It was a short-lived affair, but he had filled my every expectation, raised me out of the vacuum of morbid loneliness, and was now summarily washing his hands of the romance, pulling the rug out from under my life. It was totally unexpected, and I was devastated.

It was not the first time, nor the last. During this period, I thought that women and the comfortable world of straights, the mainstream, were forever my competition. In reality my romances failed because I chose my close counterparts, who were the most closeted, wary and anxious souls, still unable to handle their sexual destiny. They were the trial-balloon type, too often detouring into heterosexuality, so the disappointments were becoming predictable and redundant.

It was a bad time. Nothing was fun. The world was tinted blue. I threw in the towel and gave up the personals. And hope. At least for the moment.

2 5

- - - - - - - - - -

LAST SUMMER, I stopped in at a storefront Chinese restaurant in the city for some take-out. When I stepped from the steam-heated street into its cool and brightly lit interior, I decided to eat my chicken and broccoli at one of the small Formica-topped tables instead of taking it home. A waiter showed me to a rear banquette, and I took my seat against a mirrored wall, next to a young man of about Chris's age.

I'm not sure who started the conversation, but while we sat elbow to elbow, sipping tea and waiting for our orders to arrive, we began a friendly, neutral exchange. I think it started with a discussion of a dish the waiter was bringing to a nearby table, then moved on to the neighborhood, and finally into more personal territory — his new apartment, family on Long Island and job as a Wall Street trader.

He was subtle, but there was something about his manner that convinced me he was gay. As we talked, it occurred to me that Chris would like this young man, who, coincidentally, had been born in the same month of the same year. Chris had just ended a relationship and was feeling the usual side effects of the newly single again, and I began to look at this young man as someone my son would find simpatico, who might pull him out of the blues-singer mood that had played all summer.

This young man seemed wholesome, educated and sincere. It goes without saying that mothers of gay sons carry with them the unremitting lead weight of worry about The Plague. If there is a day in which that illness does not in some way flit across my conscious mind, I can't remember it. Like a little something hard to breathe in the air or the noise of gunfire nearby, it is something I have to live with and get used to, something that forebodes and threatens and never quite goes away. One could say it is the looped red ribbon I wear, whether I am wearing it or not.

And so I looked at this young man as the mother of a homosexual son would — wary, critical, but somewhat reassured. A nice boy, well brought up. He seemed like one of us. If that sounds snobbish, one has to remember that what is familiar seems less threatening, and that it is not so much a question of being exclusive as "what is unknown is unknown." There were never any guarantees, but safe and familiar is how he looked.

One does not ask, "Are you gay?" of a stranger in a restaurant. One does not ask, "Are you gay?" of anyone, anywhere, for that matter. It is not like, "Are you by any chance Armenian?" or "Are you a Republican?" and although it seems to me the query should be just as innocuous, it is a powder keg of a question, a setup for a reaction that can range from discomfort to humiliation to the grapes of wrath.

Treading gingerly, as our tandem meal progressed, I mentioned that my son was exactly the same age, and then I added, "He's gay." My dinner companion brightened perceptibly. "So am I," he volunteered. Bingo! I continued, "You remind me of Chris. You seem so similar. I wonder if you'd like each other," and so on, until the young man, apparently also currently unattached, decided he wanted to meet Chris, gave me his card and told me when would be the best time to call.

This little matchmaking story brought a smile to anyone I told it to, and in a way it was a milestone. It marked the end of a transition from my mindset of less than a decade before, when the old me would have been stricken at the very idea that "dating" could be a term used to describe a relationship between two men, especially if one of them was my son.

Less than ten years before, at about the time Chris had graduated from college and hadn't yet started graduate school, we were invited, as usual, to the Dorans' annual midsummer pool party. The Dorans were hospitable, entertained gracefully and in every way exemplified what is solid and praiseworthy about American life: the well-oiled cooperation and indivisibility of the family unit. The Doran children, beginning in childhood and proceeding through adolescence and on into adulthood, were always on hand, ready to behave most graciously and tirelessly as hosts at every gathering.

Getting my three children to attend one of our own parties, keep up smiling chatter throughout, let alone roll bacon strips around water chestnuts, was tantamount to my getting the checkbook balanced — a long shot. So, the Doran children's savoir-faire, small talk and demonstration of collaborative skilled party labor was the embodiment of good upbringing in the polite society I respected and admired. The Dorans' hosting detail always included Russ, whose interests centered very much — at that time I would have said a bit too much — on the traditionally feminine arenas of domestic management: the kitchen, interior and exterior home decor and local gossip. He was fun, impossible to dislike, a gentle boy, and the first thing one noticed about him was his giggle and his fluttering eyelashes.

Walking into the Dorans' house, whether on this occasion or for any other social celebration, being warmly welcomed and somehow made much of, always put us at ease. Here was Chris's best friend, his "second family," and now, in a way, ours.

Behind the yellow clapboard colonial house was the blue crystal swimming pool surrounded by grass and umbrellas, under which guests sat with their drinks while platters of this and that circulated. A few of the younger generation splashed in the pool, presents got opened and applauded, and the sobriety of the hosts and guests became slowly deactivated. The party cheer mellowed us all in varying degrees; at one of these gatherings, perhaps this one, a guest, overcome with pixilated hilarity, leaned back a bit too far and toppled backward, folding chair and all, into the grass. It was all reminiscent of a Jacques Tati movie — fun and broad slapstick. Chitchat flowed like the aqua vitae, and instant intimacy flowered among the guests.

It was in this atmosphere that another guest and I were sitting together, it was dusk, and a few gin and tonics had reduced her restraint. And, since I was laughing too much, probably mine. This guest must have felt a strong fellowship between us, because she leaned toward me as Russ went by and, lowering her voice, said, "He's very faggy, isn't he?"

I stopped laughing. If she had tipped her glass and poured its ice cubes into my lap, I couldn't have sobered up faster.

Russ was Chris's confidant and constant companion. When he was home from school, they talked on the telephone twice a day. If the guest's comment chilled me, it had nothing to do with my fear that this could be more than a friendship; it had to do with how Russ, and consequently Chris, might be perceived. If this friend of the Dorans' (and ours) had picked up something about Russ, it was not outside the realm of possibility that Chris was also the object of some similar speculation. Whatever vibes he'd sent off in elementary school might be being picked up in adulthood far and wide by the neighborhood scanners. In any case, Russ and he were together so much, seen as buddies, birds of a feather, it would surely be a case of guilt by association. I saw the shadow of suspicion about his sexual identity as an extravagant threat to Chris's reputation and his future, imagined — still, in the early eighties — possible ostracism, conceivable difficulty in finding a job, even the potential danger of physical attack. Much greater a blemish on my character than those fears was the ache of my embarrassment, my feeling (at this late date!) that having a homosexual son would reflect badly on our family.

It now seems appalling that this was the me of only ten years ago, but I have no excuses. A friend who lives nearby, whose world was much like mine, has a son Chris's age. The son grew up to be an environmental lawyer and was much more "visible" from a very early age. My friend always had a different attitude. "He's what he is, I wouldn't change him," she recently said. "He and his companion are planning a sort of wedding ceremony, and I'm shopping for a dress."

These kinds of revelations add to my shame. Those should have been my sentiments, that should have been my voice. When

Chris reached maturity, I no longer could blame my attitude on my youth and inexperience. By the time he graduated from college, our family was well respected in the community, we could no longer plead insecurity, so what was I thinking? And what sort of a mother had I been all these years anyway? It's my life's dark mystery. Shakespeare said it better than I could: "A peace above all earthly dignities, A still and quiet conscience."

Perhaps the need for a quiet conscience has some bearing on how far my own pendulum has swung in the other direction, my intemperate wish to make things so right for Chris that I would reach out to a stranger in a Chinese restaurant. As it turned out, Chris called the boy, they met for a drink, went on to dinner, had a pleasant evening — and never saw each other again. It was a blind date made not in heaven but here on earth, where unfortunately relationships work as imperfectly in the gay world as often as they do in mine.

26

- - - - - - - - - -

HETEROSEXUALS HAVE no corner on the agony and ecstasy of romance. The pounding heart, night dreams, anxiety, the intrusion of thoughts of the beloved during every waking minute, the need to hear his voice, speak to him, and see *that* face are not limited to lovers of the opposite sex. Cupid is an equal-opportunity archer, and he hit my heart's bull's-eye with his sharpest arrow. Just when I'd given up the hope of ever getting out of the dim solitary of my personal life, into it came the sun, moon and stars.

I'd inched laboriously along, socially and in my first job, through the years until graduate school, during which another, better me had emerged. I began to recognize myself as a decent human being and as a homosexual. It was no longer a paradox, although I was still afraid of what the world would think if it knew, and so I was still and forever in hiding. My two years at Columbia had turned me into more than a man with an M.B.A.; it had given me a transfusion of self-confidence, a new face in the mirror. I'd been president of the Marketing Club, made many friends, felt well liked and altogether sturdy. This new feeling of worthiness must have been generally visible and grounded in reality, because right after graduation I was offered jobs in some Fortune 500 companies at solid starting salaries. I felt my family was proud of me, especially my father. Although he never told me directly, I heard him bragging about me now and then to others. It was a circuitous way to get a compliment, but just the same, it certainly sank in.

I settled on Lever Brothers, which had the advantage of being in the center of my universe and twenty miles from my hometown. It's where I'd wanted to work always, in a glittering skyscraper on Park Avenue in New York City, and suddenly here

I was, on a high floor in my ultramodern cubicle, the dream ful-filled. I had become a first-rung corporate executive, working on products with multimillion-dollar budgets, learning what went into the formulation of cleaning granules, liquids, cakes, mak-ing advertising decisions and rubbing elbows with some of the world's brightest minds in the world of soap. It was exhilarating, competitive, enlightening. Here was a world with its own dress codes, pecking order and company eating place, efficient, prof-itable, glitzy and ever so slightly deceptive.

I learned that the spirit of Machiavelli lived on in the cos-mos of marketing. Take product "restaging," which often meant an old soap was given a new spin at the least possible cost, and just within the boundaries of honesty and government regulation. How could we say it was new and cleaned better without spend-ing too much money? And what did "better" mean anyway? We highly paid, newly minted M.B.A. junior masterminds were spending eight, nine and ten hours a day on these projects. There were criteria that had to be met to prove the claims the company made in advertising. Sometimes we increased the level of chemi-cals known as F-dyes to the detergent. There was no doubt that the wash came out looking brighter, because F-dyes were fluores-cents that literally deposited dyes on clothes which gave that per-ception, despite the fact that fabrics were fading over time any-way. Now we had the right to label it "NEW" for six months and to say the product cleaned better. As soon as the six months were up, the "NEW" went off the label and the high level of F-dye, which was expensive, went with it.

Another semantic manipulation I learned at Lever was the ap-pellation "Unscented," which did not for a minute mean the soap had no scent added. It described a detergent that was not given a fragrance to make it smell different from its base smell, but was routinely given a masking fragrance to cover its real and pretty awful chemical odor. "Unscented" products often smell as floral and as fragrant as those that are perfumed. To get more confus-ing, "Fragrance free" meant really unscented, but what consumer knew that? The reality was that there was plenty of psychological legerdemain prevailing here. It was also very much in keeping with the rest of my fishy life, but in the workplace, at least, I got happily right into it.

It was challenging work, and all nine of us, hired at the same time and subtly and implicitly in competition with one another, toiled long and hard hours. Lever Brothers was a marketing- and sales-driven company, so we were high in the hierarchy of departments and bunched together at lunch in the company cafeteria. Dressed in our obligatory uniform of gray or navy blue suits, white or blue shirts and silk ties, we were tacitly regarded as up one notch from the finance people. We were the company elite, but while I felt important and productive, there were always the conflicts of my second life and the awareness of the unspoken qualifications for real career advancement. I saw that the fast track often included hobnobbing with the higher-ups in an after-hours personal way. One of the "fair-haired" favorites I strongly suspected of also being gay nevertheless played the game — of golf, of women — every so often bringing a girlfriend around for the boss to see. I found that sort of deceit impossible. In the company cafeteria, and in fact everywhere, even making conversation was a struggle. One colleague might say, "My husband and I are going out to dinner," another might sigh, "I just met this gorgeous woman and I'm taking her to see *Cats*," and someone else might announce, "I just became engaged." I would confine my conversation to talk about the stock market or the latest piece in the *Times* business section. I couldn't even relate to the guys when they talked about last night's basketball game, but although I worried about my career longevity, I did get along well with all of my coworkers, and I am friends with some to this day.

When my parents repossessed their Fifty-fourth Street pied-à-terre, I found myself a small studio on lower Park Avenue. It was on an upper floor in a good building and had just enough room for a pullout couch and the two wing chairs inherited from my grandmother. The previous tenant had built a sleeping loft and storage drawers, so despite its limited floor space, I hung some family portraits on the walls, brought in four of Grandma's dining chairs and a little table, and began to feel comfortable in my more modest new home.

After my disappointing experiences with the personal ads in the *New York Native* and a few false starts in new relationships, I joined a gay dating service. For a fee, they promised introductions for the duration of six months, and they really delivered: over the next weeks I met an Episcopal minister, a medical student, a teacher of music theory and an emergency room doctor with four children, still going through divorce. While none of these "took," I made some new friends, and one of them tipped me off to a brand-new concept in meeting people. It was a telephone dating line, the first of its kind, and it was free.

It worked this way: You called an 800 number, got connected to one person and, after ten minutes, were automatically cut off. Or, if you chose to hit the pound key, you were instantly connected to someone else. It was magic. The first person said, "Hiii. How are ya? What's your name?" A deep, unctuous voice. I made up a name, Bill. "So, what do you look like, Bill?" It went on in that vein long enough for me to think, Forget about this person, he's only interested in the length of your penis. Then I'd press the pound key and go on to the next voice. It was very exciting, didn't cost a dime and I could remain forever anonymous. Obviously, I could tell some people on the line were not giving their real names either. Still, I kept hitting the pound key and I'd say, "I'm Bill, I'm career oriented, I'm five feet eleven and I have brown hair," and suddenly, click, I'd get disconnected. I'd guess the person didn't like brown hair or the sound of my voice, but it worked both ways. I'd do the same thing to someone else because he was talking dirty or was unpleasant or was a homophobe who had gotten wind of the dating line and was croaking, "You faggot, you pervert," in my ear.

The first week I spoke to many people but never gave anyone my number. And then one night Devon got on the line. He was a year younger than I, seemed artless and genuine, and although I didn't have the nerve to give him my number, he gave me his in case we got cut off, which in fact did happen. I called him back immediately, and from eleven that night, we talked until two in the morning. He said all the right things: he was willing and interested in having a serious relationship and still being undercover, all I could imagine for myself at that time. Devon was witty, open, hated gay bars as much as I did, shied away from effeminate men and sounded intelligent. By the time we hung up, I was convinced he was my soul mate, and was already titanically charmed.

We made a date for the next day. It was very daring of me, completely out of character, but I had him come up to my apartment. In our three-hour conversation the night before, I'd decided he was not only absolutely straightforward but also a little scared and naive, so I felt confident I wasn't taking much of a risk. Most people meet under the circumstances of a visual impression first, so it's usually chemistry followed by deciding whether or not you're compatible. This encounter was exactly the opposite: we already knew we had everything in common, so I was in a fever pitch of anticipation and hope by the time the doorbell rang.

To this day, I remember clearly that wash of emotion when I looked through the peephole. I couldn't believe how good-looking the person on the other side of the door was. He had reddish-blond hair, blue eyes, just a few freckles, the sort of face you'd see in front of a stucco house if you were driving through County Cork. My instant reaction as I turned the knob was "He's not going to like me."

Oddly enough, here in full and living color, Devon was not the same fellow I'd talked to the night before. In my little living-dining room, sitting erect in my grandmother's wing chair, he was so nervous that the conversation was stilted and uncomfortable. He stayed only an hour because he had to rush off to someone's birthday party, never made eye contact with me, and I was sure I'd batted zero — until he called me the next day. We started seeing each other.

The reality was that not only was he uncomfortable with gay bars, but he was completely inexperienced — had never kissed another human being outside his family, had never dated women

NOT LIKE OTHER BOYS

or men and still lived at home. His mother had died of a stroke recently and he'd been the mainstay of the family, helping to manage the emotions of four younger siblings. He didn't get along with his father, who had started his career as a firefighter and was now high up in municipal government, and who abided by the atavistic standards of the small Irish American enclave in which the family had lived for two generations.

Devon came from a different world, and had arrived in mine trembling with insecurity. He had gone to Catholic schools from kindergarten through college and didn't know many people who weren't Irish Catholic. Never mind; unlikely a pair as we were, we clicked beautifully and both soon went head over heels.

Freud wrote that what people need to be happy are two things: work and love. Suddenly I had them both, a great job and my Romeo-and-Romeo love story at last! I was ecstatically, blissfully, marvelously happy, bouncing between my days at Lever and my evenings with Devon. He also had a good position, worked as a market analyst for a chemical company, and as he became more secure professionally, his confidence in himself and our relationship also grew. We lived out all the clichéd romantic scenarios: had our song, "Never Gonna Change My Love for You," sung by *our* vocalist, George Benson; had our Special Moments; our particular, significant, meaningful chicken dish (by candlelight); we exchanged gold signet rings, accompanied by the usual emotional hoopla. With my encouragement, Devon moved out of his father's house into an apartment in Brooklyn I helped him furnish. Close as any married couple, we spent seven nights a week together in two apartments, and still it was all hush-hush. Paradise or no, this situation was becoming increasingly uncomfortable. The need to tell my mother was particularly strong; she and I had a close relationship, and to hide such a big and important facet of my life from her was weighing on me heavily. On one occasion she left a message on my answering machine. I didn't return the call until I got the message a day or so later, and had no alternative but to tell some cover-up lie.

It was the first fly in the ointment of my relationship with

Devon, but not the last. Under the best of circumstances, same-sex relationships are fragile. The His and His towels are emblematic of the confusion of roles determined by sex in prior generations: Who carves the turkey? Who gets ahead, who stays behind? Who takes the lead and when? Who sits behind the steering wheel, who takes out the trash? Call it competition, insecurity, jealousy — in Devon there was a tragic seed that grew into a mighty oak. The bliss had an expiration date, but for a long time I couldn't and wouldn't believe it. It was my first authentic, down-to-the-marrow love affair. Perhaps the "NEW" stamped on bottles of Wisk and boxes of All, removed with its brighteners in due course, should have taught me more than marketing strategy, but I was young, innocent and not very alert to irony. I was in love, deeply, madly and blindly. I really did think it would go on forever.

27

WHEN CHRIS BROUGHT Devon to the house to meet me, I thought of him as just another of his new friends. He strongly reminded me of the eponymous Archie of that comic strip — same freckles, reddish hair and ingenuous face, and as manly as any army recruitment poster. Anyway, I was not thinking then about Devon's sexual orientation and had no clue, no suspicion that he was not heterosexual. I found him good-humored, polite and respectful. What I really loved (and love) about all Chris's friends is their steadfast interest in whatever I have to say. No matter how long-winded, trivial or humdrum, they are all ears through my meandering reminiscences and anecdotes, laugh generously when the humor is marginal, and seem completely involved and attentive. Has this to do with their sexual orientation? Is motherhood held in higher esteem by non-heterosexual men? I don't know the reason, but gay men and mothers seem to have as natural an affinity as cheese and crackers, and Devon and I were no exception.

At the time Chris and Devon were emotionally entangled, I was distracted by the slow and horrendously painful unraveling of my marriage. It seemed to leave me out of touch with everything but my own sore heart. It was so incremental, so up and down, the feelings so inconsistent that I can't put a time or date to the beginning of its actual extinction.

All marriages have some bad memories, but the University of Vermont weekend seemed to be a marker, a black arrow that pointed precipitously down. It had not exactly to do only with Chris, but then again, it had much to do with children. There is the current marriage-counselor wisdom that children cannot break up solid marriages. Maybe so, but most marriages are not made of iron. Even the solid ones have fault lines along which lie a whole mishmash of covert blame, suppressed anger, contused ego and years of accumulated emotional bruises, much of the stress due to offspring. As children get older, the unpredictable complications can throw a marriage off balance. It is like a dancing couple who start off in step until the bandleader begins to improvise. The couple go on dancing, but the beat gets lost, the steps go awry. Statistically, couples in first marriages without children don't divorce at the same rate as those with progeny. This morning's television news announced a new statistic: thirty-five percent of marriages in which there are children are seriously troubled. It gives one pause to consider the gamble: a good marriage or a marriage with children?

In 1980, less than three years before Chris's college graduation, Bob and I had traveled together to Eastern Europe. For twelve years he was a member of the Young Presidents Organization, and through that worldwide association of CEOs we visited many of the world's marvelous nooks and crannies. We went to Spain, to Hong Kong, to Acapulco, to name a few favorite destinations, and the YPO did it in rich-and-famous style, every luxe detail planned to give the most sybaritic pleasure and the least stress to the vacationing young presidents and their very, very lucky spouses.

Eastern Europe was slightly different. This was not a cushy junket, but surely one of the most edifying, and somewhat disquieting. My passport showed the country of my birth, Czechoslovakia, so I had some misgivings about traveling back to my old hometown. Would Czech officials recognize my American citizenship? The communists were still in place, there were stories of people being detained, rooms being bugged, and I had little interest in spending two vacation weeks under this potential red cloud.

Bob took care of everything. He made certain that my occupation, "writer," did not appear on my visa to frighten communist officials, made many calls to the travel agent, conferred with a representative from the U.S. State Department. Wanting me to be comfortable and safe, he arranged all of these details quietly, to surprise me and ease my anxiety. Here was more evidence of his concern for my welfare and, typical in good times, of my pure-hearted envoy.

Then off we went, one of twenty-five couples, on a two-week journey into the dreary ambience of the Eastern Bloc. I'd expected distress as we traipsed from Vienna to Budapest to Dubrovnik to Zagreb to Bucharest and finally to Prague. While many of our trips bring me the happiest memories of our inherent closeness, affinity and rapport, not only were these destinations depressed and bleak cities, but while we were in Yugoslavia, Tito died and lights dimmed, music stopped while the whole country mourned, the food was often less than good and some of the bus jaunts were too long — yet there was not a hint of my husband's dark side. This trip was one of the consequential adventures of my married life, an indicator of our *agape;* in the thousand and one ways two people have to agree, we were in accord, and he kept the whole group, especially me, laughing all the way. The daffy, concerned and paternal man with me was, after all, the real thing, the good sport, the decent, solid husband who would forever care for and about me, would be at my side until we turned decrepit and the last light went out. He was then, in my view, mostly an angel, and in those days I was still worried that he would get a stroke or heart attack, go before me, that I would lose him.

At about the time of Chris's college graduation, Alison was going through a hair-raising adolescent rebellion, possibly a cause, more likely an effect, of domestic turmoil. It lit a match to the fuel of whatever tensions already existed, leading to an implosion. Chris was not going the way of a normal heterosexual, at that point Kirby's career was falling short of expectations, and now Alison's teenage behavior became unspeakable; Bob's glowing dreams for his children had surely been singed by reality.

Bob's unresolved conflicts with his own gruff and uncommunicative father, who had died some years before of what I now believe was Alzheimer's disease, probably played into all of this in ways that are, to me, still mysterious. In *The Life of Samuel*

Johnson, Boswell quotes Johnson: "There must always be a struggle between a father and son, while one aims for power and the other at independence." This was certainly the situation in the workplace, but otherwise, while old Joe Shyer was alive, father and son seemed as unconnected as two circles in geometry that intersected only at point A: the family business. Nevertheless, his father's illness and decline seemed to have powerful aftershocks for my husband. This simple man Joe Shyer, whose explosions were chronic, loud, but unhazardous, who was capable of arguments but not conversation, who had little depth but great generosity and enormous family loyalty, wielded more power over his son from the grave than he had when he was alive, alert and in authority. Perhaps, more inarticulate than unfeeling, he had died withholding the words of affection and approval for which his son had waited a lifetime. Sometimes, when Bob spoke of his dead father, his eyes would brim with tears. I never could figure out whether it was with love or with anger.

After his college graduation, Chris moved back home for a brief spell. With Alison now at boarding school and Kirby living in his own apartment, we were suddenly a threesome. Chris was an innocent bystander, the extra pair of ears, the third chair at dinner. I always felt as if Bob thought three was a crowd and saw his son as an intruder. Possibly the warmth and closeness of our mother-son relationship didn't sit well with him either. There were now, consistently, ridiculous dinner skirmishes, most often in restaurants. They usually erupted during the main course — after the vodka with the little onion in it — and dealt with absolutely nothing substantive. Part of me thought my husband's fire, directed at me, was actually subconscious discomfort about his son, too often on hand, without a manly sport or girlfriend in sight. It became a predictable tableau, one dinner after another contaminated with vapid and pointless small wars.

Once, because I disagreed with him about the type of lettuce in the salad at a local restaurant, Bob, deluged with anger, lifted his hand into the air and, with the side of his palm, karate chopped my wrist, which was lying flat at the side of my plate. Poor Chris, caught in the middle, kept refusing to moderate or take sides, and my humiliation at being literally slapped in public was overshadowed by sympathy for my son. This was his home life, and for the moment the only life he had.

This logjam of emotions became a way of life. It wasn't just the dinners with Chris that set us off. He had moved out, but Bob nevertheless started not to feel at home at home, and found relief in only one place: out of town. Although fitfully loving and glued together by life, we seemed to be two people talking different languages, allergic to the very sight of each other. On the other hand, we were still a couple, intermittently the best of best friends. Things between us got temporarily better later, when we were renovating the apartment on West Fifty-fourth Street. We were bonded by the endeavor and our increasing frustration with a bungling architect. Bob saved me the trouble of getting exercised by letting him have it on the telephone, as ever my Hotspur hero. We looked forward to the novelty of part-time city life.

"When the apartment is finished, I'm going to move in alone," he began to say, just when I was sure we were back on the loving track. It was a joke. "Oh, sure," I always replied, speaking as I would to a child who insisted he'd be joining the circus soon. He and I went to pick out the bedroom furniture, and he bounced around on a mattress to see if it was firm enough. "I'm moving in there," he might say to friends at the same time I was choosing our lamps or the marble for the bathroom. Everyone laughed. When he told me, "I need space," I was appalled he'd use this cliché seventies phrase and, de facto, mean it. Could I have stayed married to and loved a man all these years who could look me in the eye, in the midst of what had again become a cataclysmic marital crisis, and actually talk like a comic strip? Of course no one took him seriously, least of all me.

"What day would it be most convenient for me to move out?" my husband, ever the considerate spouse, wanted to know.

* * *

It was the first day of spring, it was 1986, and I was going to my Thursday morning tennis game. A white van arrived as I was leaving. When I got back from my game, the van was gone, and so was my husband. He had taken with him his clothes, his tennis racquets, suitcases and other miscellaneous items, including a large oil painting of a tennis player we had hanging in the living room, his favorite. He had packed up everything with the help of the fellow with the van from his factory, and headed for the space he needed. He did not take with him even one photograph of his children, and this oversight seemed the ultimate blasphemy. Later, I guessed he'd meant to retrieve more things at some future time, intended this as a temporary evacuation. Chris pointed out that Dad had a photo of his children on the desk in his office, and so I took it another way: we love our children equally, but somewhat differently.

"I'll bet you one hundred dollars he'll be back by Labor Day," my closest friend said.

I took the bet, and we shook hands on it. At that time, another friend, who had recently been divorced, told me about being alone. She said, "Since my husband left, and I have no one in the world to account to, I call the cat from work and leave a message telling him what time I'll be home. I tell him what he'll be having for dinner and sometimes what we'll be doing after dinner. Then, when I get home, I play back the message. It's so perverse, and it's so satisfying."

No divorce for us, thank you very much! I imagined it was just a bad phase; all long marriages go through rough spots; we'd go for counseling. I was sure Bob would see the light, change his ways, see the madness of leaving his greatest and most valuable possessions, a caring best-friend wife, a solid family. Surely we'd work it out.

In the meantime, I leaned pretty heavily on all my children, and especially Chris, who was not only emotionally available but was also often on hand physically. That auxiliary seemed to include Devon these days, and he offered particularly enthusiastic support. He helped me move into the pied à terre I rented when my marriage broke up, was thoughtful enough to shop Hallmark for Mother's Day, my birthday and whatever other occasion he thought demanded it. For the relatively short time that he stayed on the scene, I saw Devon as an engaging, beneficent friend. And nothing more.

28

- - - - - - - - - - -

MY EMOTIONS RAN deep about my parents' separation, but I did not feel responsible for my father's leaving. For quite some time, my brother and I blamed our sister, whose adolescent mutinies were causing not only sparks but conflagrations between my parents. I'd seen the tumult at home, but with Alison now doing well at boarding school, peace seemed to have been restored. So I was shocked, surprised and angry that my father gave up — just like that — and moved into the city, leaving my mother alone in the house. I didn't know there was someone else he was going to. He took me aside and said, "Maybe we'll work it out, but things are getting too tough. We need space and I'll be back in a few months."

I believed him; it seemed impossible that he wouldn't return. And later, in fact, he did.

One night my father called to offer me two tickets to the musical *Sunday in the Park with George,* which one of his plastics suppliers had given him as a gift. Dad was going out of town or had already seen the show; in any case, I happily accepted his offer and arranged to meet him to pick up the tickets at my old Fifty-fourth Street apartment, which in the past year had been renovated and was currently my father's sparsely furnished home.

I weighed the risk, and decided to take Devon with me. I very much wanted him to meet my father, although I was nervous about the flip side — my father's meeting Devon. My perception was always that something might shine out of Devon's eyes when he looked at me, that there would be some slip of the lip, or some lavender aura around our heads would give our secret away. This paranoia extended to other situations and was definitely a corrosive factor in our relationship. Devon and I worked within three blocks of each other, and after I got him to move out of his father's house, we spent many weekday nights at his place. Still, I didn't want to be seen with him on the subway, going to work. I felt someone might see. That someone might talk. That someone might blight my job, alert my family, blow my cover and ruin my life. I was still closeted at the time and would have felt uncomfortable being seen having lunch with the same man too often. Devon didn't see it my way. He was exceedingly insecure, and no matter how hard I tried to convince him otherwise, he felt I was ashamed of him. It was one reason I wanted to introduce Devon to my father, to convince him that I wasn't hiding him.

The concealment was weighing on me in another important way. I was not only deceiving my father, my colleagues, the world, I was still hoodwinking my mother. I felt the time was coming when I would simply have to do it. It might be easier now that she was alone; I would have to tell her.

My tension when I rang Dad's doorbell was running high. Introducing a lover to a parent is inevitably major stress, and playing some kind of just-pals role did not make it any easier. I needn't have worried. My father was distracted by the logistics of getting to the airport the next day and gave Devon a detached and not unpleasant how-are-you-nice-to-meet-you sort of greeting. We stayed long enough to exchange information about the show, look at a new lighting fixture, discuss the weather, and we were out. During that meeting I felt like I was an understudy in a very long play, going on for the first time and trying hard not to forget my new lines.

Devon and I were at the height of our romantic relationship. I went to sleep dewy-eyed and woke up exhilarated, living in a fog of contentment for the first time in my life. Yet destructive weeds were already pushing their heads into our hermetic little Eden. Devon's insecurity was constantly growing new shoots. He was testing and testing me, calling me morning, noon and night. He had never had a relationship before ours, and hated that I was a bit more experienced than he. Jealous of my prior romances, he often threw my (very limited) past up to me. "Why couldn't you wait for me!" he'd rail repeatedly. If we weren't spending the night together, he might call and accuse me of one thing or another; I'd have to run over and talk to him at all hours of the night. He tested me for months, threatening to break up over some slight. Sometimes when he was angry about something and needed to talk to me, he would call my office. I worked in a not-so-private cubicle, and the call would go through a secretary. I had no direct line, and each time she would say, "It's Devon Payne on the line," I would feel panicky. I'd get on and say under my breath, "I can't talk now, I'll call you later," but Devon would insist, "No! I have to talk to you *now!*" I'd hang up and he'd call right back. I couldn't raise my voice, and by the way I whispered into the receiver, it was surely becoming more and more obvious to my co-workers that this heated conversation must be a lovers' quarrel. The telephone secretary knew it was a male voice, and I was certain that it was only a matter of time before the gay skeleton in my closet would come dancing out all over Lever Brothers.

I was working on some big projects at the office and putting in what we called "face time," staying late and coming in early, not only to work but to create the impression that I really cared about the project and my company. The competition was intense, and maintaining that image was imperative if one expected to move up in the corporate hierarchy.

Devon would frequently ask, "Whom do you have more allegiance to, your office or me?" If I'd waited my whole life for an all-consuming love, I hadn't figured on how all-consuming it could be. When I got him to move out of his father's house, out of his comfortable Irish neighborhood, out of his old life, he became even more dependent on me. Once we began to be together seven nights a week, disparities in our style of living became increasingly apparent. Devon was extremely methodical about his record and videotape collections and loved to fiddle around by himself. Having me with him all the time kept him away from these solitary activities, which translated into misplaced anger toward me and a wish for a little privacy and distance. At the same time, he didn't want to let me out of his sight.

If he was going to be cleaning his apartment or going through his files, he wanted me safely sealed in my own place, preferably doing the same thing, and definitely alone. When we joined up later in the day, he wanted to know exactly what I'd done and to whom I'd spoken on the telephone. He didn't like my friends, didn't want to be with them, but didn't want me to go without him to see them either.

It was a Saturday and he wanted to spend the day alone in his apartment doing a major cleanup. Later that afternoon, I got restless and went out, but didn't tell Devon where I was going or with whom. I kept it to myself because I knew what had happened on just such occasions in the past. He might sound agreeable about my plans on the telephone, but then, feeling pathologically nervous and jealous, would rush to be wherever I was.

On this one occasion, I naively figured if he didn't know where I'd gone, he'd get everything done in his apartment and might even begin to shake off the tenacious green-eyed monster.

By the time he called, I had already gone out to meet a mutual friend, Janie. Her sister and sister's boyfriend were in town, and the four of us were in Janie's apartment when Devon started calling. I should have instantly taken the phone and told him to join us. Instead, I told Janie privately, "Please don't tell Devon I'm here. He'll just get upset and come flying down, and we do need this time apart. Let's just go out to dinner and have a pleasant evening." It sounds deceitful, but it was really pragmatic; he didn't want to see Janie or her sister, didn't want to spend time socializing, but he had to know where I was. It was also true that although I loved him deeply, I was beginning to feel too encapsulated, and needed more elbow room in the relationship.

Janie told Devon that she was going out to dinner at a Chinese restaurant on Second Avenue, knowing it would not be Second but Third, so that he could not track us down. This was another mistake, because throughout that dinner I thought of nothing but Devon, worried that I'd taken part in misleading him, agonized about what I would tell him the next day and generally regretted not having invited him along.

Then, about halfway through our dinner, Devon's face appeared at the restaurant window. It was a storefront place with a glass-enclosed sidewalk dining room, very common in New York City. He must have scoured blocks and blocks of Chinese places before finally hitting pay dirt: we were sitting smack in the window and impossible to miss.

Devon was wearing the striped button-down shirt I'd given him for Christmas, looking ready for work, not for battle, but his freckled face had gone pink and his eyes were ferocious. The scene proceeded like a silent movie without a piano player. There was no dialogue. Devon stalked into the restaurant. I was aware of everyone at the table freezing, chopsticks in air, as he came barreling through the place toward us. I imagined a thousand eyes on us as he zeroed in on our table, stood staring at me like a madman, then lifted his arm, made a fist and, unbelievably, let it fly into my face. The punch hit my cheek and landed at the side of my mouth, slightly chipping a lower front tooth.

Despite the blow to my head, the pain in my face and mouth, and the public embarrassment, what is telling about this entire episode is that my first thought was, Now they know. Until this moment, Janie's sister and her boyfriend had seen Devon and me as buddies. Now, clearly, they saw the relationship for what it was, and what we were. Although I was becoming more at home with myself as a gay man, not so much worried about what people would think of me, I was obsessed about a leak. Who else would know, who would they tell, where would it all end? I wanted to be in control of who got the word and who didn't. That revealed secret was, for me, the really grave side effect of the punch in the face.

There was more to come that night. I went home, unsure of what to do about our relationship. The rational part of me wanted to end it instantly, but the emotional part still clung to some hope of reformation. My heart kept making excuses for him. As I opened the door and let myself into my apartment, Devon, who had been hiding in my loft, waiting in the dark, jumped me. He came flying out from his ambush to attack, and without a word he began pummeling me.

I suddenly had what felt like twenty motorized fists pounding my head and chest. Violence is to me what a rooftop is to an acrophobic, and I was scared out of my mind. I didn't know if I was going to be murdered or just wake up in pieces at the hospital. I had no choice; I started punching back. Acting out some kind of third-rate saloon brawl on the rug in my apartment, we landed on the floor, knocking over one of my grandmother's wing chairs, rolling over the coffee table and breaking the bulb in a floor lamp. My strength came out of my anger, and I punched Devon hard in the face and got some results. For two weeks after that he had a black eye, the first and last one I ever gave anyone. I suppose it could be said that I won, and when the fight ended, I screamed at the top of my lungs, "It's over! Get out!"

It wasn't that easy. As Devon's temper slowly waned, he became remorseful and began yelling, "Please, no, no!" I was still frightened and absolutely resolute. I didn't know what else he was capable of, so when he got near enough to the front door for me to push him out, my relief felt like a death row reprieve.

Under these circumstances, it seems hard to believe that we could reconcile. But I was still in love, and love follows its own decrees that have nothing to do with wisdom or logic. Misunderstandings, lies, fistfights, maybe even murder don't seem to drab the colors of those emotional firecrackers, and the object of my affections remained stubbornly embedded in my heart and thoughts. Still, I wouldn't take his calls for weeks, and while this was a release and a relief at work, the first anniversary of our relationship was looming. After much going back and forth, I decided to take Devon back in time to celebrate the momentous event of our year together.

As a surprise, he arranged a helicopter ride and an elegant dinner on our day. He told me to be home from work early, but all the cliffhanging behind-the-scenes circumstances of our breakup had taken their toll at my job, and I had to work long hours to catch up, which is why I was late coming home on that evening.

I missed the last scheduled helicopter, but we did have a grand dinner at a French restaurant in Greenwich Village. Devon behaved himself, took his disappointment in stride, and we spent much of that evening planning our future. Although the fight had sobered me and I was already having serious second thoughts, I didn't want to end it and started talking about therapy, to maybe help him and us. We were planning to buy a Tudor City apartment together, and I put down a deposit of thirty-five dollars to borrow the co-op plan, the first step in that direction.

My procrastination in returning the document was based on my vacillation about going ahead with the purchase. There it sat on the table day after day, week after week, a reminder to Devon that I was hedging, and obviously not ready to buy an apartment with him.

The air got heavy between us, and every small thing became a feverish issue. Finally the crisis came: it had to do with a new gray suit of mine Devon had borrowed to wear to a wedding. He'd spilled red wine on its lapel and then, perversely, it was *he* who became angry. Increasingly defensive and furious, he began screaming, not about the suit but about the apartment we were going to buy — about everything. It escalated to such a pitch that I ordered him to pack up his things and move out. This time my motive was self-preservation, the dank fear that the fight could turn really violent.

I was through. As soon as I could, I had the locks changed, and a few days later I came home from work to find my apartment sealed shut and impenetrable. Devon had gone to the nearest hardware store, bought Krazy Glue and squeezed it into my locks. It cost me hundreds of dollars to have them drilled through so I could get into my apartment, and I will be forever grateful to the locksmith for doing the job without asking me any questions.

During the following year, Devon sent me fifty letters and a videotape begging me to take him back. Getting him out of my system was incredibly hard, because despite his violence and malice, I was still emotionally tangled, too. It was easier to get over him by not having any contact at all, but I still kept hearing this and that about him from our mutual friends, who carried stories back and forth and kept some small embers still burning. At the end of a year, I called Janie and told her to tell Devon that it was absolutely over for me and that I would prefer not to hear any more about him from her. To my surprise, he called and thanked me for putting a definitive end to it, breaking the bond between us once and for all.

He was my first love, and for too long I was somehow branded by that relationship. I thought I would never again feel the way I'd felt about Devon, that no love could run as deep.

I suppose the fire had never really been put out, because less than two years ago, and nine months out of a relationship, I found myself inquiring about him, hesitating, putting it off, and at last dialing his number. I told myself that now that he'd turned thirty, he'd certainly have matured. By this time he'd have dated others and gotten experience. Now we could pick up again as adults, now it could work, and just perhaps, it might be destiny after all.

He sounded glad to hear from me. We met, and it all came back in a rush, that nameless, mysterious plasma that travels between the head and the heart. I still loved him, and I convinced myself it was going to be a solid Us from then on. For two or three weeks we played out the recycled romance, and then the telephone call came. "I don't think it's going to work," Devon said, giving me many immaterial reasons. This time he got to do the breaking up, and I bled more than a little. But then a bit more time passed, and a profound thank-you is what I thought I owed him. I'd finally sorted out the memories, saw the person instead of the illusion, and was once and for all free of the recollection as well as the man.

2 9

- - - - - - - - - -

IN THE OLD black-and-white movies Chris has always loved watching, Bette Davis, Loretta Young, Rosalind Russell or some lesser legend announces, "I want a divorce!" She has heard her husband sweet-talk someone else in his sleep, found him with lipstick on his collar or someone else's glove in his glove compartment, and off she goes to her lawyer's, usually in a glamorous hat and with a gold cigarette case she snaps open and shut. There is a fiery-anger scene, a quick crying spell and either a reconciliation or a trip to Reno. Then it's a done deal.

I never did see an old movie, with or without a divorce, that didn't have a happy ending.

In full-color, contemporary real life, there are marriage counselors, bad dreams or insomnia, drugstore prescriptions, support groups, the empty side of the bed, the dog's waiting at the window, friends asking questions, children — even grown ones — traumatized, grandparents frantic and disbelieving. There are forensic accountants, lawyers brimming with testosterone, and for years and to this day, casual acquaintances one meets in the library or on the tennis court, offhandedly asking, "How's Bob?" Telephone calls for him continue, the mail with his name on it has to be forwarded, then slowly begins to dwindle, and friends start to whisper in your ear, "You know, I never did like him." Others have sighted him. Once, at the ballet. At the *what?* It all boils down to science fiction: the old guy turns into a totally different person, but looks and sounds the same as the old guy.

Our old/new Bob did come back, but not right away.

In the meantime, ideas for the magazine stories that had always rolled out of my head, as easily as marbles out of a sack, seemed stuck up there. The blank screen of my computer more often than not stayed dark and user-unfriendly. All three children called, if not every day, every other. Chris was seeing Devon at the time, but wrapped up in my own series of tragic tableaux, I didn't know what Devon meant to him. When two young women friends are always together, one doesn't think much of it, but two young men? How could I have missed it? They were inseparable.

The fresher air of the eighties had blown away some of my old views of homosexuality. Most enlightened people began to understand that, as someone once put it, "there are as many different types of homosexuals as there are Presbyterians." Football heroes, politicians, highly respected surgeons began emerging from their closets. That handsome lisp-free hunk of hunks, Rock Hudson, now dying of AIDS, had always epitomized male sex appeal. Stereotypes wobbled on shaky ground. William Hurt played a homosexual in the movie *Kiss of the Spider Woman,* a part most actors would have declined even a decade before.

One fine Saturday in June, I found myself, by total coincidence, on Fifth Avenue, witness to one of the annual Gay Pride parades held in New York. I was mesmerized. It went on and on, this triumphant cast of thousands. And for every gay man and lesbian marching, dancing, skating and riding by, there were a thousand more at home, at the supermarket, in the park, in Cincinnati! Was half the world homosexual? And the audacity! It was part freak show and the other part — my life. On a flatbed truck, rolling merrily and unflinchingly along, were a bunch of middle-aged heterosexuals, men and women, looking suburban and mainstream, like a part of some double-digit college-reunion celebration, gray-haired, bespectacled, waving at the onlookers, so very neighborly and unaccountably, undeniably cheerful. The banner hanging impudently off the sides of the truck read, "Parents of Gays and Lesbians." I registered Richter-scale amazement; how could they? But something in me stirred. My suspicions about Chris, which had waxed and waned over the years, slid firmly into place. At moments like this, I was dead sure I'd been right on the money from the first, right from kindergarten.

* * *

Once, long before, on the Metro-North station platform in Larchmont, I'd seen a man on the opposite side of the tracks. He was wearing a sheer flowered skirt under a leather bomber jacket and a hat with a ribbon tied under the chin. "Do you see what I see?" a neighbor standing next to me on the platform asked. Until then, I hadn't spotted this poor, sick soul parading on the empty platform across the way. Now, in full view of the people waiting for a late morning commuter train not thirty feet away, the man lay down, lifted his skirt and began masturbating. We were more amused than shocked. "No wonder they call them queer," my neighbor quipped. "His hat doesn't match his skirt."

Yes, we had a good laugh. For all I know, the railway masturbator was a heterosexual, but it was part of the ingrained image of the gay man — capable of outrageous alfresco behavior, a public nuisance. Or a school custodian taking students to the boiler room, maybe someone's funny old uncle you had to watch around little boys. What had I — and everyone else — been thinking of? I'd seen the gay life as Greenwich Village bars, lisping men and shady twosomes in the back seats of porno theaters, and my images were as typical of my day as Jell-O molds and carbon paper. We were greenhorns and dupes, most of us, and scared to death it could happen to one of our own, God forbid, one of our flesh-and-blood children.

It was Thanksgiving, and I had prepared the conventional overabundant turkey dinner, had roasted, baked and cooked my brains out, had served it as always by candlelight in our wallpapered, wainscoted, chandeliered dining room, but this year was different. It was 1987, the culture and I had come a very long way, and there were other, radical differences. My portrait, in its heavy frame and with its little picture light above it, still hung in its place on the dark red wall, but Bob's had been removed and another picture hung in its place. For the first time in thirty years, he was not in his chair at the head of the table. His seat was occupied by his older son.

Looking in through the leaded glass windows from the street, one would have seen what looked like a glowing dining room, filled with a prototypical, happy American family celebrating that most Norman Rockwell of holidays. One would have noted the silver-haired grandfather, the robust young-adult children, a few assorted friends, the darling Westie begging at the foot of the table, a picture worthy of the cover of an old *Saturday Evening Post*. Not visible were the ghosts, of my husband's parents, of my mother and of the ghost of my dream — "love within a family, love that's lived in" — my family all under one roof, healthy, happy and unified.

With the guests gone, the children off with their friends, the dishes put away, the kitchen and house seemed preternaturally empty and silent. The dog was fast asleep, tired from having stuffed herself with table tidbits (her holiday tradition) and subsequently thrown up (also her tradition). I was wiping the butcher-block table in the dinette when Chris, the last remaining guest, walked in. He stood there looking strangely uncomfortable. Obviously, he had something on his mind.

For a moment he stood watching me, and then, clearly agitated and edgy, went to the refrigerator, filled two glasses with ice, poured us each a glass of water. He pulled up a chair and sat down. The ceiling fixture over the table cast light in a sort of puddle, shadowing the rest of the room. My son sat in this home-made spotlight, the dark all around, fidgeting. Then he looked intently at me. Something was up; the air was thick with it. I got very nervous and stopped wiping the table, and I thought, Whatever it is, I don't want to hear it.

"Mom, I don't know how to tell you this," Chris began.

30

- - - - - - - - - -

"MOM, I DON'T know how to tell you this."

It certainly wasn't spontaneous. A first parachute jump is how it felt: that yawning door, the empty hazard of space into which I had to leap, all alone. I hovered, waited, moved psychologically forward and back, hesitated once more, all of that, standing frozen in place in the kitchen. There seemed no putting it off any longer. As if a bell had sounded, a starting gun had been fired, I felt the push and hurtled forward.

"I have something to tell you."

My mother was moving around the table, looking tense, looking — angry. That's when I asked her to sit down. She didn't want to, just stood there, her face cemented in this not-now expression I couldn't quite read. I came close to panicking, backing out.

I'd prepared myself for this moment. Possibly all my life. Most recently, I'd tried to read what I could about how one was to break The News to parents. The current wisdom had it that one had to be comfortable about oneself before springing it on the nearest and dearest. In other words, one should not say, "Please accept me." The idea was to be firm. "There is nothing wrong with me, but this is how I am" was the way to go. It has to do with the two stages of coming to terms with one's homosexuality. The first is to totally acknowledge oneself as gay, the second is to feel free to tell the world. I was inching toward self-acceptance, wasn't quite there yet, was over the hills and far away from telling the world, but felt the pressure to reveal myself to my mother because of Devon. The secrets I was keeping from my mother were also becoming like weights sewn into my time with him. The overload was becoming intolerable.

I'd listened with every cell whenever I was with my parents and the subject of homosexuality came up, tried to determine how they felt about it, how they might react. Once, I'd heard them discussing a man from our country club. It was rumored that his older son, an aspiring actor, was gay. "It serves him right," my mother said, referring to the boy's father. What exactly did that mean? Was having a gay son a punishment? Or was it a retribution for this man, who had the reputation of being a self-important bigot? I never did get a firm read on this. The one and only gay and mature visible member at our club was the object of *everyone's* derision. Unfortunately he was an alcoholic, a sad sack of a fellow who was either hunched over a glass at the bar or on the beach baking on a towel, oiled head to toe, in both senses of the word. That man seemed always in the corner of my eye when I was there, and his being gay embarrassed and upset me. It was as if his homosexuality was factored heavily into everyone's opinion of him. Not "a loser and, incidentally, gay," but simply, the club queer.

I'd had many conferences with Julia, then came out to other friends, perhaps as a dry run. Mostly I got a "So what else is new?" reaction, and invariably, "It doesn't make a bit of difference." One good college friend became inexplicably distraught. It wasn't until much later that I realized that somewhere, locked in the back room of her imagination, she'd held out the fantasy hope that someday, over some rainbow, she and I would wind up a happy couple on a honeymoon. Generally, though, my homosexuality was not headline news, and that was heartening, but friends were not parents, not my family. I had an old school chum, who was close to the Dorans, try to sound *them* out to see if my mother had ever said anything that might give a clue as to whether or not she'd guessed my secret, but these baby espionage steps got me nowhere.

So, on that Thanksgiving Day, frightened to death, I approached my mother, hoping my parachute would open. It was easier somehow now that my father wasn't there; I was ten times closer to my mother than to him, and at that time my brother and I were also very angry with him for leaving. Still, although she was more accessible, it terrified me to think I might destroy the warm relationship I had with her.

My concealment was not only a heavy burden then, but — what I couldn't predict at the time — a barrier to what has become a much deeper kinship, the no-secrets-no-lies friendship we have now.

With what I saw as some reluctance, she finally did sit down. I'd put a glass of water beside each of us, like a prop, or maybe preparation for a swoon or some other physical emergency, and as we looked at each other over these untouched glasses of water, I got it out at last. "I'm gay," I said. It is impossible to record the feelings I had as these words, bottled up in me for as long as I could remember, came out of my mouth.

I would describe her face as going through a metamorphosis so subtle that I might have said, "I could be allergic to shellfish" or "My feet hurt." On the other hand, a good Hollywood director might have done a close-up of just such an expression to reveal controlled inner upheaval. I saw something soften, there was sort of a give, the muscles around her mouth seemed to relax, the anger — she says now it was worry, not anger — dissipated.

I could see it wasn't easy, sensed all the energy going into keeping herself steady, but she didn't spin out of control or, what I was really afraid of, cry. "I've suspected since you were five — even earlier," she said. That momentarily floored me. A lifetime of subterfuge and she'd guessed it all along? And all these years, not a word from her? Did that mean I was obvious? Did that mean she thought it was so awful she couldn't mention it? And if she knew, did my father know? What did he think? My mind seemed like a hopper out of which unspoken questions were tumbling: Had she told my grandparents, friends, neighbors? Who knew, who didn't?

She asked my question. "Who else knows?"

I named my friends. She'd discussed it with no one except her own mother, who had died with the secret. And my father, who she told me didn't want to believe any such thing.

Now she said that I wasn't to worry or be upset. Times were improving, attitudes — hers too — were radically changing, and though circumstances might be hard for me sometimes, they could also be tough for everybody, and I could count on no better or worse a dealt hand than my brother or sister, born straight. All the while she spoke, I knew she meant her words as she said them, but wondered if her attitude toward me would change anyway. I'd seen it happen again and again. Even as she accepted my homosexuality in theory, could she handle seeing me with Devon? Would it upset her to imagine me as sexual with another man? Would she always worry now about AIDS? I felt uncomfortable discussing sex in enough detail to alleviate her fears. And I had the wild and passing thought that she might worry about my sharing drinks with other men, using the same glass or towel. People responded in unexpected, god-awful ways, treating us all like latter-day lepers. Of course, she wouldn't, would she? Then again, who could tell, even about one's own mother?

How would she now respond when people asked her if I was dating? And could I stop her from telling other people?

It was a long, charged conversation, and my mother did come through. "Listen, Chris. It's all right," she said. As parents' reactions to spilled guts go, this was a parachute that had opened relatively smoothly, and although we are not a gushy, hugs-and-kisses family, with two sets of elbows steady on the butcher-block table, the cushions of affection and support stacked up in our kitchen that Thanksgiving night as palpably as goose down. A soft landing: I left my mother's house very much intact, stuffed with turkey and dressing, overwhelmed with relief and gratitude.

31

- - - - - - - - - -

WHEN CHRIS SPOKE the words "I'm gay," it was something like touching the burner on an unlit stove that turns out to be red hot anyway. Although I'd suspected, with varying degrees of certainty, that Chris would turn out to be what I'd felt was a probability almost all his life, I still wasn't prepared. The spoken confession on that Thanksgiving Day came with its unforeseen fiery sting. The lightning burn of a NOT MY SON! zigzagged viscerally through me, as did the knee-jerk hope that there might be some reprieve, a way out. This, after a twenty-year preparation for this moment? I suspect I had mastered the possibility that my son might be a homosexual, but here was the reality in situ; it was not conjecture, not a maybe, but fact. My shocked system teeter-tottered, struggling to come to terms with the fixed and final actuality.

The scene took place in the eating area of our kitchen, where we sat facing each other over two glasses of water on a butcher-block table. One would think surroundings would go unnoticed in times of enormous emotional upheaval, but for some reason they remain as firmly entombed in memory as the language used to impart the news. We were sitting in the pool of light cast by the modern chandelier that hung over the table, the rest of the room dim except for the light over the sink. The kitchen had just been cleaned, the silver put back in its drawer, the platters, gravy boat, trays and bowls in their places in the cupboards, all the turkey detritus distributed or wrapped in foil in the refrigerator. It was as if everything had been slicked down and purged of all distractions to prepare us. There was nothing to look at except my son's face. "I'm gay" sank in, deep and deeper.

I would have rather had the chandelier above us fall on my head than let him know that for a flit of a moment I recoiled. It took a minute to run my wits under the cold and soothing water of logic until his words cooled off in my head. Then, in an unexpected twist, a new brand of relief kicked in. I had no more reason to try to fix "it," change him, lie awake nights wondering, or give his sexual orientation another second's thought. It was no longer my business — not that it had ever been. It was over. My son was gay and so be it. A psychological cage door opened, the fait accompli freed me on the spot, and lo and behold, I felt liberated.

"Look, Chris, I've guessed this since you were five. Or maybe even four."

He leaned toward me, looking intense. "*Four?*"

"It's nothing new. I actually discussed the possibility with your kindergarten teacher." Another absurd side effect was my delight with my own perspicacity. Wasn't I clever to have guessed so early? I was an excellent mother-detective, wasn't I? The I-told-you-so compensation temporarily obscured the shame. I'd spent the last twenty-five years as a cloak-and-dagger homophobe.

But in the final crunch, I'd behaved decently. And why not? He was the same boy, a son anyone would be proud of. He was obedient, reliable, compassionate. He loved his family, was ambitious, hard-working, thoughtful and veracious, as everyone who knows him well would confirm, despite what might read like a mother's hyperbole. In any case, darling or dud, star or flop, he was my son.

With the cat out of the bag, we talked. I suppose I rattled on. I'm not sure how firmly I believed what I heard myself saying, although I believe it now. His sexual orientation didn't matter to me and wouldn't matter to anyone who knew him. His life need not be second string. "There is no reason you can't lead as fulfilled and happy a life as your brother and sister." The unspoken postscript was "If you're careful and stay in good health, and if you don't let the world of bigots intimidate you."

I thought he would be more pleased than he was that I hadn't fainted or torn hair out of my head. Other parents might have needed resuscitation after such news. Instead, he seemed more abstracted than relieved. "All that time and you never said a word." He was not upbraiding me; it was more a statement than a question, but I took it as mothers take things grown children casually throw out — not casually.

"But Chris, what could I have said if I wasn't sure?"

What indeed? I have given this so much thought; it is a question I've been asking myself for years. At that time, I couldn't have gotten myself to ask point blank, "Are you that way?" but somewhere along the road I could have said, "Mr. Jones and Mr. Smith are among the nicest couples we know." I could have pointed to other boys, obviously gay, and commented, "Joe marched in the Gay Pride parade. I'm sure his parents were proud of him." I could have hinted that I knew a boy just his age who should have made his sexual orientation known to his parents, who had already guessed anyway. I should have shown disgust with anyone who made a derogatory remark about this (or any other) minority. In other words, I should have made the path to disclosure as smooth and free of the ruts of fear as possible. It would have been a subtle way of taking his hand, letting him know that he was absolutely fine as is, and guiding him to self-acceptance and revelation as painlessly as a parent could.

I can't altogether blame society, with its changing values, for my holding out for so long. No heterosexual couple prefers to have a gay child. But my view has changed — I think it's called a shift in the paradigm — and it pains me now to hear questions put to a new high-tech generation: "If you were pregnant and there was a test that could determine sexual orientation, would you have an abortion if you were told your child was going to be born homosexual?" For me, in the sixties and seventies, it might have been a temptation. Today? It distresses me to think that anyone is left on this enlightened planet who would choose to end a pregnancy on that basis. Although it is inaccurate to claim that as a group homosexual men are better company, have more charm and are somehow *nicer*, from my perspective there is a touch of truth here. Since they have been chronically persecuted, the targets of pink triangles and police clubs, the vitriol of the religious right and discriminatory legislation, the perennial victims of street crime, vandalism and general malevolence, I see gay men as vitally bruised, consequently often more humane and sensitive than the mainstream rest of us.

All those years when Chris was growing up and he wanted to join me in the kitchen, I barred the door, refused to show him how to cook or bake for fear of reinforcing traits we thought feminine. I didn't take him to art museums or teach him to sew on buttons either. I think of my young self clipping and stunting him like a bonsai plant in a shallow pot, and if I had his life to live over, he would have more height and breadth. He would not have had so many chapters filled with heartache I can hardly bear to read. I suppose like many people of my generation, I deserve to have my brain washed out with soap, but it's a long evolutionary process and I'm still learning.

As a result of that Thanksgiving Day conversation, I tried to understand what is not easily understood: the dark mysteries of sexual attraction. His feelings toward men are as baffling to me today as they were on that evening, and so are all the logical and not so logical yearnings implicit in erotic desire. I left the main turnpike of my thinking for the perplexing hinterlands. Why men and men? And why, for some men, only women who are red-headed, overweight, tattooed? *Chacun à son goût,* but why do we select a him or her, or do we really, any more than we choose to be depressed or jealous or hungry?

After his disclosure, Chris and I became closer than ever, but there was a stumbling block. My son wanted my complicity in his secret. This put me in the awkward position of having to keep a confidence I didn't want to keep. And this secret had extra weight: it obligated me to lie when people asked, "Is Chris dating? Who is he seeing?" I'd always been able to say, "No one at the moment," but now I knew there was Devon. It also kept me from sharing a most seminal facet of my life with my closest friends. I am by nature open and had established a warm relationship with a few men and women who shared their lives, no holds barred, with me. It pained me to hide what I now wanted to lay right on the line.

Worst of all, for those who might guess Chris's sexual orientation now or in the future, it implied that I was embarrassed by him and hiding the truth on that basis. The hard fact was, I was not a bit ashamed of him. It was me I was ashamed of.

It fell to me to tell my daughter. Chris and I decided his sister would take comfort from my reaction. I would be setting an attitudinal example: although hit by this bolt out of the blue, I was remaining composed, unfazed and philosophical. I hoped my daughter would take her cue from me.

It was three weeks later. Alison was home from college for Christmas vacation. Although she is an outgoing and very sociable girl, her wellspring is her family, and at that age, her older brothers were her deities. It was late in the evening, the same setting, the same butcher-block table. The beverage on this occasion was coffee in striped mugs, and the perpetually unfinished *New York Times* crossword was lying between us, Alison's pencil poised in her hand above it.

"Alison, I have something to tell you," I said.

She was busy filling in the Across or the Down and was distracted enough not even to look at me. "What is it?"

"It's Chris. Your brother. Alison, he's gay."

It got her attention. Her head shot up. "No," she said. She put down her pencil and looked at me, and her face crumpled the way it had when she was three and had fallen off her tricycle. "No!"

"I know it's tough to hear, but it's okay with me. He's still Chris, the same boy in every way. It's just a declarative sentence that takes some getting used to."

"Oh, my God." Alison looked devastated. As in the old tricycle days, I felt I should pick her up, walk her around the room to soothe her. "Oh, Chris." Her voice was cracking, her lower lip trembling. "It's not okay! It's not okay!" Her shoulders sagged and she looked as if at any moment she might throw herself across the table, her head in her arms, and sob her heart out. It took another few minutes before I was able to talk her through what I saw as an extraordinary and unexpected responsive outburst.

"This is so sad," she kept saying. "Terribly sad. Now it makes sense. No wonder he never had a girlfriend. No wonder he got mad at me whenever I asked him why."

I misconstrued her visceral reaction. I thought she was distraught to the point of tears because her brother had come crashing down a galactic distance in her estimation, or possibly because she was still in her sensitive teens and didn't want to be identified as the sister of a gay brother. But her acceptance of her brother's sexual orientation was immediate and unconditional. She was upset, she later explained, for Chris, for what she knew instantly and instinctively he must have gone through all the hidden years of his life. Her compassion tore her apart, and when she thinks about what it must have been for him, it still does.

32

- - - - - - - - - - -

HAVING BEEN courageous enough to bare my soul to my mother, and then to my sister, it would seem logical that I'd call my father and brother and finish the job. Clearly, my father was the more daunting. I'd grown up being afraid of him, but now I was a full-grown, mature, already balding adult, so what was I waiting for? Maybe it was my excuse to myself, the procrastinator's stock in trade, to promise I would come out all the way as soon as my job at Lever Brothers began looking less like unrequited slavery and more like a sturdy career, as soon as things with Devon got better, as soon as I got on higher, and therefore safer, emotional ground.

My parents' separation was dismal, a hard concept for all of us, and that New Year's Eve I gave a party at our house for all my old friends — and Devon's — on the assumption that the family home would shortly be sold, that it would be my last chance to entertain the old crowd here. It would be sort of a poignant, celebratory swan song. As it happened, Devon and I had one of our final, awful and, in hindsight, awfully John Cleese-y skirmishes that night. Although on the surface it had to do with who was bringing the carrots, it was really about his friends versus mine, and on yet a deeper level, a reprise of Devon's jealousy. His fixation was that my friends, and therefore I, were in some way of a higher caste than his.

The fight was resolved, as usual, and — shades of my father! — Devon became apologetic, loving-sweet as the evening wore on, but the handwriting was on the wall, and reading it day in and day out began to affect my work at Lever Brothers. Simultaneously, things were becoming political there, with (I thought) too much emphasis on memo writing and not enough on productive idea-generating. I was in a general malaise and, after our breakup, decided I'd had enough of my cramped and difficult city life and needed to lick my wounds in my hometown. With money I'd saved from my Lever salary I bought a co-op apartment in the heart of Larchmont. It was small, but still two or three times the size of my city studio. There would be the comfort of my old haunts and friends, especially the Dorans, with their forever open-door policy, their warm aloha kisses, the we-love-you status quo. With the crumbling of my own family, it was my cozy haven, a domestic scene warmly peopled by Russ and his sisters and the comings and goings of their new boyfriends and husbands, a fire in the fireplace, and always the conviviality of ice cubes clinking in glasses.

But suddenly I stopped being invited. It was incomprehensible; my home away from home seemed to have closed shop as far as I was concerned, or was it that the Dorans were too busy for party-ing these days? Russ, now working full time for his father, made a too brief appearance at my little housewarming and never seemed available when I called.

In June, my mother got her annual invitation to their summer pool party. The invitation, which had always been addressed to my parents "and family," was now addressed solely to my mother. We mulled this over. Was it an oversight? What was cor-rect protocol here? We gave them the benefit of the doubt and stepped over a social boundary: my mother called Mrs. Doran. "Isn't Chris invited?" she asked.

"Well, of course he is!" Mrs. Doran answered without hesita-tion. If we'd put her on the spot, she managed to jump off it gracefully and fast.

And so, as always, I went.

It was the usual local group, many from the Dorans' country club or church, a few neighbors, an elderly relative or two, my generation mixing affably with the older one. There was always wonderful food, mountains of it, a swimmer or two doing a lap or two, the rest of us socializing around the blue pool under sun umbrellas, with twilight slowly falling over lawn chairs and con-versation lighter than fizz. My recollection is of bleeding madras and suntanned noses, ladies slapping the no-see-ums on their freckly arms, bare feet in Top Siders, cigarettes glowing like fireflies, everything adding up to my pastel summer comfort zone.

Almost as soon as I arrived at the Dorans' on this perfect Sunday afternoon, I sought Russ out. "Is something wrong?" I asked, finding him at the kitchen sink.

His no seemed wishy-washy, his manner evasive.

"We have to talk, Russ."

"Not here, not now." He seemed terse, but not unfriendly. At these parties, he was usually busy being bartender, waiter and major-domo, and was now bustling about, refilling the ice bucket, wiping the counters and generally staying in energetic motion.

"Wait a minute. What's happened? What's wrong?"

"This is not a good time. Call me at the office next week and we'll talk then," he said under his breath. Something was off, I could smell it in the air as distinctly as the chlorine, and I became increasingly uneasy.

He managed to avoid being alone with me the entire rest of the party.

It's hard to remember how many times I called him after that Sunday. He was always too busy, said he'd call back but never did, and that was finally, painfully, unquestionably the end of a friendship that until then was among the closest and best I'd ever had. If I passed a Doran or two in town, and I did every week or so, they'd wave, never stop, and since it always gave me a pang, I'd try never to go by the yellow clapboard house. I was baffled by the Dorans' behavior but had my suspicions, though it wasn't for months that Jack confirmed them. Jack was a long-time mutual friend and one of our crowd, also gay, and he related a conversation he'd had with Russ when — months before the Dorans' pool party — he'd told him what he thought Russ already knew.

"Chris is gay?" Incomprehensibly, Russ, now a grown man, unequivocally effeminate and of questionable sexual orientation himself, was astonished. There was an eye-blinking, stolid silence.

"And Devon is his companion," Jack continued.

"I have a problem with that," I am told Russ finally responded.

NOT LIKE OTHER BOYS

"And of course," Jack said, "I'm gay too."

"I never had a clue."

Is it possible Russ hadn't even guessed? I'll never know, because the backlash went right across the board, and after that conversation, he ended his relationship not only with me but with Jack and Jack's companion, another school friend, as well. It wasn't until a year or two later that I heard Mrs. Doran's reaction to the news of my sexual orientation.

She'd always called me her adopted son, a part of the family, and never greeted me without a kiss. I felt bonded to the Dorans, my affection for them running as deep as a blood tie. I'm told Mrs. Doran now said to a friend, "I always liked Chris, but under the circumstances, I'd really never want him to swim in our pool again."

So, I was down and out in Larchmont, having broken off with Devon, the Dorans, and losing contact (mainly because of Devon) with the few gay friends I'd had before in the city. I worked late hours at the office with little result and did not feel in good enough shape psychologically to bare my soul to my father. I kept putting it off and off, until one bad year had staggered by.

I will get no sympathy by revealing that it was another Christmas vacation, that my brother, sister, mother and I took a winter trip together to Davos, courtesy of my generous father, that in that extraordinary Swiss abode of the gods of skiing, I felt both exhilarated and sad, energized and benumbed. It is possible to feel very bad where it's very good, to schuss down gleaming white Alpine slopes on the slickest, newest Christmas skis by day, fill up on Swiss delicacies at dinner and curl up into an ongoing wretchedness at night. My brother, sister and I barhopped together, bumping into the sort of American and foreign student and postgrad types we'd known all our lives. While my siblings took up with members of the opposite sex over their glasses of Ravella or Coke or beer in the quaint après-ski spots in town, I hung back, waiting for something or someone to cross my path and put my life into working order.

* * *

We were back from Davos, the time was right and ripe, we had gathered at home for my mother's birthday, and she was urging me to get it over with, but I couldn't seem to get my mouth to put the words together to tell my brother. I asked her to tell him for me, she resisted, but finally we compromised.

As we three sat together in the den after the birthday dinner, my mother said, "Kirby, your brother has something to tell you."

My brother, distracted, the remote control in his hand, turned to me, but my mouth refused to give birth to those little everlastingly gestating words.

"He's gay." My mother brought them to life, made them — made it — sound as matter-of-fact as if she were reading the fiber content of a new coat.

"What?"

"I'm gay." I said it this time.

My brother's demeanor ordinarily gives new weight to the word "unflappable." He is the external stoic of the family, going about his emotional business where no one ever can see it. "You're *gay?*" he said now, jaw dropped, eyes wide, as flappable as I've ever seen him. "How long have you known?"

"My whole life."

He shook his head a few times, like someone just coming out of hypnosis. It had never dawned, not a single inkling. In all our growing-up years, not a clue. And this despite a conversation he'd had with a friend not long ago that he related to me later. The friend had asked, "Is Chris dating anyone?" "No." "Is he gay?" Kirby had given it some thought, possibly a nanosecond's worth. "Hmmm. No, I don't think so," and never let the possibility enter the pathways of his consciousness again. We had lived under the same roof through childhood, much of adolescence and intermittently afterward, been on vacations and in camp together, eaten thousands of meals at the same table, watched movies, listened to music and jealously eyed each other's birthday presents. We'd shared grandparents, Christmas trees, the television, a dog and a cat. Nowadays, if we didn't see each other, we were in constant touch by telephone. If it was incomprehensible that my brother had remained, in my sister's word, clueless, it was also comforting. The dream of the closet case was bountifully fulfilled; I wasn't showing!

My resolve to be Out varied from day to day and hour to hour. I may have desperately wanted my close friends to be full confidants when I got up in the morning, but by the same afternoon, the fear of losing those friends would have me doing a full U-turn. If I had no choice but to be gay, I wanted the world to stay out of it. Based on my years of exposure to people's reactions, I thought life would be easier in hiding, with just a small circle of people with access to my closet.

It is only recently that I did my psychological one-hundred-and-eighty-degree turn. My revelation was something like the Magic Eye, those pictures in which other pictures are concealed, until suddenly one's vision acknowledges what's been there all the time, and sees the new configuration very clearly. It's not us in the homosexual community who are deficient. It's those who condemn and deride us, those who are ignorant and misinformed who should be scorned and ridiculed. It is homophobia that should be in the closet.

My brother just sat there, recovering from his thunderbolt of shock. We had, after all, just spent a Swiss ski vacation together, had been inseparable these last ten days. What must he be thinking? Like a shot of penicillin, I suppose the news took a while to take effect, because it was much later that Kirby told me he'd broken down on the way home that night and cried. Truly wept. My imperturbable, stoic brother had shed tears thinking about what I'd had to go through to hold it in and hide it from everyone all these years. For him it had particular poignancy, because he thought I must have had an enormous struggle to put up a front so painstakingly that he never suspected. And now, recovering from the bombshell, he had a few questions to ask.

"When are you going to tell Dad?" was the first.

Since my parents' breakup, my father and I had strictly a restaurant relationship. We met for dinner — almost always sushi —

talked about my job, the food and what had to be done to his car or mine. Our conversations had no depth and were completely impersonal. Before, when he was living at home, our exchanges seemed to have to do with what my mother wanted, needed or thought, or to have some imperative built into them. "Did you call your sister?" "Did you bring the luggage down from the attic?" "This belt doesn't fit me. Do you want it?" "Did you remember to make a dentist's appointment?"

There was not one common thread except a mutual interest in business, and that hardly came up until he left home. In my life as my father's son, we actually never had any kind of conversation, so it was especially difficult to think about sitting down with him face to face and giving him the gruesome word. What was my father's reaction going to be? Was he going to kick me out of his apartment? His temper was so horrible that my fear of him, even as an adult, was as involuntary as the pupils of my eyes dilating at dusk. I was creating all sorts of imaginary scenarios, writing dialogues in my head, predicting his level of probable shock. A stroke did not seem outside the realm of possibility. I was so afraid of how to go about it that I devised an escape route, a gentler way out.

I always thought I'd work in the family eyeglass business one day, but did not consider it an option this soon, only two years out of business school. I thought I would gather more experience before making that move, that it would be my ultimate career choice. I suppose I saw myself stepping in when my hair was gray or gone, taking charge when my father had begun to dodder. A few job interviews — I was determined to leave Wisk and Dove — convinced me that I'd learned quite a bit at Lever Brothers, that since my destiny was clearly the family business, it might as well be now. And so, in presenting the fact of my sexual orientation to my father, I took a circuitous route, a sort of back door through business that would lead to the main gate of my identity.

I called and asked him if we could have dinner, said I wanted to discuss something with him, and arranged to go to his apartment first. I didn't feel comfortable making my announcement in the public arena of a restaurant, where God only knew what sort of passion and sizzle could be played out in front of a crowd of sushi eaters. My imagination was running wild as I sat in what used to be my old living room and my father sipped his usual drink or two and made small talk about traffic and his current aches and pains.

It was another leap into incalculable space, riskier and more fraught with danger. I wanted to back off, get up and run, fly or evaporate out of my father's apartment. All this despite the roundabout speech I'd very, very carefully prepared.

My father had gotten up for more ice or another drink and was about to sit down on the couch again. It seemed the right moment, because we were not face to face and I didn't have to look directly into his eyes. I had tried always to live up to his difficult standards: even when we were kids wisecracking at the dinner table, we could never measure up. My father's eyes would get cold and steely, making it clear to us that our jokes were never as funny as his. Getting him to laugh was an almost impossible goal. It was as if I'd been stretching all my life, wanting to get it right, to do better than my siblings. In some way I needed to make it up to him for the fact that he would know that I had failed him by having homosexual feelings.

"I wanted to have dinner with you because I'd like to come to work for you," I began now, my heart in my mouth. "And I thought you ought to know before I did that, that I'm gay."

He sat down, his face momentarily stunned, as if I'd just pulled a gun out of my pocket, but the look came and went in an instant. He seemed to recover his balance, but I kept talking to fill with words the grim space of his charged silence. My father, not knowing what to say? It was a new experience. The stone face, the groping for a response, was chilling. I think I said, "It's no one's business." I began trying to soothe him by mainstreaming myself, keeping both visible feet in the straight world. I thought it would calm him, that it was what he wanted to hear. "It doesn't matter. I'm not seeing anyone right now," I continued. This filling-the-void chatter, the obedience to my father's standards, came thick and fast out of my mouth.

He cleared his throat and finally found his voice. "You know, your mother always thought that, but I didn't believe it." A hollow pause, eyes averted. "But you're careful, aren't you? You've got to be very careful." The question, decent and caring, was so typical of the good, antipodal side of Dad.

"You don't have to worry," I said.

Then he said, "I have no problem with it."

That was a merciful, beautiful sentence with poetic cadence for my ears. If only he had stopped there, but he didn't. "You know, gay or straight, I don't care — as long as it's not those crazies. The ones who march." Then, the afterthought. "It doesn't matter, no one has to know. It's no one's business." If he was trying to come off as a liberal, he was off by at least one generation. "As long as it doesn't show," he said.

I was breathing normally again and thanked him, though in retrospect, it was generous on my part. He hadn't fainted, screamed or thrown me out, and I was relieved. I told him it was difficult to be speaking up, that it was probably better that it had taken me so long to come forward, that the struggle I went through, my repression and inhibitions, possibly saved my life in a time of HIV and AIDS. I thanked him for helping me be more masculine as a child, and he was very pleased by that. At the time, I saw my whole life stretching ahead in the role of a man who could "pass." I saw it as a distinct benefit that I would be straight-seeming, that unlike my childhood, I would be exempt from victimization because I wasn't "obvious." I thought this would help in my business life and was grateful that I wasn't "that way" — that I hadn't turned into one of the "crazies," the ones who march, those who were anathema to my father.

Ironically, since I'd lived in this apartment, he had been getting circulars, announcements, pamphlets and all sorts of gay-related mail addressed to me, but he still had not wanted to face it. He thought it was a phase and hung on to the life raft of possibility that Julia was my girlfriend. In all fairness, I think he figured I'd stop going in the wrong direction for my own sake and not for his; it's what happened so often in his generation. Maybe he thought I'd make myself fit in because I had, after all, struggled to be mainstream all my life. In any case, I got his message. He wanted it kept quiet, didn't want to have to see it.

So it is to this day.

That night my father and I went out to dinner together and talked only about business. For the moment, the subject of my sexuality was as dead as the raw fish on our plates. Later that evening I tried to call him, to see if he was alive and well in the aftermath of truth, and got a busy signal for hours. Did that mean he was calling a girlfriend? My brother? Was he on the telephone on some unrelated matter? Did he take the phone off the hook? Was he crying? He's never told me, I never wanted to ask, so I suppose I may never know.

33

<hr style="border: none; border-top: 1px dashed #000; width: 30%;">

AT THE TIME I was writing this, I came across a "Dear Abby" column in a local newspaper. It appeared on June 11, 1994.

> Dear Abby: This may be silly, but I need an answer. I have three sons, ages 5 and 2 years and 10 months old. "Ricky," my two-year-old, loves to play with dolls . . . Some people make wisecracks when they see Ricky with his dolls, but he would rather play with dolls than cars or trucks. I have never thought there was a problem, but some people say it would make him "funny" when he gets older.
>
> . . . Ricky's "babies" are girl babies — he even tries to feed them. He watches me with his baby brother and mimics everything I do. Is this a bad thing? Or is it good for a boy to act so maternal?
>
> Concerned Mommy

> Dear Concerned Mommy: If you are really concerned that this will cause your son to have homosexual tendencies, you need not give it another thought. Homosexuals are born, not made.

Oh, dear Abby, where were you thirty years ago?

On all sides of me now — on the street, at our country club, in every supermarket, shoe repair shop, ice cream parlor and video store, in cars stopped next to mine waiting for the light to change — my line of vision is crowded with mothers and their small boys. When I see them, I see me then, and I feel blossoms of regret and sadness. When the men I call my boys were really boys, here were my chances, at least one missed every single day, to toot my sons' horns instead of trying to mute them. Now here are the mothers who used to be me, with their priceless, ephemeral opportunities still stretching ahead of them, while mine are long since gone. It is not just their chance to give a hug instead of a slug when the boys want to try on lipstick, or a kiss when they want to be shown how knitting needles work. Here are their bountiful possibilities — today, tonight, tomorrow at breakfast! — to ratify, support and applaud the harmonies of their sons' spirits instead of condemning whatever score they want to follow, to give them an extra pat on the head for being whoever they are today or might turn into tomorrow. Here is their fleeting scrap of time to get it right, not to hold back, not to abandon them. If I had it to do over again, this time I would open every faucet of affirmation full blast, knowing that from a mother's heart there would never be an overflow.

Dear Concerned Mommy: Playing with dolls is not a harbinger of homosexuality, any more than a football scholarship assures that a boy won't fall in love with the homecoming king. But whatever will be, will certainly be.

Bob and I sat in the now familiar office of Dr. Lowey, our marriage counselor, hoping he'd come up with the right formula to make things good again. I think counseling is a tricky skill, something like fancy baking. One wrong ingredient and the cake may have to be thrown out. Bob said once that if it weren't for the marriage counselors, we'd still be together, and although that may not be the case, Dr. Lowey did dig up ingredients that should never have been stirred into our sessions. The accumulations of old wrongs and new infractions were piling up as quickly as items at a checkout counter.

"But you blame Bob for Chris's homosexuality," Dr. Lowey said, eyebrow up in what I saw as an accusatory moue.

"No, I don't." Surely I had in the past, but no longer.

"You think it's his fault."

"Not anymore. But, doctor, what do you think? Do you think homosexuals are born or made?"

"Not important what I think."

"But I'd really like to know."

"I believe they are born that way," Dr. Lowey said.

Oddly enough, I was now also seeing a psychiatrist independently, to help me cope with the trauma of our separation. Dr. Gloverman was an Upper East Side doctor connected with one of New York's finest hospitals.

Not more than seventy-two hours ago, I'd been sitting in *his* office, and he'd asked me if I blamed my husband for Chris's sexual orientation.

"Do you think homosexuals are born or made?" I asked him.

"Evidence points toward the likelihood that they are made," he said. He cited studies of same-egg twins, who were not identical in their eventual sexual orientation, but who were genetically undifferentiated in every other way. It sounded perfectly logical and valid, and I have no sound scientific counterarguments to support my position, but by this time I had enough firsthand quotidian experience behind me to draw my own conclusions. Can any of these experts know more than the mother of a boy like Chris? My vote is with dear old Abby. With her homespun wisdom and syndicated quick-fix answers, she is right on the money. Born, not made.

Pinwheels of anger filled my head during the marriage-counseling sessions. An entirely new level of fury was building in me. I felt as if I could do what I'd never done before in my life — pick up objects and throw them, right now, like one of the plants in the window or the counselor's coffee mug, never far from his hand. I wanted to scream into the air of this colorless room or run out of it, while the thousand and one issues were dredged up, the ancient history of wrongs that didn't seem so wrong until they were reexamined here as we were burned each in turn by current events and accusations of old, long-buried slights. (Incorrect, revisionist, unfair!) I had my laundry list of complaints as did Bob, who felt I had no respect for him and wasn't making him happy. How was this exhumation supposed to help? My husband and I, basically in accord for thirty years, now could hardly agree on anything.

Nowhere was it more obvious than in the struggle about revealing (or concealing) Chris's sexual orientation. For one thing, I felt that trying to pass as heterosexual put Chris in the worst limbo of loneliness; now he belonged nowhere at all. Also, I wanted to have the right to discuss my son with intimates of my choice. I'd held in his secret so long I suppose I needed the catharsis, and it certainly made me feel more honest. These confidants would not include any of our remaining aged and infirm parents or step-grandparents, at least for the moment. Bob and I did see eye to eye on that.

As far as discussing it with our close friends, it was, "It's nobody's business!" I watched Bob's tic come and go as his anger leapfrogged mine.

The counselor's white flag waved in vain.

"I refuse to lie!" I said.

"Your friends don't have to know!"

And so on.

To my consternation, Chris, for his part, continued to insist I tell no one. It is a sinister irony that of all my children, Chris is most like his father. It's not only a question of his bone structure, hair and physique that mark him as his father's son. He has been spookily stamped with Bob's mannerisms and best traits — plus some dividend attributes like diplomacy and peacekeeping. It came as no surprise, then, that he took this position, and that we argued over it. I imagined that many of our friends had guessed anyway, but for the time being, Chris won. I respected his wishes and kept my mouth shut.

During all the fifty-minute hours Bob and I sat there in Dr. Lowey's office, I behaved quietly and peacefully, as if I were being interviewed for a job and my life depended on it. Which, of course, I was. I was fighting for my position as wife, but why? Perhaps I had outgrown the job description. Perhaps I had indeed lost respect for this angry and unlettered man, however goodhearted, conscientious and decent he was. Perhaps I only wanted the job for its benefits — family unity and the idealized dream of mother and dad becoming grandma and grandpa, presiding at the same Christmas dinners, accepting each other's eccentricities and flaws and tantrums, laughing at each other's jokes, and resting side by side under adjoining granite through all eternity.

Our eternity was coming quickly to a close. A few reconciliations, followed by packed suitcases and more soul-wrenching goodbyes, weekly sessions with yet another expert, and at last I learned what I now know: the person who wants to leave a relationship casts the bigger vote. And when a family gets torn into "Dad's apartment" and "Mom's place" instead of "home," when there have to be two Thanksgivings and several calendar jugglings for every other holiday, every child, though fully grown, carries his share of the loss. New beginnings don't guarantee happy endings; when assets, friends and photographs have to be divided, and after all the accumulation of memories and years, the impedimenta are so heavy that there are no big wins, even for the one who cast the bigger vote.

Late in the summer of 1989, after the final scenes of my marriage had played themselves out, Chris, ever sensitive and compassionate, agreed to take a short trip with me. We chose Maine, because lobsters, blueberries and the magnificent coastline beckoned, and because neither of us had ever been there. I was especially fragile that summer, and careful not to tread in beautiful places where old memories might lurk, so off we went, to Bangor, Penobscot, Bar Harbor.

On one of the first evenings of our vacation, we were upstairs in a two-tier restaurant in Bar Harbor, halfway through our Maine lobsters, when there was a shriek from a table not far from ours. There followed a frenetic commotion, the swoop and flutter of something sinister and black in the air above us, and a flow of blood to my head. My mother always assured me that they are sweet little creatures, our mammal friends. Maybe mother knew best, but I am totally terrified of bats.

I jumped up out of my chair and let out a strangled cry. "Let's get out of here!" I am not stupid enough to imagine that the bat was aiming right for my hair, but then again . . . "Chris! Come on, let's go!"

To the rescue: my son took me by the arm and sat me down again. "It's only a bat," he said. "Harmless, nothing to be afraid of. Calm down, Mom." Et cetera.

My tower of strength was amused. He held me down while the restaurant staff expelled the ominous intruder. I simmered down, somewhat. It struck me that what we had here was a radical role reversal. My son, now my protector, was not going to let that wannabe vampire get me — which was a far cry from my trying to stop the world from getting my son. This was the child I'd always considered in jeopardy and my duty to protect, the object of my worry and concern for twenty-odd years. Now I became aware that I'd been leaning on Chris these last few years, not to protect me from airborne fauna, but to keep me safe from my own black emotions, which for the moment were more threatening than anything creepy flying above. What fate had dished out to me terrestrially turned out not so bad when Chris was at my side. He was my defender, companion and, of late, all-around pal. My son and I, having grown up together, created a bond I'd never imagined or expected. We were most compatible companions. On this trip we did some hiking in Acadia National Park, ate blueberry pancakes in Northeast Harbor, took a ferry ride through the Cranberry Isles. We meandered through those hokey village shops so dear to my heart and bought books for a dollar at the Bar Harbor Library book sale. On this trip, Chris safeguarded me not only from a black bat but from the fuzzy dark thoughts that were hanging from my psychological rafters. He had become that "masterpiece of nature," a best friend. And he still is.

I went to several meetings of PFLAG, Parents and Friends of Lesbians and Gays, an organization for people who have nothing whatsoever in common except that they love someone who is not heterosexual. The first gathering I attended was not long after Chris's disclosure. It was held in a church basement in Manhattan, and I was struck by the heterogeneity of the group, which represented a cross section of human beings — all colors, all classes — so unlike those in my peas-in-a-pod suburban neighborhood.

We sat in a semicircle on folding chairs and spoke our lines: "My name is Lois, I have a gay son and a lesbian daughter." "My name is Tom. I'm gay, I just found out that my brother is also gay. My father has threatened suicide." "I'm Rhoda. My husband is gay, he has a lover, the lover is always hanging around our house. I don't want to lose my husband, just his companion. What should I do?"

The stories were funny, poignant, redundant, heartbreaking.

In the Westchester PFLAG group, the crowd was smaller, somewhat more homogeneous, and the revelations were not that dissimilar from those I'd heard in the city. "I knew from the time my son was two years old and kept straightening the fringes on the sofa," a mother reported, deadpan. Another said, "My son and I were watching an old James Bond movie on TV one night, and guess what? We both have crushes on Sean Connery." Many tear-stained laughs in this room! Rose, the facilitator of the Westchester group, has been heading it for ten years. "It's not uncommon to realize his sexual orientation when a boy is three. It seems to be the 'magic' age. And we feel it's definitely genetic, familial. I knew early on with my son, too," she said. "My own brother was gay, and I saw how my mother treated him. To her, he was a leper. It was her Catholicism. When she was dying, I begged and pleaded with her to please make her peace with her son. She never relented, rejecting him with her last breath. It was so horrible, final, and sad. I'm the exact opposite with David. I feel he is unique and marvelous, I'm lucky I had him. I vowed I would accept my son as he was — and did, from day one, and so did his father. I told him recently that not only did his sexual orientation never distress me, he had enriched my life, opened me to new experiences I never would have had. He is the best of my four children, my reward for motherhood!"

The PFLAG meetings are not only support systems, they are

real and living theater: One gay man reports catching his own father cruising in a gay neighborhood. A wife discloses that she is keeping the fact of her son's homosexuality from her husband to "spare" him. A young man is the son of a gay father and lesbian mother. Ironically, neither is dealing well with his homosexuality. I listened to these stories, heard a gamut of responses to the declarations of disclosure, noted that parents of my generation were often unable to come to terms with what they saw as the tragedy of their lives. What was an eye opener here was that people who are enlightened, open-minded and liberal, who may find homosexuality perfectly acceptable in the world at large, cannot deal with the reality of it in their own children. "My son enriched my life" was Rose's heart-stopping, amazing p.o.v., and it was my epiphany. The assertion was true for me too, one hundred percent.

At PFLAG I learned to stand firm against what often seems like majority opinion, to see more clearly that what's wrong with homosexuality is only society's view of it. James Baldwin wrote: "It is a great shock at the age of five or six to find that in a world of Gary Coopers you are the Indian." "Indians" are extinct, even in Hollywood these days, but the point is, whether we call him Chief White Feather, Native American or Faggot, the targets of prejudice need their advocates. When I'm with friends, the Gary Coopers, and they use defamatory tags or homophobic throwaway lines, what do I do?

Within the last three months, out of the mouths of people occasionally in my company:

"The highlight of my weekend was dancing with a fag at my cousin's wedding."

"There were four queers blowing smoke in our faces at the table next to us."

"AIDS is God's punishment for homosexual behavior."

Do I jump in and condemn the remark and the person who made it? Do I shut up for the sake of diplomatic relations, do I object strenuously, or proselytize? I don't want to be thought of as someone around whom people must constantly watch their verbal steps. On the other hand, it must be my mandate, from this point on, to protest the defamation of the Indian in our world of Gary Coopers. I suppose I should have started long ago, confronting the mothers and fathers of the boys who were ragging Chris. I might have mentioned that it wasn't about our rocks or theirs, trespassing, or boys will be boys. It was and is about the geography of acceptance and integrity, and whether we are black, white or in between, cowboy or homosexual or both, the world will sleep better when we get to that estimable place, one and all.

34

- - - - - - - - - -

IT WAS NOT very long ago. I was sitting on a French-provincial chair in a chandeliered, candle-lit, moire-draperied restaurant in this midwestern city. Working in the family business is not as easy as people assume, and as usual I had to put in the extra push to be the best of the best, just to feel I wasn't letting my father down. Still, I'd come a long way since Lever Brothers. I'd learned the ropes and was definitely now feeling up a few rungs in his world. As two waiters in black tie hovered over the table, distributing tasseled menus and pouring French wines, I admit I was feeling pretty rosy.

My official title was Director of Marketing, but little by little my responsibilities stretched into tangential areas. I became understudy for my traveling father and also a jack of all in-house trades: financial analyst, strategic planner and all-around troubleshooter.

My uncle and I had flown to this city for meetings with the executives and staff of one of the largest retail eyeglass operations in the United States. We were there to educate and pump up the employees of the chain stores, many hundreds of them, into pitching our twelve new Sophia Loren frames, and my purpose specifically was to come up with a creative and effective marketing plan.

The preparations were months in the making, the expenses staggering. Sophia prefers to have her photo shoots done near her home in Geneva, so our entourage of about eight, including her favorite photographer, a hair and makeup stylist, a fashion stylist who chose the more than twenty thousand dollars' worth of clothes she would wear in the pictures, and assorted other personnel flew to Switzerland. There Sophia endured several days of costume changes, with each outfit chosen to coordinate with a certain eyeglass frame. Out of hundreds of photographs several were chosen, to appear in catalogues, ads and other promotional materials. The last step in the marketing preparation involved going to the stores where the photos would appear, to determine what size or type of display materials were needed and to wine and dine the customers.

We'd had a fruitful day, finished our meeting with the chain-store bigwigs and were now sitting down to a posh dinner. The party included their buyers, responsible for thousands of dollars of our business every year, as well as the CEO of the company, the vice president, and their wives. With the business of the day completed, the dinner took on a much more sociable texture, and conversation veered toward the personal and the mundane of vacation plans, industry gossip and today's tabloid news.

"I brought my son to a basketball game last night," one of the group was saying, and someone else followed with, "I just read how they think Magic Johnson got AIDS. Not from a woman, not from drugs."

With that, a buyer threw down her napkin. "No! Not Magic Johnson!" It was a wail that sounded to my ear like the cry of a woman whose dog has just been hit by a truck.

The vice president chimed in. "Oh, no! Magic is my son's idol! I don't want to tell him that! He'll be *crushed!*"

Now the president moaned, "What next!" His eyes rolled, and it was clear that he meant, What's left? All our heroes are destroyed!

To a heterosexual's ears, these may seem innocuous, no-harm-intended comments that straight, red-blooded, mainstream men and women are quite within their rights to make, but to me they sounded insidious and cutting. What exactly were these people saying? That a basketball player was still a hero if he'd caught AIDS through promiscuous sex or drugs but was a fallen icon if he'd had a relationship with a man? If Magic Johnson was no longer a hero because he might be suspected as gay, where did that leave me?

There I sat, feeling consequential one minute and like a shriveled dead duck the next. Here I was, a fully actualized gay man who they were depending on to help make them hundreds of thousands of dollars. If they found out I was gay, what then? In the optical industry, many consider gays the dregs of humanity — strange, because the same narrow minds are buying frames created by, or named for, the ubiquitous, talented and famous homosexual designers.

And while remarks about other minorities are considered déclassé, homosexuals are still fair game, whether they are titans or hustlers, dukes or drifters. If the company's vice president had said, "Imagine my son's disappointment when he discovered the basketball player turned out to be a Jew," would that not sound despicable? But would it really be so different?

Am I angry now? When I was a child, I had a child's perspective, always looking at myself to see what was wrong with me and what I could do to change myself, to conform, to make my family proud. These days, especially during encounters of this sort, my perspective spins on its heels: when I hear an outrageous and overtly bigoted slur, I can dismiss it as coming from an unenlightened redneck boor. And when the insult is subtle and is spoken quietly in polite company, it drills the deepest. It sends a message to my very seabed, that no matter how hard I try or how successful I become, once I let my sexual orientation be known, I will still be considered a white Magic Johnson, and in the trash heap of human life.

Who wouldn't be angry?

It is said that homosexuals are members of the only minority who do not have the unequivocal support of their families, and the situation with my father is a case in point. Recently, when my brother was getting married and I was going to be best man, I made it clear that I would be bringing my companion. In a somewhat embarrassed way, my father said, "You know, my friends Tom, Dick and Harry from the industry are coming to the wedding and bringing their wives. What are you going to do?" He meant that it was a sticky issue, that we might both mind if they knew. It seemed a fair question, but not quite. My father seems to enjoy the fact that I can pass, and his position was and is that business relationships might be jeopardized, that these friends might talk and some sort of shadow would fall across our company's image and ledgers. It's as if he has two sets of ears, one caring and understanding, the other all business. For the time being, the business ears are larger and, without a doubt, more keen.

Another, more crushing indignity came when he missed an opportunity to support me at work. An employee on our managerial staff went into the shipping room not long ago and handed one of the clerks a package of frames. Someone overheard him say, "Take care of this today. The fag wants these sent in a hurry."

I immediately reported this outrage to my father. What I wanted was an apology, and more: specifically, a confrontation in my father's office, in his presence. Although I assumed my father wouldn't speak out, I thought he would encourage me to say what I wanted to say: "If you have a problem working for a gay man, you are free to leave. And if you ever use the word 'fag' under this roof again, you can clean out your desk and get out."

My father's response to this request was pacific. For once, I might have enjoyed a show of the usual fury. Instead, he said, "This man is not working for *you.*" And then he added, "I don't know if you want to address this issue. I'm sure they talk about me behind my back too, call me an asshole and whatever else they can think of, but you have to rise above it. It doesn't matter what they say behind your back as long as they get the job done. I don't know if you want to draw attention to your homosexuality." Calm. He was very calm.

There was doubtless some sound logic to this spin control, but I wanted more from my father. Advocacy, outrage, a rush of blood to his face, at the very least. *Something.* He is my father, isn't he? But he wanted the issue dropped, and his indifference cut deeper than the homophobic vilification. It stays and stays with me.

35

- - - - - - - - - -

SOMETIMES THESE DAYS I feel my heart has grown too big for my body. It is filled with remorse and regret for the past, yearning for one more conversation with my departed parents, crammed with love and worry for my three children and particularly for Chris, on his own in a difficult world. It bulges too with pity and feeling for my globe-roaming ex-husband, who recently came back to Larchmont and tried to reclaim two old chairs from the attic of our old house, which I had just sold. One does not have to be a psychiatrist or marriage counselor to look into his soul and find some vestigial yearning, some subconscious desire to enfold our past. He turned out to be a family man to the core, a born-again father to his three grown children, and to have a pure heart, which I suspect is also filled with remorse and regret, and like mine, crowded to overflowing.

Our son's life started from a cell, his father and I gave him his name, his genes, his tuition, but it can't stop there. There is no more blame and no more reprehension. We were simply human, amateur parents, very much victims of our culture and our time. Now we have to give our son his dignity, make up for all the marauding affronts and disparagements that went before, and both watch over him penitently for the rest of our lives.

Our love may come from different directions, but his father and I still both have this in our blood: we would give up our lives for this son. We love him that much.

36

- - - - - - - - - -

IT WAS YET another business dinner. A customer turned to me and asked, "Are you seeing anyone, Chris?" Perhaps she intended to introduce me to a sister or friend or cousin. I squirmed. "Yes," I said.

"Oh. What's her name?"

My father was at the table. The shadow he throws is very large; I made up a name.

The woman asked, "And what does Janie do?"

The lies coming out of my mouth piled up. My dinner was spoiled.

That was the instant in which the footprints of my life changed their direction forever. Never again. Not for the sake of the business, not for any sake, would I call my male companion Janie. I would wear no sandwich board proclaiming my sexual orientation, but never a dodge or lie would cross my lips. I am gay, but the path ahead must be unveering and direct from now on.

I spoke to my father. I explained that I'd gotten past hiding, that my sexual orientation should have no bearing on our business relationships, and recited that cliché line of lines, "I am who I am." He was, predictably, not delighted, and there are now a thousand and one subtleties, those smaller and larger gnat bites of commission and omission that flit in and out between us: my companion's picture cannot appear in a frame on my desk, and although I serve on a trade-association committee and should certainly be in attendance, I have not been invited to the couples-oriented annual industry convention. In words unspoken I have been told that my private life has got to stay private.

And so, although I am now definitively Out, I am also just Outside. At work and in life, between my father and me, there is a certain meridian of silence that is as clear a signal as a raised eyebrow, a pink triangle — as unequivocal as purple on Thursdays.

In all fairness, he has come a long way. Other gay men have been banished, disinherited and alienated from their fathers, and mine is trying to be even-handed and accepting, to treat all three of his children alike. I have a colossal storage bin of gratitude for the life he provided for us all. My childhood memories, although laced with melancholy, are magnificent and extraordinary in many ways, thanks to his generosity.

Yet being accepting falls a bit short of being my advocate. Telling me to roll with the punches is not like throwing one, or wanting to, when I am reviled or stigmatized. Supporting me is different from expecting me to conform to community standards when they're repressive, unenlightened and unjust. I don't expect my father to march in parades or wave flags, and I can't expect him to change society, but I want him to stand behind me. I guess it's his homestretch for him to go, and will require the most effort. Although he's getting closer, he is not quite at the finish line. When he gets there, no matter when, I'll be there waiting for him, not only because he's my father, but because I love him.

If I inherited my father's digestion, my mother's chin, my grandfather's ability in math, an assorted potpourri of genes from ancestors going back through several countries and many generations, doesn't it follow that this conglomerate has produced this me package that was imprinted in the womb? I was born with a left eye through which I have only peripheral vision. For this developmental error only the gods of mismanagement are to blame. It's a small, annoying deviation about which I am not angry, an impediment I've adapted to and work around.

By the same token, I point the finger of accusation at no one for my sexual orientation. It's the way it is, the way I was born, a differentiation I've adapted to. The world is changing, sometimes too slowly for me, but the way it spins is really no one's fault. Neither am I. I'm the product of genetics, the sum of atoms and neurons and cells that divided, the random me I'm stuck with, and although it took many years, I've worked around not being able to fall in love with a woman. If my mother and father took a few crazy twists and turns in raising me, I forgive them. Now we're together, often in proximity and always in spirit. Our little heterosexual and homosexual family conglomerate gets along; it turned out to be possible after all. I've landed on my feet in that warm space between contentment and optimism, where life is good and the air I breathe seems fresher and cleaner. I look with pleasure at the sensibilities of my contemporaries, who are much more open-minded and open-hearted than their parents, and who without a doubt will make fewer mistakes in the next generation.

With some exceptions. Last month, I invited my old college friend, Megan, now the mother of two babies, to a party at my house. She asked how many guests would be gay, how many straight. I told her it might work out about half and half. She called back a day or two later, saying she'd be coming but her husband would not. "He wouldn't feel comfortable in that sort of crowd," she said, sounding apologetic. It made me sad. What message will that father be sending to his children? I was thrown back to my days in school, the bullies, the obstacle course of humiliations. Will his boys be picking on the likes of me in a few years?

But he is atypical, I think. I'm hopeful that for the most part my contemporaries' children will not be cooped up in the maximum-security lockup of conformity. Individuality is nature, and nature seems to be winning. At long last.